To

Ray Hiebert

with fond and affectionate
regards and gratitude
for valuable instruction in journalism
when I was his pupil.

Cuban Journal

Mohammed A. Rauf, Jr.

Cuban Journal

Castro's Cuba as It Really Is—
an Eyewitness Account
by an American Reporter

Thomas Y. Crowell Company / New York / Established 1834

Dedicated

with affection and respect

to

ERWIN D. CANHAM

Contents

1. A Visa to Cuba

THE ringing of the telephone bell yanked me out of my reverie.

That morning there was nothing much doing in the News Room of the *Cleveland Press*. I had just finished a background story on events in Finland, and I figured that the rest of the day would consist of waiting for something to happen. I was busy making plans for the date I had for that evening with one of the girls in the office, and I was debating with myself whether I should take her to a movie or invite her to my apartment to listen to records.

But the telephone call dispelled all thoughts of girls marooned in my apartment. The caller was Earl Richert, editor of the Scripps-Howard Newspaper Alliance, Washington, D.C. This is a chain of eighteen papers, including the *Cleveland Press*, and Richert directs its foreign coverage, sending his men on reporting safaris to the far corners of the world.

"Mo, my friend," he said, cool and suave, "I want you to go to Cuba, and write a series on how the people live five years after the revolution. Do you think you can do it?"

There is no denying that his words sent a thrill through me, for all reporters dream of assignments involving danger and excitement, and I am no exception.

"I'll go," I told Richert. "I'm willing to try." He ordered me to fly to Washington pronto for further discussions. I said that I would, and he hung up. Louis Seltzer, editor of the *Cleveland Press*, and my immediate boss, thought that the idea was great. He told me to go home and start packing.

I was still excited about the assignment as my plane gained altitude.

But when it leveled off and I sat gazing at the clouds as it droned its way through them, my thoughts turned to my past career as a reporter.

A native of Lucknow, India, I came to the United States, the fabled land of opportunity, in late 1958, to struggle for journalistic recognition. My first stop was in Washington. I enrolled at the American University, and got myself a job as a copyboy with the *Evening Star*. From that position I gradually rose to become an embassy reporter and feature writer. In 1961, I won an Asian Foundation scholarship to the Pulitzer School of Journalism at Columbia University, New York. After graduation, I returned to the *Evening Star* for a few months, and joined Scripps-Howard in October, 1962. I worked with three of its newspapers: the *Cincinnati Post*, the *Fort Worth Press*, and the *Albuquerque Tribune*.

But all that was now in the past.

Richert's reception of me was cordial. He narrowed his eyes, wrinkled his forehead, leaned his balding head toward me, and began expounding the problems of the assignment to Cuba: "You know very well, Mohammed, that Cuba is barred to American correspondents. To get there, they first have to get the State Department's permission, which is not easy. The next problem is to get a Cuban visa, which is almost impossible; and the final problem is to find a plane going to Cuba. But we think that, because you are an Indian, these problems would be less formidable for you. Anyway, we want you to begin trying. Take your own time and do the best you can."

Those were all the instructions I got. How to proceed? The incongruity of the situation was appalling. Cuba is only ninety miles from Florida. In other days, tourists on a whim flew over for an afternoon of gambling—with no passports, visas, formalities of any kind. But now going there appeared next to impossible.

Of course, as an Indian I had no need to check with the State Department about my trip, and I hoped that also because of my nationality it would be easier for me to get a Cuban visa. But I was well aware that as a *reportero* working for American newspapers, I would be running a risk of being arrested. I realized that I would be an object of suspicion to the Cubans, that they would keep me under constant surveillance, restrict my movements, and that the people would be afraid to talk with me. I decided to apply for a visa as a tourist and not as a journalist, and to play down (and even deny, if possible) my association with Scripps-Howard. I realized that that would make things doubly difficult for me were my true identity discovered, but I decided to take the chance for the sake of the story.

Cuba has no diplomatic representation in Washington. Cuban affairs are handled by the Czech embassy, housed in a limestone building, carefully shuttered, on Massachusetts Avenue. I obtained the visa forms there, but a rather uncooperative aide sullenly told me that I would have to wait several months for an answer. I suspected that he knew I was a reporter.

I telephoned the Cuban mission at the United Nations in New York, because all missions to the U.N. have diplomatic status and are authorized to issue visas. I asked to speak to the head of the Cuban mission. A secretary, speaking English with a strong Spanish accent, asked me the reason. When I told her what it was, she said that too many persons were applying to the mission for visas, and that the mission's policy was to deny all requests.

I was left with no alternative but to leave the U.S., travel to a country which had diplomatic relations with Cuba, and apply for a visa at the Cuban embassy in that country.

My first choice was Mexico, because it is one of the few countries in Latin America that have extended recognition to the government of Fidel Castro. But, since I was an Indian, I needed a Mexican visa to cross the Rio Grande. I presented myself at the Mexican embassy in Washington, and asked for the visa forms. The clerk, who was sitting behind an iron railing, looked at me from over his glasses and asked me why I wanted to go to Mexico. My mistake was that I told him the real reason. At once his demeanor became frigid. He said that I was free to fill out the forms, but that they would have to be forwarded to the Mexican Foreign Ministry in Mexico City for action.

"We have no arrangement with the Indian government," he said, "whereby our embassies can issue visas to our respective nationals."

"But this is ridiculous," I protested. "Why can't you call your Foreign Ministry on the telephone? I'll pay the cost of the call."

The clerk glared at me as if I were planning to run away with his wallet. He said, "No, I can't do that. And I won't do that. We don't do things that way."

"But why are you flinging so much red tape in my face? I don't come from a country that is unfriendly to you," I said, trying to keep my temper down.

"I know you don't. And that is why I say that your application will be very sympathetically considered by our government. I think you will get the visa, but give our government some time—two months, at the most."

I realized that there was no point in arguing with him. I carried my case to the minister-counselor, but was met with more foot-dragging. This was a jolt, but still it was nothing compared to what was still to come.

The second country in North America that has diplomatic relations with Cuba is Canada. With Richert's approval and with my fingers crossed, I took a plane to Ottawa. I did not need a Canadian visa, since both Canada and India are members of the British Commonwealth, and the citizen of one country can enter the other without a visa.

I checked in at the Ritz Hotel on Banks Street in Ottawa. The next morning I took a cab to the Cuban embassy, on Sherwood Drive. It is a small building, well hidden behind trees and shrubs. There seemed to be no one about. A sleepy clerk told me in broken English that the embassy issued only diplomatic visas and for a tourist visa I should apply at the Cuban consulates in either Montreal or Toronto.

That night I took the train to Montreal, and got myself a room at the YMCA. I arose early the next day, and dressed myself in my Indian attire for my first visit to the Cuban consulate on Sherbrook Street. I decided to wear my Indian attire because I thought it would help create a better impression on the consul. It consisted of a pair of white jodhpurs, a knee-length jacket buttoned to the neck, and a close fitting *toppee* of black velvet. The outfit didn't seem to cause much surprise on the streets of Montreal.

Sherbrook Street is one of the fashionable streets in Montreal. The Cuban consulate was in a three-story house. The bell was answered by a man in shirt sleeves. He was in his early forties, over six feet tall, and sturdily built; he had uneven teeth and a small moustache. He did not seem to be an unfriendly person, but he definitely was surprised at my get-up. Apparently, never before had anyone called upon him wearing such things.

"Who are you? What do you want?" he asked me rapidly in very good but highly accented English.

"I am an Indian and I want to go to Cuba as a tourist," I answered, making every effort to appear casual. "I have come to you for my visa."

"Come back next week," he said. "We are moving to another place and the consulate is closed."

He would have shut the door in my face, but I wedged into the room a few inches and smiled as broadly as I could.

"May I talk with the consul anyway?" I asked.

"I'm the consul. But I can't—"

It was my turn to be surprised, but I did not let him finish the sentence.

"Oh, you are the consul. I am so happy to meet you," I said, and without waiting for him to extend his hand I took it in both of mine and shook it.

This threw him off somewhat. He asked me to come in.

"You see, my wife and I are packing. I can't even ask you to sit down," he said, pointing at papers piled on chairs and filing cabinets assembled in one corner.

"That's all right, Mr. Consul," I answered. "We can talk standing up."

"Why do you want to go to Cuba?" he asked with suspicion in his voice.

"Because I have heard so much of your country," I replied with a straight face. "I want to see things for myself. I personally am a great admirer of your Fidel Castro, and I think the future of all countries lies in producing men like him."

I do not know what made me say that. I said it unthinkingly, spontaneously. But the consul was obviously pleased with my answer. He gave me his name—Rogelio Guillot. But he had no authority, he said, to issue a visa to an Indian. I would have to write to the Ministry of Foreign Affairs in Havana for it.

"If Havana tells me to give it to you, I'll give it," he said.

I was loud in expressing my disappointment. "But, sir, isn't there some way by which the process can be hurried?" I asked.

"Come to my new office in the Ville Marie in three days and then we will talk about it," he said.

He did not ask me anything more. I decided not to overstay my welcome.

It was mid-May when I arrived in Montreal. Summer had set in and the weather was perfect. I realized that I would have to stay in the city for many weeks, and, frankly I did not mind that at all. Montreal has many things to offer, and I spent the next several days sightseeing.

6

Most nights I was in one of the many nightclubs in the city. At first I did not know a soul, but friends weren't difficult to make, nor were dates hard to get. I was able to do a story for the *Cleveland Press* on the terrorist activities of the Quebec Liberation Front. The terrorists were very active. I visited the family of a night watchman who had been killed by a bomb. I bought pictures of several bombing incidents from the *Montreal Star*. My editor was well pleased with what I wrote.

Ville Marie, a new forty-nine-story office complex in downtown Montreal, is one of the most beautiful buildings in the world. Guillot had gotten himself a two-room suite on the twenty-third floor. I called upon him a week after my first meeting with him. His furniture had been delivered only the day before, and he was in the process of arranging it. He was being helped by his wife—a lovely woman with dark, flashing eyes, and long hair. Guillot introduced me to her, and said: "We are very shorthanded. We had a clerk, but he has gone back to Havana. We are expecting a new one."

"Well, I could help with the typing, if you want," I replied.

"No, no, thank you. We can't let you do that," he said.

I went ahead, however, and helped him lift the desks and put the books in the shelves. I let him do all the talking. There were constant interruptions. A Canadian padre who wanted to go to Cuba came in, and there were other callers. Several times I answered the doorbell.

Toward the afternoon, I again raised the visa question. Guillot still had not asked me anything about myself. Now he wanted to know what I did for a living. I said that I was a student in Ottawa and worked at odd jobs. He questioned me no further, but repeated that I would have to apply to Havana direct for the visa. And, he said, the best way for me to expedite the procedure was to request it by reply-paid cablegram.

At this point the two separate names given me by my family came in very handy. I am Habib Akhter Shaida Ali, and I am also Mohammed A. Rauf, Jr. My passport bears both names, but I write under the second, and hardly anyone knows me by the first. I decided to use the first in my cablegram. I figured that if the Cubans had any file on me because of my byline stories (all anti-Red), it would be under the name of Rauf.

That evening I sent the following cable to Minrex, the code for the Ministry of Foreign Affairs, Havana:

Am student from India. Wish to spend summer in Cuba. Request tourist visa. Reply care Cuban consul Montreal.

Ali

And now began a long wait for an answer. I kept calling upon Guillot. I would spend long hours in his office reading Castro's speeches and other Communist literature. Several times he and I had lunch together, and several times I accompanied him on his errands. Once I went with him to the bank, and while he was cashing a check I stood at the door, eating an ice-cream cone. I must say that I found him to be a very funny man. When his wife was not with him, he was free with his comments on the girls that passed us on the street. It was a treat listening to him.

He still had not received any office help, and he and his wife were running the consulate. There was not much work to do—only a few letters and cables to answer, and some forms to fill out. Guillot was sending all the other consulates a circular letter informing them of his new address. I helped him address and lick the envelopes. There were several occasions, too, when I went to mail his letters. He was a confirmed Communist, but not of the type that considers a non-Communist worse than an insect. He spoke to me feelingly of the good things which, he said, the revolution had done for Cuba. I listened to him politely and agreed with him in every instance.

But there were several occasions when I was subjected to long questioning sessions. One afternoon I was waiting for Guillot when a Cuban walked in. I told him that Guillot would soon be back.

"I don't mind," he replied. "I'll wait."

"Here are some magazines you might want to read," I said.

He looked at me quizzically. Something in his face made me think that he was more than a casual visitor. He had such an aggressive air about him that it automatically made me put up my guard. He asked me abruptly and harshly what my name was. I told him, and I realized at the same time that it would not be well for me to ignore him or be rude to him. I noticed that he was watching me keenly, and a sixth sense told me that if I showed any signs of nervousness, I would be lost. I therefore remained very calm. When the questioning came, I was prepared for it.

Q: What are you?

A: I am a student.
Q: Where?
A: Ottawa.
Q: Where in Ottawa?
A: University of Ottawa.
Q: What do you study?
A: Economics.
Q: What is your textbook?
A: Flintstone's *Economic Theory*.
Q: Who is your professor?
A: Philip Graham.

There were more questions like those. Every one of them I answered without any hesitation or appearance that I was unsure of my answers. I must have succeeded; the man seemed satisfied with my replies. At the end of about fifteen minutes he threw a smile at me and said that he hoped I would get my visa.

"How do you know I am here for a visa?" I shot back, realizing that he had been planted upon me.

"I know. There is no other reason for you to be here," he said.

"I hope that while I am waiting for it, Señor Guillot will let me do some work for him," I said.

"Good spirit!" he said. "Everyone in Cuba works."

At this point Guillot walked in and my session with the man ended. They talked with each other in Spanish, and then the caller left. I could not even get his name.

I must say that this man was not very smart. He was absolutely naive. He tried to appear tough, but it was easy to see that he was putting on an act. He took all my answers at face value. As far as I know, no effort was made to check my veracity. For instance, a single telephone call to the University of Ottawa would have revealed the fact that the university had no student named Ali. The man quizzing me did not know that there is no person called Flintstone, author of *Economic Theory*. (The only Flintstone I know is the one who appears in a comic strip of that name.) My interrogator was unaware that Philip Graham was not the name of a professor but of the publisher of the *Washington Post*, who had recently committed suicide. I had been reading about him and I just happened to remember his name.

Three weeks passed, and still I did not receive an answer to my cablegram. I said to Guillot that I wanted to call Havana on the telephone. He thought it was a good idea and suggested that I call the visa section at the Cuban Ministry of Foreign Affairs. He did not know the name of any one person I could speak to.

The next morning at nine I went to the office of the Bell Telephone Company and asked a long-distance operator to get me Havana.

"Havana?" she asked in surprise.

"Yes," I said.

"Havana?" she repeated. "In Cuba, you mean?"

"Yes, the very same one. None other," I answered.

"Okay, mister. I don't know what you want there, but I'll try. Though you'll have to wait a long while."

She called New York. From there the call was referred to Miami, Florida, and I was told that it would be several hours before the connection to Havana could be established. I pulled up a chair, and settled down for the wait.

There were magazines to read, and there was always someone, usually of the opposite sex, to talk with. But the whole day I waited and got no connection. My operator buzzed Miami several times, but to no purpose. At five in the evening I went home disappointed but with a couple of telephone numbers of girls working in the building.

The following day, too, I showed up very early. This time I suggested to the operator that she try reaching Havana via Mexico City or Georgetown, British Guiana. The hunch paid off, and at about three in the afternoon, I got my connection.

"Hulloo," a female voice said, loud and clear.

"Is this the visa section?" I asked.

"*Sí señor.*"

I identified myself and said what I wanted.

"*Sí*, we got your cable, and . . ."

At this point something went wrong with the connection, and the rest of her sentence sounded like steam hissing from the spout of a kettle.

I hollered for the operator. Mercifully, after about fifty seconds, the line cleared.

"You understand, Señor Aalee," the woman said.

"No, I don't. I didn't follow what you said."

"I said call again tomorrow morning and talk with Señor Otero."

I asked why I couldn't talk with him at once. But the line went dead.

The next morning I called again, and this time I was able to get Havana after only one hour. The man, Otero, whoever he was, acknowledged my cablegram, and assured me that a reply would be sent to me in a week. I tried to talk more with him, but either he hung up or I was cut off.

The reply, when it was delivered to Guillot by cable five days later, was that no visa could be given me. It was curt, brief, and mentioned no reason for the refusal. Even Guillot was surprised.

I sat down and wrote Minrex a long letter of complaint. I stressed that I was a friend of the revolution, and that I was most eager to see the great works being undertaken by Castro, and that it was improper of him to deny me the visa. I urged a favorable reconsideration of my case and requested that Guillot be instructed to issue me the visa. So far, apart from the cable, I had made no written request for a visa. Guillot now had me fill out the proper form in triplicate. A snapshot of me was pasted to each copy. Two copies were sent by registered air mail to Havana. I paid for the postage, and Guillot let me personally take the envelope to the post office.

There was no point now in waiting in Montreal. I promised Guillot that I would keep in touch with him by telephone, and returned to Ottawa to see whether anything could be done there. I talked with and stood lunch to several newsmen, diplomats, and officers of the Canadian Ministry of External Affairs. But they were unable to give me any lead. I also made a regular practice of calling at the Cuban embassy. Once I did get to see the ambassador. He was polite, very nice; but he said that he was unable to do anything.

One person at the embassy with whom I was able to get along very well was a Mr. Hendershot, a Canadian, who did most of the paper work. He claimed that he was a man of power and authority. It was not my place to contradict him, but I found that the only authority he had was that he could call Guillot long-distance without getting the clearance from any superior officer. Every time he called, Guillot told him that the matter of a visa for me was still in the works and that I should not give up hope.

In Ottawa I found plenty to write about for the *Cleveland Press*. I had no difficulty getting press credentials and a pass to the Parliamentary Press Gallery. The Liberal government of Lester Pearson had just been installed, and I did several stories on it. I even managed to get an interview with Paul Martin, Minister for External Affairs, and do a long piece on him. I was given a byline for every story, and my picture appeared with most of them, but there was no way for the Cuban diplomatic staff in Canada to know of these stories. One of my stories was published in the *Washington Daily News*, another Scripps-Howard newspaper, but I was given no byline for it. I also was able to do a story for the *Ottawa Journal*, but only my initials appeared at the end of it.

One afternoon I bluntly requested Paul Martin to ask his ambassador in Havana to get in touch with the Cuban government about a visa for me. He referred my request to the head of the Cuban desk in his department, who decided that such a step would go counter to diplomatic protocol.

When I was not doing a story or scurrying around for the visa, I was out enjoying the many river beaches in Ottawa. It was fun taking a dip in the Ottawa River, sailing up the Rideau Canal, and visiting Rockcliffe Park. Many evenings I spent sitting on a bench on Parliament Hill and watching the placid flow of the river and the city lights around me as far as the eye could see. I was unsure about getting a visa, but having a girl by my side when I sat enjoying the view and the breeze always seemed to lessen the disappointment.

I kept calling Guillot on the telephone every three or four days, and I visited him every second week. We would lunch together and discuss world politics, but still I was getting nowhere nearer my visa. On several other occasions during visits to Montreal I was subjected to impromptu quizzings, always when Guillot was out. On one occasion, a rather undernourished Cuban with an oily face came in and introduced himself as Señor Rodriguez. For a while we sat facing each other. It was clear that he was trying to size me up, and I had the uncomfortable feeling that it was all very deliberate.

He asked me what I thought of the United States. I answered that it was a lousy country, and that all it wanted to do was to put the whole world into some kind of economic noose. I was asked whether I had ever been in the United States. I answered that I had gone there as a student, but that what I saw of life in that country disgusted me. I was asked my opinion of the Bay of Pigs invasion. I said that it was dollar diplomacy in action, and that if Cuba were to be invaded again, I would join the Cuban army to help repel the invaders.

Very soon I lost my dread of my various interrogators and began to enjoy them. No Cuban officer was ever smart enough to leaf through my passport and check my entry stamp into Canada, which clearly showed that I had only recently left the United States. Frankly, these Cubans reminded me of small-time juvenile delinquents playing Lavrenti Beria.

Otero never wrote me directly, but I kept dropping him pleading letters. Twice I cabled for a reconsideration of my request, and twice more I called Havana on the telephone. Once I got the connection, but there was no one available who could speak English. The second time, a girl assured me that she would convey my request to Otero, who was on a tour with Fidel Castro. But I was getting a bit fed up with all this and was losing hope.

I had come to Ottawa in mid-May, and now it was July and I had nothing to show for my efforts.

July was ending when I traveled to Toronto to urge the Cuban consul there to take an interest in my case, because by now I was sure that Guillot, although he had the rank of consul, was just a glorified stamp clerk of the Cuban government in Havana. The Cuban consulate in Toronto was near the City Hall, not far from a burlesque theatre. It was on the third floor of a dilapidated building. I called at ten in the morning, and no one was there. The place was locked. I called at twelve. It was still locked. I called at two and this time the door was opened by a very thin man of about twenty-five, who had a sly, furtive look on his face. I recalled that face; I had seen it a few times in Guillot's office. On no occasion had I been introduced to the man.

He showed me into a dingy, stuffy office. He was the only occupant. I explained my case to him, and he subjected me to a lot of quizzing, along the pattern with which I had become so familiar. He asked the same questions, though he was a bit harsh in his manner, and I gave him the same answers. He called Guillot on the telephone, and was told that I should not become impatient.

I was now almost sure that I had run into a dead end. I was told by the head office that if nothing happened in three more weeks, I should give up the idea of going to Cuba and return to Cleveland.

Early in August I visited Toronto again, and from there made yet another telephone call to Otero. This time, something happened; something totally unexpected. My heart actually skipped a beat when I heard a woman's voice say that my visa application had been sanctioned and that I was to pick up the visa from Guillot.

I lost no time in flying back to Montreal. Guillot had gone home. I called him there, but he was out. I kept calling until ten at night. Finally, when I was able to talk with him, he said that he had received a letter sanctioning the visa, and that he would give it to me in the morning.

I was up most of that night. I didn't go out anywhere, but I just couldn't sleep. At eleven the next morning, Guillot put the visa stamp on my passport. He charged me a four-dollar fee. One big hurdle was now crossed. The other one—that of finding a plane to fly me to Havana—loomed ahead.

2. To Havana—via Madrid

THE office of the Sabena Airlines in Montreal is located in the same building as the Cuban consulate. The day after I got my visa, I went there to buy my tickets to Havana. I had no difficulty. A very pretty clerk put all my tickets in a folder, handed them to me, and said: "Here you are, Mr. Ali. You are now all set for your trip. Tomorrow, Sabena flies you to New York. At Idlewild you catch a Mexican Airlines plane to Mexico City, spend twelve hours at the airport there, and then board a Cubana Airlines flight to Havana. That will be twelve hundred dollars and thirty cents round trip, please." I paid the money.

"How about my stay at Mexico City airport?" I asked. "Will I need a transit visa for it?"

"If you don't leave the airport, no," she answered. "We have checked with the Mexican consulate here. They told us that if you don't stay more than twenty-four hours, don't leave the airport, and if you have a ticket on a connecting flight, you don't need any visa."

"Is that true for all nationalities?" I asked, remembering my last encounter with the Mexicans.

"Why, of course. Your worries are now over, Mr. Ali," she said, flashing a bright smile.

The next day, about two o'clock in the afternoon, I landed at Idlewild, and took the terminal bus to the Mexican Airlines counter. A woman clerk examined my tickets, checked my bag, and put it on the conveyor belt. Just as she was about to issue my boarding pass, the manager of the counter appeared from an inner office and stopped her from doing so.

"Do you have a transit visa for Mexico?" he asked. I said no. He said he could not board me, because I was Cuba-bound, and so I had to have the transit visa. "The Cuban planes are never on time," he said.

"Sometimes they are several days late. If this happens, you will be stranded in Mexico City."

I informed him of what the Mexican consulate in Montreal had said about my not requiring a visa. But he refused to budge and said with infuriating hauteur: "Go back to Montreal and tell them at the consulate that they should read the rules more carefully."

I tried to switch my ticket to another airline that had a flight that evening for Mexico. Again I was refused. I was left with no alternative but to fly back to Montreal. I arrived there well after midnight, weary and exasperated. I was immediately accosted by officers of the Canadian Immigration department. They had been informed by the Mexican Airlines in New York that I was trying to board their plane illegally. It took me an hour to explain my position. By the time the airport limousine dropped me at the YMCA, I was more tired than I had ever been in my life.

The next morning I stormed into the Sabena office, all set to chew everybody's head off. I was referred to the Mexican consulate, where I was received by an elderly man who repeated to me what had been told to Sabena. I related my experience in New York. The man shook his head resignedly, and said: "Well, if our airline says so, it must be so."

I realized that nothing would be gained by losing my temper, but I lost it, anyway. The man heard me out politely, and said: "If you can wait about two months, we think we can get you a visa." Stupidity such as this, I decided, was surely genius in reverse. In spite of myself and everything, I laughed.

I retrieved my money from Sabena, and returned to Ottawa to see what could be done there. A friend told me to try the Trans-Canada Airlines. Attendants there said they could fly me directly to Mexico City and arrange a twenty-four-hour stop for me, because, they said, they had the authority to issue stay permits for the airport to their passengers who had tickets on a connecting flight. I bought the tickets.

But when I arrived in Montreal to board the flight to Mexico, once more I was turned back. A clerk said that the airline had been deprived of its authority to issue stay permits to passengers whose ultimate destination was Cuba.

Once more it seemed to me that I had run into a blank wall of red tape, regulations, counterregulations. I called Washington, and once more it was hinted that I should go back to Cleveland. I begged that

I might be allowed to try for three more weeks. I was determined to follow every avenue.

For instance, I learned that two Cuban planes, carrying medicine, flew every week from Toronto. I failed to get passage on any of them. I learned of a weekly KLM flight from Paramaribo, Dutch Guiana, to Havana. KLM in Montreal did their best to get me on it but were told that it was for diplomats only. I thought of making the trip by sea. From Thomas Cook & Son I learned that there were no passenger ships going to Havana from any port in the world, but that with luck I might secure passage on a freighter.

For the next two days I wore my legs out going from dock to dock in Montreal looking for such a freighter. I spent two evenings at the Sailors' Club hobnobbing with men familiar with the Caribbean. I hoped they would suggest something. I bought them many, many rounds of beer, picked up a lot of seamen's lingo, but got no new leads.

My wanderings in the dock area, however, brought me to the office of Montreal's harbor master, Captain R. J. Ligtermoot. I explained my case to him and asked for his help. He traced for me two freighters, the *Camagüey* and the *Bahia Santiago,* of the Cuban Lineas Mambisas, both due to sail that month from Quebec to Havana. Consul Guillot, though, refused to give me passage on either of them. He suggested that I could apply to Havana, but warned that I would have to wait a long while for an answer. It was with a sickening feeling that I left his office. The list of avenues I could explore was getting shorter, and the three-week grace I had been allowed by Scripps-Howard was ending.

One evening I had a date with a friend I had made in Montreal, Jacqueline Murdoch, who worked at the Reddy Memorial Hospital. I was waiting in her apartment for her to get ready, when I happened to pick up an atlas that was lying on a table. I casually opened it and found myself looking at a map of the Atlantic Ocean. Naturally, Cuba was the first place I picked out in the map. As I was staring at it, I noticed how very close Haiti was to Cuba. At once, the idea came to me to fly to Port-au-Prince, the capital of Haiti, and take my chance on a fishing boat or trawler from there to the Cuban port of Santiago de Cuba, about fifty miles away.

I returned to Ottawa and obtained a Haitian visa. The Haitian chargé d'affaires, Mussez Pierre-Jerome, assured me that there were excellent chances that I could find such a boat or charter one for a small amount.

But an experienced officer in the Canadian Ministry of External Affairs warned me that even if I found the boat—and it was by no means certain that I would, he said—the chances were that I would be arrested by the Cubans as a CIA agent or that Cuban gunboats would blow my vessel out of existence.

I inquired about freighters from Kingston, Jamaica, which is also not far from Cuba. I was told by the British High Commission that no contact by sea existed between the two islands. Then I learned from shipping circles that if I could get to British Guiana, I would be able to find a freighter there, because Fidel Castro and Cheddi Jagan, the prime minister of British Guiana, were close friends, and there was regular trade between the two nations. High Commissioner R. S. S. Gunewardene of Ceylon, whom I knew very well from Washington, gave me a warm letter of introduction to Jagan. But Scripps-Howard vetoed the trip because of the element of chance in it.

Now I had only ten days left of the time-extension given me by Scripps-Howard. I toyed with the idea of taking my annual vacation and spending it in a continued search for a passage to Cuba. But there seemed to be no more routes I could aim for. Unless, of course, I could come up with something really unorthodox.

I learned that the Czech Airlines and the Russian Aeroflot had service to Havana from Prague and Moscow respectively, but, first, one had to get to these cities. This I did not try to do. I learned, however, that Czech planes had refuelling rights in Gander, Newfoundland, and were allowed to pick up passengers there under very special circumstances. A permit from the Canadian government was required for it. I tried to obtain such a permit but could not.

I also learned that the Spanish Iberia Airline flew one plane a week from Madrid to Havana. It was the only free-world airline still going to Cuba. I made up my mind to travel to Madrid and catch this plane, even though the cost for the round-trip was $1600. I informed Scripps-Howard of my decision and asked for more money. I got in touch with American Express in Montreal, and told them to make all the bookings for me for the evening of August 16. All my tickets were made out, and all day on August 16 I waited for the money.

At 4:00 P.M. I got another big jolt in the form of a telegram from Scripps-Howard, saying that it had canceled the whole project and that I was to go back to Cleveland without any more delay. To say that I was disappointed would be an understatement. I stalled on returning to Cleveland, and, since Richert was on vacation, I wrote to Walker Stone, the editor-in-chief:

> It is true that I am suggesting a very unorthodox route to go to Cuba. But it is no more unorthodox than Lenin's assertion that the quickest road between Moscow and Paris is via Peiping.
>
> It is true that sending me via Spain would cost you a lot of money. But this reminds me of the occasion when that famous reporter Richard Harding Davis was in Florence, in 1896, and James Gordon Bennett [of the old *Herald*] wired him to cover the coronation of Czar Nicholas II, and Davis wired back: "They don't run penny buses to Moscow."

After having dispatched the letter, I called Scripps-Howard on the telephone and said that it should send me the money and deduct it in installments from my weekly paychecks.

This open defiance could have led to my dismissal. For six days I waited for an answer. I didn't really know what to expect. The answer could be anything. But when it came, it was that Stone had given in to my entreaties and that the money was being forwarded to me.

I lost no time in having American Express get busy with making the bookings for me all over again. This time they arranged for me to fly from Montreal to Paris, change planes there for Madrid, stay in Madrid for three days, and fly to Havana via Santa Maria, in the Azores, and Bermuda. I liked the arrangement, because it would enable me to see a bit of Spain, a country I had always wanted to visit. Paris, I did not much care for.

But did that mean an end to my travel problems? Not quite. Something unexpected happened. It had to do with the plane's stop in the Azores. This group of islands lies some hundreds of miles from Europe in the mid-Atlantic Ocean. The islands are owned by Portugal. The Iberia Airline had no office in Montreal, and booking on the plane to Havana was made by American Express through the Iberia office in New York. I called the Iberia office manager in New York to double-check my reservation, and he raised a new problem.

He said that although I did not need a visa to fly through Santa Maria, I might have trouble with the Portuguese authorities there because of my Indian nationality. He said that this could happen because the Portuguese were still angry at the attack by India upon Goa. That tiny Indian territory was formerly Portuguese. In 1961, Indian troops marched into it and took it. Since then the relations between the two countries have been bad, and Indians are denied entry to Portuguese possessions. The manager said that he would not allow me to board until I had something in writing from the Portuguese consul in Montreal authorizing my passage through the Azores.

I called upon the Portuguese Consul, Fernando M. Silva Marques. He was very nice and very polite to me. He said that I did not need a transit visa, but that he was willing to give me one if I could wait a fortnight for it. I said that I did not have the time and suggested that I write him a letter explaining my problem. He could then write me a reply that no transit visa was required if I stayed within the airport. He agreed with the suggestion. I borrowed writing paper from him, wrote my letter, and he immediately dictated the appropriate reply to his secretary. I read the reply over the telephone to the Iberia manager in New York, and he was satisfied.

Now, at last, my travel problems were over. Now, at last, all the hurdles were crossed, and I was free to fly out of Montreal to Europe.

At this point, I should pause to let the reader know something about the luggage that I had selected for myself, and the precautions I had taken in this matter. Securing the visa and the airplane reservation were just the beginning. The real assignment was to come now.

I had been preparing for my trip by discarding everything bearing a "Made in U.S.A." label. I had bought four Canadian shirts, two pairs of slacks, and one full suit, and had been wearing them to rid them of their newness. But I took care that the "Made in Canada" label stayed on each item. It was the same with everything else I carried. My ball-point pen was Canadian; so were my shaving things, and my writing pad bore the words, on the flyleaf, "Printed in Canada." I also bought a Canadian trip diary. On the address pages I wrote in just the friends I had made in Canada. I arranged with some of them to forward mail from me to Richert.

My whole point in taking these precautions was that I wanted it to appear that I had no associations with the United States. European journalists who had visited Cuba reported that anyone coming from or having anything to do with the U.S. was automatically a suspect.

As yet another safety measure, I changed all my American dollars into Canadian dollars, although I had to take a beating in the exchange rate. I decided to carry only $500 with me.

I also bought a copy of Marx's *Das Kapital* and a few other books on Communism. I wrote my name in each, underlined various passages at random, deliberately broke the binding of one, and spilled coffee on another. The idea was to make it appear that the books had been read— and enjoyed. These I placed on top of all my things in my one suitcase. My friends had suggested that I grow a beard, but that I refused to do.

I knew full well what would happen if the Cubans discovered that I was a reporter for American papers disguised as a tourist. I would be arrested immediately. I would have no friends, no acquaintances, nothing to fall back upon. The Cubans would, of course, make a big play of my arrest, and no doubt Scripps-Howard would set into motion powerful diplomatic forces to get me free, but still many weeks would elapse before I would be released.

I did not know any Spanish, nor did I try during my stay in Canada to learn any. I was told that half the people in Cuba knew English, so I would have no language problems. But I still bought myself a Berlitz phrase book in Spanish. It was printed in the U.S., but it bore the stamp of a bookshop in Ottawa.

On August 26, when the plane left Montreal for Madrid, I had trouble convincing myself that I was actually aboard it. There had been too many setbacks, too many failures. The fact that all the difficulties were finally overcome was almost unbelievable.

I was in Madrid until August 31. I was to leave for Havana at six o'clock that evening, but there was a delay of five hours, and at one point it appeared that the flight would be canceled.

When all Havana-bound passengers assembled in a ramp to board the plane, I found that there were only eleven of us. Included were a British woman and her two children, who were going only as far as Bermuda. There was a Barcelona businessman, two Roman Catholic priests, and some minor Cuban officials returning home from Spain. We were a sad lot. There was hardly any conversation. The empty seats were piled with crates of medicine and other vital items meant for Cuba.

We landed in Santa Maria at 2:00 A.M. An armed guard was waiting for us. This was because we were Cuba-bound. The company commander issued us landing permits, and his men escorted us to the airport restaurant. They stayed with us during the 45-minute stop. We weren't allowed to wander out of the restaurant building. Next day, a Saturday, at 10:00 A.M., we stopped in Bermuda for an hour.

At 2:00 P.M. I looked down and found myself gazing upon the green fields and the blue waters of Cuba. From up above, everything looked peaceful, and quiet. Small cars plied the roads. I spotted men on bicycles. In another twenty minutes we had landed at Havana's José Martí airport.

3. My Passport Is Taken Away

THE sun shone brilliantly over the airport as I deplaned. It was reflected off the gleaming surface of a huge Russian airliner that occupied one full corner of the airport, making the other planes appear very small. It fell upon a group of some two hundred people cheering at us from an airport roof. It lighted the bold lettering of a sign which read: "Free Cuba Welcomes You." It blazoned a huge drawing of a Cuban warrior in battle dress advancing to attack. Under him were the words: "Cuba—the Free Territory of Latin America."

I noticed that most of the airport equipment in use was American. There were TWA ladders, Pan-Am motor washers and scrubbers, and TWA airport mats with "Welcome" upon them.

Escorted by khaki-clad, grim-looking guards, we entered a waiting room. It was bare of furniture except for one table, at which sat a middle-aged man smoking a cigar. He carefully checked our health certificates.

I was not wearing my full Indian dress, but had on my Indian *toppee*. This was making me an object of curiosity, but I did not take it off. There was no air-conditioning at the airport, and the humidity was very high. I took off my tie and put it in my coat pocket.

Our next stop was before a tall counter behind which sat a man in an open-neck bush shirt. An armed guard was by his side. I was the last in the line, and as he went through my passport he asked me, in English, the purpose of my visit. I said that I was a tourist. The guard heard me, and exclaimed in absolute disbelief: *"Jesu! Turista."*

The man questioning me showed no emotion. He was icily cold as he asked me what towns I would visit, where I would stay, and what exactly would be my program. I said that my program would depend upon the tourist office, and—

At that moment, a Cuban woman wearing a skin-tight dress went wiggling by. I deliberately stopped in the midst of my sentence to turn my head and ogle her, and then winked at the guard. He was not prepared for anything like this and was caught off balance. But the faintest trace of a smile appeared on his face. When the woman passed through a door, I redirected my attention to the clerk and asked him to repeat his question, which he did—not impatiently, but rather tolerantly.

"Oh, yes, I will go where the tourist office takes me," I said. "I would love to visit the beaches and your nightclubs." Then, changing my tone to one of eagerness, I asked, "Say, do you still have stripteases here?"

"We have no striptease anymore," he replied somewhat stiffly, as if the question had jarred him. But he became less rigid in his questioning and after a time he told me to proceed to Customs.

I tried to lift my passport from the counter, but he would not let me have it. "We are going to keep it for now," he said. "You can go to Immigration in two days and get it back."

"How about a receipt for it?" I asked.

"No, you will get no receipt. Don't you trust us?" he said with some sarcasm, and handed me a slip of paper bearing the address of the Immigration Department.

I realized that I was in no position to argue, and left him.

My suitcase had arrived at Customs. It was examined by a rather effusive woman officer. She was obviously impressed by the books on Communism that lay on top of my clothes.

"Ah . . . stoodent?" she asked.

I nodded.

"My son also stoodent. Habana University. Engineering. Someday build bridges."

She talked incessantly as she searched my suitcase. I was carrying an electric iron. She took it out reverently and said: "Very good. Press clothes. Ah-ha, I know."

I also had a light rubber raincoat, the kind that can be had for $2.95.

"American?" she asked.

"No, German."

"No raincoat here. Can't buy anymore."

"Why?" I asked.

"Because of them crazy Americans. They stop everything."

When the search was over I was directed to a money counter. I was asked how much money I had and was told that if I had any American dollars I would have to change them to Cuban pesos. I was assured that when I left, the pesos could be exchanged for dollars. When I said that I had only Canadian money, I was told that I did not have to exchange all of it into pesos, but only as much as I wanted. I changed fifty Canadian dollars at the rate of eighty-two centimes for one dollar. I had some Spanish money, and tried to get it changed, too, but the Cubans would not touch it.

I was told that since I was a tourist the law required that I spend at least ten dollars a day. All the cash I had was noted on a form, and I was told that the next time I changed my money I was to get the amount mentioned on the form so that a tally could be made on whether I had been spending ten dollars a day.

I was asked to declare whether I had a watch, a camera, or any gold ornament. I had none of these things. If a visitor loses any one of these things, and does not report the loss to the authorities, he is liable to get into trouble, because the government can charge him with having sold it in the black market. When he is leaving, he is required to declare that he still has all the valuables he came with. If he gives anything away, he must give the name of the recipient.

When all the formalities were over I went looking for a restaurant. The airport restaurant was closed, but a food counter, serving only coffee, was open. The brew, black as coal and very hot, was brought to me in a small toy cup. A glass of cold water was served with it. A man sitting next to me told me that the ritual was first to drink the water, then empty the cup in one swig.

"In that way, it can't hurt you. Otherwise it can be bad for your stomach," he said.

"How about some milk, and a bigger cup?"

"Milk, my friend, you don't get here. And a bigger cup is unnecessary. One small cup is enough. It has the same energy as one big cup in . . ."

He looked at me, expecting me to complete the sentence and tell him where I was from.

"Canada," I said.

"But your cap? Canadian?"

"No, Indian."

"So, why Canada?"

"I go to school there."

Mercifully, he did not prod me further.

I drank the coffee as told. It really was strong and bitter. Its price: three centimes. But it was invigorating. I wanted a second cup, but was warned by the man next to me .that that would be bad for the stomach.

An adjacent gift shop was selling 1956 Havana guidebooks.

"But how about a *new* guidebook?" I asked the woman attendant. "This one is seven years old."

"That is unimportant," she replied. "Havana is still the same." I had the feeling that she actually believed what she was saying.

I found the airport a very inactive place. There were dozens of gun-carrying guards, but no work was being done anywhere. I learned that some of the persons I had heard cheering when I landed were those due to leave for Spain when my plane took off.

The counters of Lufthansa, KLM, Sabena, TWA, BOAC, and other airlines were still there, but they had been boarded up and were gathering dust. Before the revolution, a plane used to land or take off from Havana airport every five minutes. Now, only about half-a-dozen planes land every week.

There were no buses running to the city. A guard directed me to a taxi, whose driver was the most inquisitive I have ever met. I sat in the front seat with him, and the moment he started the engine he began asking me, in perfect English, all kinds of questions about my political views.

It took me only a few minutes to realize that the probe was deliberate. It was meant to be casual, but the man was being very obvious about it. I praised the revolution, but kept mentioning women and nightclubs and such things in all my answers. I think I succeeded very well in creating the impression that I was only a fun-seeking tourist.

I strengthened the impression when he took me to the Hotel Nacional and I tipped him one dollar in addition to the five-dollar fare. Tipping in Red Cuba has almost gone out of fashion.

I knew that this hotel was the third best in the city. Persons who had visited Cuba before the revolution had spoken of its elegance, cuisine, and roulette wheel. I didn't want to stay there, because my assignment was to find out how the people lived, and that could best be done by staying in a cheap hotel.

But I went to the Nacional lobby, anyway, and was surprised to learn that the rates were only eight dollars a day. I was told that the hotel, like everything else, had been nationalized, and that the government had cut the rates. But when I asked for a room, the clerk wanted to know whether I was visiting Cuba in any official capacity. When I said no, I was told that there was no vacancy. It was suggested that I walk over to the Hotel Capri across the street. There, too, the same question was asked me and I was unable to get a room.

These hotels were in the Vedado, a semifashionable sector of Havana. I found an English-speaking cabdriver and asked him to take me to an inexpensive hotel in the downtown section. He took me to a place called Hotel Roosevelt. It surprised me that the name had not been changed. Since it, too, was full, I walked to another hotel nearby, the Hotel Lincoln. Then I walked to a third, and to a fourth. All were full.

At last I came to Hotel Royal Palm on a narrow, crowded street near the Capitol. The seven-story building undoubtedly had seen better days, but now it was badly in need of repairs and paint.

The large lobby was full; men and women sat, silent or listening to a radio. There was a TV in one corner, but nobody had turned it on. I learned later that few watch the shows. Their standard has fallen, and they contain a heavy dose of propaganda. The walls were plastered with flags and pictures of Castro giving a speech, or leading a band of fighters. There were placards containing quotes from his or Khrushchev's speeches or from the works of Lenin and Marx.

I was able to get a room in this hotel for $3.60 a day. The manager, who had lived in the U.S., filled out a long form about me, and I saw him putting it away in a box. I learned that at the end of the day all papers in that box were carried to the police station in the area.

My room was modest in size, furnished with an old, creaky bed, a dressing table, a wardrobe, and a chair. It had just one dim light, in the ceiling. A paper pasted on the wall announced that guests were not allowed to use electric fans or irons.

The linen was clean but smelled foul. This was because good soap was unavailable, and even water for washing purposes was not always plentiful. In the bathroom I found that the flush sometimes didn't work, but both shower and bathtub facilities were available. I could hear the din of traffic from the street below and could even smell the exhaust fumes of the buses.

From the window I could look inside the apartments on the opposite side of the street. Because of the heat, nobody bothered to close the windows. I opened my window and found myself witnessing a kissing scene in a rather advanced stage in the apartment opposite my room.

After a quick shower I went for my first real look at Havana. I spent three hours, well past sunset, just walking up and down the streets to get the feel of the place. I did not have a map with me and at times thought I was lost.

I was wearing Western clothes, and had left my Indian cap behind. Those who know me say that I look very much like a Mexican, and it must be true, for nowhere did I excite any curiosity. I had the pleasant feeling that I had blended myself with the people, had become just another *habanero*.

My first shock came when I stopped at a Sears Roebuck store to buy toothpaste, which I had forgotten to bring. A placard on top of the signboard proudly proclaimed that the store had been nationalized. The wooden E from Roebuck in the signboard had fallen off and had not been replaced. But what shocked me was the fact that toothpaste was rationed. A clerk asked me to produce my ration book. When I said I had none, I was told to get one. When I said I was a tourist, I was advised that the tourist office would be able to get me a permit.

"How many days will it take?" I asked.

"About four, I think," he replied.

"And will you give me the toothpaste then?"

"Not then. Ten days from today. That is when we get our supplies."

"Do you make toothpaste in this country?" I asked.

"Not anymore. The Americans have cut off the chemicals. Now the People's Republic of China is supplying it to us."

"Oh, you mean Red China."

I should not have used that name when talking with a Communist bureaucrat. They don't like it. The man glared at me and said, "What are you? An Imperialist?"

I wanted to reply to him, but I was determined not to enter into any arguments. "I'm sorry," I said meekly. "I should have said Socialist China."

"There is only one China. The other is only an American state."

"Yes, yes, of course," I agreed.

The store had few things to sell, and most of the shelves were empty. I thought of asking why, but decided against it.

I had difficulty finding a place to eat. The time was now eight o'clock. I went to a restaurant and was told that all food had been sold.

The only thing left was some sort of soup. I ordered some but didn't touch it because it had pieces of pork in it, and it's against my religion to eat pork.

I went to another restaurant. All it had were some hard rolls and mango juice. I learned that if you want to eat out you must arrive at a restaurant no later than seven in the evening. In a dark, smelly alley I found an Arab restaurant. It was small, but clean, and I had a dinner of lamb curry for four dollars. I remembered having a similar dinner in Port Said for sixty cents. The owner told me that he had come to Cuba from Lebanon fifteen years ago and had become a citizen. His wife and mother did the cooking. His restaurant was one of the few not nationalized.

By now I had had enough for one day. I returned to my hotel, hot and sweaty after the long walk. I decided to have another shower. When I discovered there was no water in the tap, I called the manager, who said he would send some right away. What I got was just a jug of ice water.

T 4. An Encounter with Russians

HERE was still no water in the tap in the morning. I asked an attendant where I could take a bath. His reply was: "The ocean is very near. If you want a bath, go to the ocean." I was supplied with a cake of soap. It was not sweet-smelling, but at least it lathered, and I used it to clean my teeth also.

I learned that water was cut off in the downtown area on Saturday nights and Sundays, because the pumping station was not running at full capacity. Its machinery was worn out, and replacements were hard to get.

When I left my hotel for the day, the first thing I saw was a government truck distributing water to the people. Women and children were crowded around it with buckets and canisters. Persons too old to come to the truck would hire a Negro or street urchin to fetch water for them, usually for five cents a bucket. It was one of the few forms of private enterprise still open in Cuba. A family could take as much water as its containers would hold. A militiaman was supervising the distribution, and it was obvious that he lived in the area, for he knew everyone that came near the truck.

Wanting to taste the water, I went to a woman and made a sign to her. She gave me a drink in an empty cigarette tin. The water was very brackish.

My first concern was to get some breakfast. I went to several restaurants. Nowhere could I find eggs, milk, toast, or butter. All these things were rationed. The only thing available was the toy cup of coffee and cans and cans of mango juice at twenty-five cents a can. The juice was locally produced and processed. The cans were small and I drank four of them.

In Montreal I had been told by Guillot that in Havana I should report to the Cuban Institute of Friendship for the Peoples—or ICAP, as it was commonly known. A branch was located at the Hotel Riviera, and I took a cab to it. The man in charge asked me whether I was a government guest. I said no, and he told me that he could not do anything about arranging sightseeing for me.

"But señor, I have come here to see the progress made under Castro," I protested in mock chagrin. "I don't know where to go, what to do."

"You go to INIT and they will take care of you," he said. "INIT" are the initials of the National Tourist Institute. When Castro took over, one of the first things to be nationalized was the tourist industry.

I had risen that morning with a bad headache. I had hoped that the morning air would cure it, but it hadn't. When I asked where I could buy aspirin, the man gave me two from a bottle in his desk. Cuban men seemed to have a habit of carrying aspirin.

I asked where I could get a decent breakfast, and was directed to a lunch counter at the hotel. There I had two eggs, one small piece of bread, and one real cup of coffee with condensed milk in it, all for $1.20. That was the only time I was to have eggs in Cuba. At the Hotel Riveria every kind of food was available, because the place was occupied mostly by visiting foreigners, and the government did everything to create a good impression regarding the prosperity of the country. I asked the waiter for sightseeing suggestions. He said I could go visit Miramar beach, and in the muggy weather that seemed to be a good idea.

The beach included a very large recreation center. It used to be an exclusive club before the revolution, but now it had been nationalized and declared open to all. The entrance fee was twenty-five cents, but when the guards learned that I was a tourist, they let me go in free. The place was crowded. Men, women, and children were there by the hundreds, splashing about in the water or lying in the sun. The children played in the sand, but few had toy buckets and spades; they were using small wooden boards to pile up the sand for their castles.

Lockers were free. I found an empty one, changed into a bathing suit, and set out for a stroll. As I walked among the people, a wonderful feeling of relaxation began to steal over me. The events and anxieties of the past three weeks had left me exhausted. The beach did much to soothe my nerves. The sun was brilliant; the breeze sweetly cool. I was looking for a quiet spot where I could do some swimming and lie by myself in the sun. It did not take me long to find such a spot. It was at the far end of the beach. No one seemed to be about. I swam for a while, then I lay down on the sand and fell asleep.

I don't know how long I slept. Maybe an hour, or less. But I was awakened by men and women coming into my part of the beach and engaging in the usual beach games. I opened my eyes, and saw that all of the newcomers were Russian. I realized that I was in a portion of the beach reserved for them. Later on, I was to discover that all beaches and restaurants have sections set aside for the Russians. They seldom fraternize with the Cubans.

There were about fifty Russians at Miramar beach that morning. Most of the men were tall and well built, with blond hair and blue eyes. Also, most were in their late twenties. Some had skin-diving equipment with them. Quite a few of them had cameras around their necks. The women were young, too; most of them were wearing one-piece swimming suits, but a few were in bikinis. All looked trim and athletic. Very few women got into the water. Most of them only joined the beach games or lay in the sun. It was tantalizing to see them run to catch a ball, as their russet brown or chestnut hair blew behind them in the breeze, or got into their eyes, causing them to pause to throw it back. Laughing, chatting aloud in their native language, spraying each other with water, they were a gay relaxed group. As some of them ran past me, their faces showed that they were surprised to see me sitting on the sand, watching them closely, but they did not bother me.

When a beach ball came bouncing my way, I caught it and tossed it back. A man, who mistook me for a Cuban, shouted *"Gracias"* over the noise of the surf, and ran away. I ran after him. He was one of a group of four men and three women who were tossing the ball back and forth. I got into the circle and waited for the ball to be thrown to me. I was ignored. Once when it came my way I sought to catch it, but a young Russian caught it first. The whole group then moved away a few yards, without anyone's saying a word. I didn't let the snub bother me but went looking for other Russians I might talk with.

Some distance away I found three men who were taking pictures of each other. I asked whether any of them knew English. When one of them said he did, I extended my hand to him.

"Glad to meet you," I said. "I am from India."

"What are you doing here?" he asked, with more bluntness than could be considered idle curiosity.

"I am a tourist," I replied, ignoring his crudity.

"Tourist!" he replied, wrinkling his brow. "Tourist from India?" he asked in absolute disbelief.

"From India," I assured him. Then posing dumbness, I asked, "Are you a Bulgarian?"

"No!" he shouted in real astonishment as he gave me a hearty slap on the back. "I am from Russia. From Roos, as you say in India. I was there once." He repeated in Russian my question to his friends, and they all burst out laughing.

"Are the three of you students?" I asked, still appearing very dumb and wide-eyed.

"Are you one?" he countered, without saying yes or no.

"Yes," I said.

"Where?"

"I study in Canada and I am here for my vacation."

"I see you have been in Canada very long," he said. "You say 'vacation' instead of 'holiday.' Only in America and Canada do they say 'vacation.'"

I was surprised, and somewhat uncomfortable, at the man's alertness.

"Yes, I have been there several years," I answered, appearing as casual as I could.

"How do you like it?"

"I don't."

"Then why don't you leave?"

"I will be leaving soon. I want to study in Cuba."

I don't know what made me say the last sentence. It came out without any prior thought, and I was gratified that it created a good impression.

"What do you want to study?"

"Economics. Do you study economics?"

"No, I am a technician."

"What kind of technician?"

"You are too inquisitive, my friend. Come let me take your picture."

I posed for him, shaking hands with one of his friends. He wanted to know my name and where I was staying. I told him, and asked him his name.

"Yuri Gagarin," he replied. At this, the other two Russians laughed

33

and he laughed, and, seemingly overjoyed with the joke, they skipped away from me.

I walked to the areas of the beach where the Cubans were. The crowd had grown. But I noticed one big difference: things such as potato chips, pretzels, popcorn, beer, ice-cream cones, and popsicles were not in evidence. Also, nobody had a transistor radio. You can't buy one in modern Cuba, and even if you have an old one lying around somewhere in the house, you can't get a battery for it.

I noticed that most of the men and women were wearing homemade bathing suits. Factory-made bathing suits are scarce, and so are towels. Few bathers had any with them. They just dried themselves in the sun. Sunglasses were also rare. They were badly needed, because the glare was strong, but they just weren't available. Many women who wanted to take a dip were hesitant about it because they didn't have bathing caps.

I also noticed that men and women, although they swam together, didn't cuddle or hug as they might, say, at Coney Island in New York. I was to learn that such public demonstrations of affection were frowned upon in revolutionary Cuba as a decadent, bourgeois practice. This was the line that was given me, in later conversations, by ardent followers of Fidel Castro. "Time for love will be when the socialist revolution is complete. Today we have no time for love," one of them told me. But this did not mean, as I was also to learn later, that love has gone out of fashion in Cuba.

Music was being blared over a public-address system. Once I recognized a melody from *The King and I*, but the other tunes were new to me. They were interspersed with announcements on the "achievements" of the revolution. Most of these were in Spanish, but one in English that I remember said:

"We have wiped out illiteracy. We have built seventy-five thousand new homes. Our army is strong enough to resist any invasion. We cannot be subdued. Our people are united. . . . "

The food at the beach restaurant was good, though expensive. I had a steak lunch which cost $2.50. A roll, a piece of avocado, and the usual toy cup of coffee were served with the meat. Since the restaurant was state-owned, I wondered who got the profit. Under private enterprise, any restaurant charging that price would be out of business in no time.

I was impressed by the facilities available for physical exercise, though a lot of the equipment was improvised. For instance, bamboo poles had been set in the ground, and ropes hung from them. Young men were swinging, Tarzan-like, from pole to pole. As I watched, one of them even let out a Tarzan yell, but he was stopped.

I tried swinging from one pole, but I could not catch the rope on the other pole and, to the loud laughter of the watchers, I fell sideways on the sand. I tried several more times, and in the end was able to swing across three poles. But it was tiring, and when skin began to peel off my palms and knees, I gave up. There were other, less taxing, pastimes. Mud dunes had been erected and a very low tunnel connected one to the other. The trick was to run through the tunnel in record time.

These exercises, excellent for body-building, were very popular with Cuban youths. They were a part of an organized drive by the government to make the young healthy and strong—even those who were not in the army or the militia. Heard very frequently was a saying by Castro: "If you are a scientist or a mathematician, that doesn't mean that you should have a weak body. If our island is attacked, everyone, soldiers and scientists, will be required to get into the field to fight the enemy."

There was an amusement park attached to the beach, and I went to it about four o'clock in the afternoon. People were just beginning to come into it. It had the usual rides, but its roller coaster had broken down. From the looks of it, it appeared that it had been out of commission several years. I inquired and found that the park had been built before the revolution.

Mango juice and cane juice were the only drinks available. A small machine crushes the cane before your eyes, and as the juice flows from the spout it is caught in an empty jam jar and served at twenty-five cents a jar. There is a terrible waste of tin cans. Mango juice and orange juice are sold in these cans, and the empties are just thrown away. Thousands and thousands of them go into the garbage every day in Havana.

There were shooting galleries in the park but no gambling booths. I had just finished a ride in a miniature train when Havana was hit by a freak rainstorm, one of those wild, furious deluges that burst without warning. A clear sky suddenly becomes clouded and the rain begins to pour. This storm lasted twenty minutes, during which I found cover in a children's pavilion. A family there had arranged a party for a five-year-old child, and toy hats were being given to all the little guests.

There were balloons and streamers, and the balloons had revolutionary slogans written upon them.

Although there were dozens of militiamen on the beach and in the park, I did not take much notice of them until one came up to the bench on which I was half lying down and asked me to remove my legs from it. When I did, he patted me on the back. Later I saw another militiaman chastising someone for having spit on the ground. The militiamen were dressed in khaki and carried rifles or revolvers. They were there performing police duty, but many just spent their time sitting or wandering about. Of course they were an object of awe to the girls.

Propaganda posters were prominently displayed throughout the park. One showed CIA agents sneaking into Cuba disguised as priests, and the people were admonished to beware of them.

I found the average Cuban extremely talkative and friendly. All that was required to start him talking was to give him a topic. But when it came to politics, he would clam up, and talk only if he was sure that he was not being overheard. Ardent revolutionaries, however, would blab their opinions for all the world to hear. I often found myself closeted with one of them, and it was exteremely difficult to get away. He would ask me a question, then proceed to answer it himself.

I solved the language problem by going to a group of Cubans and asking whether one of them spoke English. If there was one, I would ask him to be my interpreter and tip him a dollar or so for his trouble.

Outside the park I came across a bar, containing a mural of the New York skyline, complete with the Statue of Liberty holding aloft the freedom torch. It was in color and had been done recently. This surprised me. Again feigning innocence, I asked a man what it was.

"Why, that's New York," he replied, looking at me as if I were demented.

"I've never been to New York," I said meekly.

"I was there ten years. Drove a cab," he said. He then made a sound like the whirring of a car engine.

I introduced myself to him more fully and asked him about his present occupation. He said that his name was Pedro and he worked as a waiter. He told me that he was married, that his wife worked as a cleaning woman, and that the two made $300 a month between them, which was just enough for themselves, their three children, and his mother, who lived with them.

"Would you like to go back to New York?" I asked.

My question startled and frightened him. His face became somewhat taut. He began talking very loudly about how good the revolution
was. I could not help noticing that his outburst was being addressed not
to me but to some militiamen who had just come in. It was obvious
that he was under great strain, and his words lacked conviction.

I patted his hand gently and left him. I did not need to be told what
he wanted to do—if only there were a way.

And so ended my second day in Havana. It had given me a good
opportunity to mix with the common people and find out something
about how they lived. I wondered what the morrow held for me.

E
5. The Fidel Mystique

ARLY in the morning the next day I was at INIT—the tourist office—located on the ground floor of the Habana Libre Hotel, the former Havana Hilton. I wanted the office to draw up a sightseeing program for me and arrange for me to visit some of the factories, housing projects, and state farms. I was met by Señor Renaldo Perruc, the manager of the office. He was in his late fifties, a quiet, unassuming man, who performed his duties methodically and managed a staff of three dozen men and women efficiently.

"But please, señor," I asked him, "can you tell me how I can meet Fidel Castro?"

"The best way to meet him is to catch him on the street," he replied.

That evening, my third in Havana, I found out what he meant by that. I was at Twenty-third and L Streets in uptown Havana. I was admiring a huge glass-fronted trade emporium that was being built by Czechoslovakia, when a large, black Cadillac appeared in the street. A flurry of excitement rose around me. I looked in the direction of the car and immediately recognized Castro by his beard and cigar.

He was in the front seat, beside the driver. Six bearded soldiers were crammed in the back seat, their machine guns and carbines protruding from the windows. Behind were two more cars—a Lincoln and a Mercury—both black, new, and full of soldiers. There were no flags on any of the cars. Nor was there a motorcycle escort. Traffic was not halted for them, and they moved slowly, obeying the signals.

People who recognized Castro began clapping their hands and shouting revolutionary slogans. Castro vaguely acknowledged the cheers with a lift of his hand, in which he held his half-smoked cigar.

I had met Castro in the summer of 1959, in Washington. He had not been in power long, and he was visiting the United States in search of economic aid. I was then a copyboy at the *Evening Star* and on my afternoon off had gone to the Lincoln Memorial to sit beside the reflecting pool and do some reading. I had not read much when Castro arrived at the Memorial to look at Lincoln's statue. I went up to him, introduced myself, shook hands with him, and we chatted briefly. In 1959, of course, nobody was aware of what really lay in Castro's mind. Everyone was looking upon him as a real revolutionary and as the liberator of his country from the Batista dictatorship.

When I had a glimpse of him on my third evening in Havana, I saw that he had aged somewhat. He appeared very preoccupied and very tired as he waved to the crowd.

During the rest of my stay in Cuba, I talked with dozens of persons about Castro. I talked with his ardent supporters and also those who did not like him or were very lukewarm toward him. Thus I was able to judge somewhat his standing with the people and to assess for myself what has come to be known as the Fidel mystique.

In Havana I discovered that he was looked upon as mysterious but approachable. Few knew where his office was. I supposed he had several, but not one was commonly known. I did my best to get at least some inkling, but I could not. I could not even find out the names of his secretaries or assistants. There was, of course, no telephone number by which he could be reached.

Nor could I find out where he lived. Everyone I asked told me that he lived somewhere in the country, eight miles from Havana, and drove to work every morning. I also heard that he had six houses located in different parts of Havana, and that his choice of a house for the night depended on the whim of the moment. The fact that he divorced his wife many years ago apparently made it easier for him to have no fixed abode. True to the custom in all Communist countries, the leader's personal life was a closed book—his tastes in food, his hobbies, his favorite reading, what he did over the weekends, when he went to bed, were unknown to the public. The Cuban newspapers and magazines would carry long accounts of Castro's speeches, they would print his picture several times in each issue, but rarely would they carry anything about his personal life.

But all of this is balanced by the way he moves among the people. Most evenings he can be seen driving around Havana, stopping at cheap restaurants, talking with the common people, asking them what they think of the revolution, and eating a simple meal with them. I was told that on a recent evening he had dropped in at the Habana Libre and spent three hours chatting with people in the lobby. They plied him with questions, and he answered them frankly or brazenly, as he saw fit. Afterward, he went to the hotel kitchen and ate a meal of rice and beans with the waiters.

He carries a supply of cigars (nobody knows the brand) in the front right pocket of his shirt and sometimes offers one to the man he might be conversing with. He carries a ball-point pen and a small note book in which he makes occasional jottings. His revolver, in a leather holster, seldom leaves his hip, and he is known as a good shot.

Some evenings he may show up at beaches and swim with the crowd. On occasion he drives to a baseball diamond and swings a bat with any team that might be playing. He wears his fatigue uniform all the time, but it is never crumpled or soiled. His beard is always neatly trimmed.

Sometimes, Havana is swept with rumors that Castro has been shot, or is dangerously ill, or even that he has fled the country and someone else has taken over the government. This always happens when he has not been seen in public for ten days or a fortnight. But always, at the end of this period, he shows up as hale and hearty as before. There was no way for me to check on whether or not any attempts have been made to assassinate him. The newspapers do not publish any account of his travels through the country, and the public never gets to know the names of the persons he meets or talks with. An account of an interview with him is published only when there is some political purpose behind it.

Again and again I was told by people from all walks of life that, thanks to Castro, their small island was now one of the most important lands in the world, and that Castro himself was one of the best-known figures. One storekeeper told me that before Castro the rest of the world thought of Cuba only as the prime gambling spot in the Western Hemisphere and an amusement spot for wealthy Americans, a bordello where both liquor and women were cheap and plentiful. Now, he said, peace or war between East and West depended on what happened in Cuba.

"But how about the hardships—the shortages, and all that?" I asked.

"Ah, that is the fault not of Fidel but of the U.S.," he replied.

"What about the lack of political freedom?"

"Yes, there is regimentation in Cuba, but it is necessary to save the revolution," he answered.

"Do you think the economic situation is improving?" I asked.

"Today we are free," was the curious answer.

"Free from what?"

"From the *yanquis*."

"But how about the Russians?"

"They are here as friends. But no matter what happens, Fidel will find a way. We have Fidel."

In those last two sentences lies the essence of the Castro mystique. People are rarely ruled by logic. They are the creatures of sentiments, emotions, unrealistic idealism. Most of the reasons advanced to me as to why Castro should continue failed to meet the test of logic.

"Batista was a dictator," but Castro has turned out to be a bigger one. "In the days of Batista, the Cuban jails were full"; they are more full under Castro. "Under Batista, the United States had an economic stranglehold over Cuba." If there was such a hold, it has now passed to the Russians. In fact, Russian control is greater. "Batista seldom held general elections; he would announce a date but postponed it repeatedly." Castro, too, has never held free elections, and he has been five years in power. "Cuba was poor under Batista." Under Castro it is poorer.

But when I asked whether Castro should be overthrown, even those who were critical of him were hesitant to say so. They pointed out that they had no alternative to Castro. I reminded them of the various prominent Cubans living in exile. I mentioned several whose names I knew. Not one was thought capable of replacing Castro. Not one was thought honest enough to take his place. Quite a few evoked positive repulsion. I was told that the return of these leaders to power would mean a return of former corruption.

Castro has succeeded as few persons have in projecting the image of a popular leader. People remember (and through skillful propaganda Castro does not let them forget) the personal sacrifices he has made. They remember how, when he was a lawyer, he used to defend without a fee the victims of Batista tyranny. They remember his years in jail. They remember his personal courage under fire. And they contrast his simple living with the gaudy and ostentatious Batista.

When Castro came to power he made grand promises, most of which have remained unfulfilled. He keeps making more. He fulfills some and makes a big show of it. But what is amazing is that quite a number of times he has publicly acknowledged his mistakes. He goes on radio or

TV and confesses his errors. The people are taken aback by it, and when he attributes the errors to lack of experience, the people tend to forgive him. They look upon his youth, take note of the American blockade, and feel that he should be given another chance.

After talking with dozens of persons, I came to several conclusions as to why Castro was still in power:

> He has given Cuba an honest government and wiped out bribery, corruption, and nepotism. I was told the story of a man who, before the revolution, had run for mayor of Havana and had spent several million dollars in the campaign. He was sure that he would be able to retrieve all the money and make triple that amount once he was elected. Castro put an end to all this; not to the extent desired, but still to an appreciable degree.

> Before the revolution, there was a lot of exploitation of the poor by the rich. There were two classes of people—the very poor and the fabulously rich. Castro ended the hegemony of the latter by confiscating their wealth and driving them out of the country. This pleased the common people. Although the poor are still poor, they feel something, however negative, has been accomplished. They are willing to give Castro time to achieve the positive.

> Castro's hold over the government and the other organs of authority and power is absolute. He is a dictator in the truest sense of the word. All key posts in the government are filled by his ardent admirers—persons who know how to interpret the mind of their master and carry out all his biddings. His men control and guide the labor unions, the student groups, and the various associations of writers and intellectuals. The defense forces are under him. His younger brother, Raul Castro, is the commander-in-chief, and Raul has never been known to disobey him. The all-powerful militia is under him. It sits in every building, and controls the country. The G-2, the usual name for the Cuban secret police, is also under his guidance. Like a giant, his figure sits astride everything.

> There is no other leader inside Cuba strong enough to take his place. Not one has the powerful appeal that he has. He is the Lenin of Communist Cuba. There is no denying that he is the momentum, the guiding force behind everything. The life

of revolutionary Cuba revolves around him. To him come all problems for ultimate decision.

Songs of extravagant praise of Castro are legion. The following, by a poet, Juan Aguilar Derpich, is an example:

Who is Fidel?
Fidel is simply Fidel. A colossus that could have come out either from Greek mythology or be the combination of all great patriots.

He is a big boy full of tenderness and understanding, deeply in love with his people; the modest giant that turns down his eyes bashfully when he hears praises and blushes all confused if they try to please him.

He is the orator full of emotion who sheds tears when he remembers the nightmares that his dear country went through; he is the fair hurricane that roars with wholesome fury against those who try to stand in the way of the successful revolution.

Fidel is not a man, he is the triumphant meek in search of a future. To assert that Fidel was born only a few years ago is a mistake, because he has always lived in the heart of every oppressed man in the world.

Magnanimous in his greatness, he knows neither hate nor revenge; he yearns only to remove all traces of pain and misery from the surface of Cuba, and to that purpose he devotes his life.

The man next to Castro in power and authority is Ernesto Che Guevara, the minister of industries. He is of Argentine birth and had been a doctor before the revolution. He joined Castro when the latter took to the mountains, and was with him in all the campaigns. The first thing Castro did on seizing power was to confer Cuban nationality on Guevara. The ordinary Cubans call him Che.

One evening I had an opportunity to meet Guevara. I was at the Habana Libre where an international chess tournament was being held. Che, an expert chess player, was there watching the games. I found an interpreter and went up and introduced myself.

He said the usual polite things about how happy he was that I was visiting Cuba and that he hoped I would enjoy my stay. I was bold enough to invite him to play chess with me. He declined because, he said, he had a reception to attend. But when I took my notebook out and asked him for his autograph, he shouted that he would not give it. His attitude confirmed to me what a Western diplomat has said—that Guevara is a man with the charm of Charles Boyer and the smile of a dragon.

I found that Che had quite a reputation for getting things done, and for publicly criticizing government officials for their incompetence. One night I heard him on TV. During one part of his speech he kept pointing at his shoes. I had a man translate his remarks for me.

Che acknowledged that shoes made in revolutionary Cuba were worse than those made before the revolution, and said: "Today, too, they are made with the same nails, the same soles, the same glue, the same leather, but today they lose their heels in half the time they used to." He called the Coca-Cola produced under the revolution "the breeding ground for bacteria" and blamed lack of quality control and revolutionary vigilance.

Che is known to lean toward the violent overthrow of non-Communist governments. He has written a book on guerrilla warfare that is much like the one by Mao Tse-tung, the Red Chinese leader. He also has written a large number of articles that are frequently published in Cuban magazines. They recount his experiences when he was a mountain fighter. One was headed "Air Attack," and described how one of his followers was able to get away from the fighting on the pretext that his mother was ill. It is simply written, and makes good reading.

But even Che comes nowhere near Castro in popular esteem. Nor is Castro's brother, Raul, considered a fit replacement. I asked Cubans what would happen if Castro were shot. All shrugged their shoulders. They were confused about it; they did not know what to say. And the impression I got was that Cuba's revolution is held together by just one man—Castro.

6. "We're the Grandchildren of Nikita"

THE children, all twenty of them, were singing:

We are the boys of the Granma*
Listen to us.
We're the grandchildren of Nikita,
And the children of Fidel.

The children were inmates of a government orphanage, and they were having their evening outing. Wearing indentical clothes, they were marching on the sidewalk like boy-soldiers—and very impressive they looked.

They switched to another song:

Open the door,
Open the thickest door.
We'll tell you how.
Who has the key
To that tough lock?
Nikita has the key.
And he gives it only
To socialist countries.

These and similar songs, translated for me by a friend in Havana, are the first to be taught to growing children in a government school or orphanage.

At one of these orphanages, a boy asks his teacher for a rubber

* *Granma* is the name of the ship in which Fidel Castro arrived in Cuba from exile in Mexico to lead the revolution.

duck. He is told to pray to God for it. He is forced to kneel before a statue of Jesus Christ and pray for the duck. No duck is forthcoming. The child is then told to ask Castro for it. He goes to a picture of Castro and asks for the duck. The moment the words are out of his mouth, a duck is given to him.

The children are taught to regard toys, and everything else, as group property. They are told to look upon a toy as "our toy," and a pen as "our pen." At one orphanage I noticed that this did not always work; children will remain children. I saw a five-year-old boy get hold of a spoon and refuse to give it up. The teacher did not forcibly take it away from him, but instead set the other boys to recovering it. And they did.

Before the revolution, schoolchildren were taught the story of Cinderella in Spanish and, at quite a few places, in English, too. The stories of Snow White and the Seven Dwarfs, Little Red Riding Hood, and others were also taught. Now the curriculum includes stories of Russian collective farms, and of Castro's coming down from the mountains to "free" his country.

Every textbook I saw had several pictures of Castro being hugged by children, of Castro giving a gun to a boy soldier, or of children standing in a crowd, waving tiny flags as Castro drives by. They also had pictures of Khrushchev, identified as "the friend and big brother of the Cuban people."

Every story in every book had some sort of political angle. Fathers were identified as heroes of the revolution. If a father was away from home, he was somewhere in the country minding the trenches or manning a gun. If he was not a soldier, he was a loyal, dedicated political worker. When he returned home, the children climbed up his lap and asked him the latest news about the revolution.

In these books, mothers were workers in "people's" factories or state farms. When they were late returning home, they were putting in extra hours to "over-fulfill" their work quota. Children were taught to look after themselves—clean their own teeth, make their own beds—while the mother was away. If the mother was also in the militia, the children were taught to help her clean her boots.

In one book I saw a girl assuring her mother not to hurry home in the evening from the factory but to stay and work more than the other women. In the same story, the child told the mother to win a medal for hard work.

In another book a young boy is shown waking up his older brother in the morning and urging him not to be late for a meeting at which Castro was to speak.

Children are taught that if both the parents are at home, they should not make noise, for the mother and father are resting "so that they can work all the better for the revolution." They are taught that their first loyalty is to the revolution; that everything that strengthens the revolution is good, and everything that weakens it is bad. Family ties mean nothing. Personal loyalties are unimportant. The only way to judge a man is to determine how good a revolutionary he is.

At one school I saw children eagerly reading the story of some workers who had been singled out for special praise by Castro. In the story, Castro was at a meeting and he asked the people to point out good workers to him. The following is a translation of his words:

> Another one got up and said: "Juan Antonio suffers from a gum condition. He has such and such a problem and sometimes his face has been swollen for weeks and he has never been absent from work."
>
> Another worker stood up and said: "This comrade was once a painter. Later he began working in one of the offices. One day we arrived here with fifteen cars which had to be painted. It was urgent that those cars be painted and this comrade said, "Don't worry, just wait until I finish my work." When he finished his office work he spent long hours until he had completed the painting of all the cars. And this comrade will just as readily work fifteen or twenty hours."
>
> While the masses were explaining those virtues, the qualities of that worker, one could not help but be impressed by all that was said, by all that recognition. Then I asked a worker, "What do you think of this worker? Do you think that he is a better worker than you?"
>
> And he said, "He is ten times better than I"—he was a young man.
>
> "And do you hope to be like him? Do you think that you will be like him some day?"
>
> And he said, "Perhaps I will. Perhaps if I improve myself, if I work, perhaps some day I will get to be as good a worker as he."

I also had occasion to visit two places that housed the *becados*, the country boys and girls brought to Havana for education and training. I learned on reliable authority that there were 50,000 *becados* in the city. The youngest was seventeen; the oldest, twenty-five. Over 80 per cent were girls.

Havana's Fifth Avenue mansions and the villas that used to house the millionaires had been turned into dormitories and classrooms for the *becados*. Boys and girls were taught separately. They had been broken into groups according to the size of the house.

On several evenings I drove down Fifth Avenue and saw these *becado* girls listlessly watching traffic. Tht idea of educating them was good, but I could not understand their utter lack of joy or verve. This was explained in part by the very strict discipline to which they were subjected.

A *becado* girl from, say, the mountains in the interior, is brought to Havana for nine months. She is given the uniform of blue jeans, a red checked shirt, and black slippers. She has only two changes of these. She is not allowed to use any makeup or to effect any but the simplest hairdo. The day consists of almost-continuous classes.

She is taught to read and write; she learns something of Communism, sewing, elementary nursing, cooking, and some handicraft. She is not allowed to mix with boys, go shopping or sightseeing or to a movie or dance. Her only day off is Sunday. Late in the afternoon, she may join a group of other girls for an outing to the beach, but she is not allowed to fraternize with other bathers.

Menus in these schools are extremely simple, and the girls do the cooking by turns. The student is supplied with no magazines or books. Her dormitory has no radio, TV, or phonograph. There is no sporting equipment. Parents are allowed to visit only on Sunday evenings.

When I saw all these Spartan restrictions, I was not surprised at the total lack of any joy or happiness on the faces of those girls. Several times I met them and tried to converse with them. Not once did I get any kind of answer, not even a nod of the head, not one smile.

Only on a formal visit was I able to draw a laugh from them. It was when I went up to the blackboard and copied on it from my phrase book the Spanish for "You are very beautiful." It drew cheers and applause. Tension relaxed for one brief moment, but descended again like a fog when I stepped back.

It was clear, however, that my mere coming represented a welcome change for these girls. I was asked my name, and so on. I asked questions, too, and obtained the name and address of one girl, promising her that I would write from Canada.

I also learned from several reliable sources that quite a few of these girls had been brought to Havana as hostages to prevent their families from joining the anti-Castro guerrilla bands in the inaccessible mountains of the interior.

The wife of a Western diplomat was able to talk with one *becado*. She asked her about her family, and the girl professed total ignorance as to what had become of it.

Havana was full of rumors that Castro had ordered the forcible removal of a large number of villages from the mountains in Oriente province. The inhabitants, whose loyalty was in doubt, were just told to pack, and they were settled in an area where they could be watched. To check their hostility further, the young girls and boys in each family were taken away and brought to Havana for "study and training."

How else can I account for the look of fear on the faces, and the absence of all luster in the eyes of these girls? Just looking at them made one gloomy. They did what they were told to do. They hid their thoughts, kept their mouths shut, and behaved as if they were mere feelingless automatons, deprived of all powers of independent action.

7. The Castro Youth

CUBA today is a hothouse of youth. On the young men and women of the country rest the hopes of Castro to perpetuate Communism in the island. The children and the *becados* described in the previous chapter will be useful in this direction ten or fifteen years from now. For the rest of this decade and the first half of the next, Castro is banking on youths who were in their early teens when he came to power and who are now reaching adulthood.

The government is forcing their development by a three-point training program—military, political, and technical—at the cost of an extravagant portion of its revenue. The result has been that the young are rampant, conscious of their importance, and proud that it is upon them that the permanence of the Communist revolution depends.

I had numerous occasions to talk with these young men and women. One evening I visited a student dormitory in Havana. It was full of special "scholarship students," who were being trained at a furious pace to fill the jobs left vacant by the thousands of Cubans who have fled the country. In Havana, eight skyscrapers have been appropriated and turned into dormitories for them. These students could be distinguished by the orange band they wore around their sleeves. I got an idea of how zealous they were toward what was being taught them when after somebody mentioned God, I found myself engaged in the following exchange:

"You know," said the student, "that there is no God."

"I am sure there is," I replied quietly.

"No, there is not," he insisted, and launched into a long harangue. "Look at the ancient Egyptians," he said. "They used to worship the Nile and the sun. Now it has been proved that the Nile is just another river and the sun is just another star."

"That's true," I said. "But you have just proved that the ancient Egyptians were wrong. You didn't prove there is no God."

"You don't understand," he replied with a snort.

I had made up my mind not to enter into any arguments with anyone, but that day I found it impossible to keep my mouth shut.

"More blood has been shed in the name of religion than for any other cause," I was told.

"Please don't confuse religion with the misuse of religion," I said.

"The biblical account of creation is all nonsense. There was no Adam. Life was born in the warm seas of this earth billions of years ago," I was assured.

"Were you there when it happened?" I asked.

"No, I was not," he shouted in reply. "But you don't have to see a thing to know that it happened."

"True. But can you point out to me one single incident from our contemporary world of a new creation of life? Why did the process stop? Why is no new life being created today?"

"The first spark of life was probably the result of some cosmic dust or light or force that hit the earth billions of years ago."

"Whence came this spark?"

"From somewhere in space."

"What is space?"

"We don't know," he replied, "but this I know—that religion was invented to enslave man. To prevent free thought."

"Under Communism do you have the privilege of free thought?"

"Of course we have."

"Have you read the Bible?"

"No. I don't want to. It's bad."

"How do you know it's bad when you've not read it?"

I countered all the arguments that were thrown at me by these fanatics by using the method of proving how little they knew about things in general, and thus how incompetent they were to act as sages.

"Do you realize," I pointed out, "that what we know today about the universe and its mysteries is the smallest fraction of what remains to be explored? When your information is so limited, how can you claim that you have the absolute truth? You are basing your conclusions on incomplete and even incorrect data."

I often caught them saying contradictory things.

"Communism stands for peace," one of them said, but he added in the same breath, "There can be no revolution without war."

Often we just rambled. We talked of capitalism, Communism, kings, India, Castro, movies—almost everything. For two solid hours this continued, and when it was over I was limp with fatigue.

I was much impressed by the study load of these young Cubans. The government supported them, but the continuance of a scholarship depended on whether a student consistently made good grades.

One student, in his second year at Havana University, was taking twenty-one credit hours according to the grading system in the United States. He was studying hydraulic engineering, but in addition was required to study one foreign language (he had chosen Russian), some history (only the Communist version of it), and Marxism. It was also incumbent upon him to attend political meetings frequently, to do four hours a week of militia duty and volunteer work on a state farm every Sunday morning.

In the dorm, the students slept on bunk beds in small, well-lit rooms. The only decoration was a picture of Castro or some other leader near the window. It was forbidden to have a pinup or the photograph of one's family or sweetheart on the wall. Also disallowed was the use of flowers, tablecloths, or anything to brighten the place.

Not every student had a desk and chair. It was considered more in line with the spirit of Communism to study in the Community Room. Each set of ten bedrooms had two of these. The first was used as a study, and the second as a game room; the latter had a Ping-Pong table and a chess set, but the students weren't allowed to play cards.

At the foot of his bunk bed, each student was required to maintain a chart, ruled off into squares. Each square represented an hour. The student colored the squares according to what he did during the day. Blue, for instance, was used to denote attendance at political meetings; green meant farm work; red meant study; and so on. At the end of every week, the chart was examined by the authorities, who thus kept a constant check on whether a student was spending his time in "worthwhile" activities.

The stiff schedule left a student little time for recreation. Only late in the evening did he have a few free hours, but he could go out only with permission and had to be back by ten o'clock. Only on Sunday evenings, if the farm work had not exhausted him, was he allowed to go out on a date. If he had a permanent girl friend, he saw her only surreptitiously during the week. She was not allowed to visit. The best way, I found out, was to see her between classes on the campus.

Clothes were free. They seldom fitted; pants and shirts came in three sizes—large, medium, and small. No one had more than two changes of clothes. Such things as jackets and ties were not supplied, and only one pair of boots (no shoes) was issued. The boots were for all occasions—to wear to classes, to drill, and on dates. Slippers were a rarity.

Pocket money was two dollars a week. Smoking was discouraged, and so the money was spent mostly on movie tickets on Sundays or on a new pair of socks. Food was reasonably good. Each meal included a cup of milk diluted with water.

Twenty-five percent of these scholarship students were girls. I found them more fanatical than boys. They were encouraged to date only good Communists. One of the girls introduced me to the Young Communists—the elite among the youths.

If a student did exceptionally well, he was allowed to join the Young Communist group. He had to apply for membership and get testimony as to his good grades, political reliability, and eagerness for work. If he believed even remotely in God, he was disqualified.

Each application was voted upon by the entire unit to which it was made. A committee was then formed to test, through prolonged questioning, the beliefs of the applicant. If the findings of the committee were favorable, the unit voted him in. Then followed an initiation period, during which the member was given special lectures while he served under some older member. He was given minor jobs, and was judged on how cheerful and cooperative he was. No one under fifteen or over twenty-seven could become a member. The fee for a student was twenty-five cents a month; for a worker, one tenth of his monthly salary.

The proudest possession of a member was his membership card. It was folded into three parts. One side had twelve squares on it. When a member paid his dues, a special stamp was pasted in as proof. The card was changed every twelve months.

Havana has been divided into sections, each of which has a Young Communist unit. The office I visited was in a large building, where I was accosted by a male receptionist. I told him I wanted to tour the place. He summoned two other party members, and they took me around. I saw the library, the lecture hall, the recreation room, the lounge, and the assignment room. I found that the library contained only books on Communism. The assignment room had charts and maps on the wall. A shelf with pigeonholes held each member's orders for the week. Assignments varied from teaching people to read to attending Castro's speeches and providing the chorus.

Both boys and girls could be Young Communists. Here again I found the girls not only more fanatical, but also more stern and forbidding than the boys. With their femininity so warped, they presented a strange spectacle.

It was imperative for each member to attend the Saturday-night reunion at which his performance over the week was examined before the whole unit. If he had been lax or negligent, he confessed and promised to do better. If someone else had caught him doing badly, he reported every incident before the group. Personal feelings or loyalty meant nothing at these reunions. The unit told the erring member to improve his ways. If he was caught again, he was punished in some way, such as by being assigned to sweep the office floors. If he was caught a third time, his party privileges were taken away for some time, though he remained a member. If the occasion arose for a fourth chastisement, he was expelled. And that could remain a stigma on his reputation for a long time.

Under the Young Communists were the Pioneers—children from seven to fourteen. Their indoctrination was through one-act plays and simple books. If a Red dignitary from another country was visiting Cuba, these were the children, all scrubbed and shined, who waved the tiny flags on the sidewalk. At the unit office I saw them gathering with their mothers for a cultural function. It was to consist of a short lecture, revolutionary songs, and a movie.

There were many mothers who were happy to have their children become Pioneers. But there were others who didn't like it, because they found their children rejecting toys and saying, "I want to make a speech like Fidel," or "I want a uniform like Fidel's." One mother told me that her eight-year-old son even wanted a beard like Castro's, and finally bought one from a curio shop.

To sum up, the youths who are reaching or have reached adulthood under Castro are studying Communism avidly. They fervently believe that it is the only truthful system in the world—the natural successor to all past systems. They are not torn by the doubts and misgivings over free enterprise that are the characteristic feature of any society where free thought is encouraged.

The image these youths have of the American young man is that of a rather obese, sloppily dressed character, whose evenings are spent not in study but in dating girls. He has a car which he uses for necking with his girl friends. He is involved in frequent smashups, wild parties, and brushes with the police. A beer can is always by his side. His most urgent concern is how to dodge the draft. He goes looking for a job, but wants a 35-hour week, and is interested first in pension plans and fringe benefits.

According to this image a large part of the reading of the average American young man consists of sex novels, girlie magazines, and newspaper comics. He is never without his transistor radio, and he wants to tune in to silly songs even when he is supposed to be reading. "But look at the modern Cuban youth," a student told me. "We study hard. We have to, because if we don't get good grades we will be thrown out of the university. We have girl friends, but no time to see them. We don't want a thirty-five-hour week; we want a fifty-hour week. We have ceased reading comics. Sex books are no longer available in our society. And if it comes to fighting, we will throw aside everything to die for our fatherland. Every day we prepare for it through military training."

One modern Cuban girl, Mayda Molina, whom I came to know quite well, will never be forgotten by me. My encounter with her, and a report on her unique life in Castro's Cuba, are described in the next chapter.

M 8. *Stood Up by a Communist Girl*

AYDA MOLINA was thirteen years old when Castro came to power. When I met her she was eighteen. She was a good example of the Cuban youth who had become the backbone of the Castro regime.

Mayda was a secretary at INIT. Her hours were from eight-thirty to one-thirty and three to six-thirty. At night from eight to eleven she had classes at Havana University. She was studying foreign affairs and hoped for an overseas embassy or consular appointment. This was her routine, Monday through Friday.

On Saturdays she worked until one o'clock in the afternoon. In the evening there was always some seminar at the university. She did not have to attend, but she never missed. On Sundays, with other students, she did volunteer work on a state farm. She was on the campus at five in the morning to catch the bus to the farm. It was late afternoon when she returned home. Sunday evening was the only time she had free. She lived with her parents at 201 Suarez Street in Havana. But she hardly got to see them, because she was away from home so much.

Mayda was short and chubby; she had dark, flashing eyes, and long, lustrous hair. She had skin the color of olives, and a personality that was alternately vivacious and subdued. She looked very attractive when she dressed up, but rather repulsive when she put on a militia uniform. She seldom used any makeup. I never saw her wearing lipstick or nail polish.

She knew English very well, and had read Shakespeare's *Julius Caesar, Hamlet,* and *Macbeth.* Shakespearean comedies, too? No.

Recently she had been in the Soviet Union as the leader of a group of Cuban workers who had been sent there on a holiday as a reward for a good performance. She knew little Russian but she was learning it fast. She was most eager to visit the Soviet Union again. Mayda belonged to the Young Communists. When I saw her, she had just been voted an exemplary member, and she was very happy about it. She also belonged to several social and political clubs. She got time off from work to attend the meetings of these clubs. She did militia duty four hours a week and knew how to handle a rifle.

Did she have a boyfriend?

"More or less."

Did she plan marriage?

"Someday, maybe. But I must finish my education. Women must work if they want to stay ahead. The revolution has given us many rights. We must prove that we are worthy of such trust."

Did she like to go out with boys?

"Yes, but I have so little time."

What kind of man would she like to marry?

"He must be a revolutionary first. With any other kind I cannot be happy, and he cannot be happy with me."

Would she like to be just a housewife?"

"Never."

When, on rare occasions, she went out with a boy, did she allow him to kiss her good-bye?

"Yes."

It was common in Cuba for a girl to be chaperoned on a date. Did she still believe in the chaperon system?

"It seems so needless. Girls are out late every night working or studying. They aren't chaperoned then. So why should they be chaperoned when they go out on a date?"

What kind of boys did she date?

"I date only boys who are helping the revolution, working hard to make it work."

I asked her to let me come with her to observe her volunteer work on a farm. She readily agreed, and seemed pleased that I was interested. The next day being a Sunday, I arranged to meet her on the campus of Havana University at five in the morning. I then asked her whether she would go out on a date with me after the return from the farm and she said she would be happy to.

I had visited a newspaper office, where I collected a glossy print of Fidel Castro. Mayda was insistent that I give it to her. I put up a show that my reverence for Castro was as great as hers, and refused to surrender it.

I pointed to a thousand-page book on dialectical materialism that was lying on the desk before us, and asked her whether she was reading it. She said yes, that she had read half of it and had only two weeks more to finish it.

I asked her whether she believed in God and in a hereafter. She said no. I wanted to know what she thought would happen to her when she died.

"Oh, first the worms will come, and then in time I will be no more than fertilizer for Cuban soil."

Had she taken part in the literacy campaign of 1961 when thousands of youths were sent into the countryside to teach the alphabet to the villagers?

Her attitude was apologetic as she explained that she had not gone out on the campaign. "But I did go on teaching expeditions inside Havana," she added.

That kind of thinking, zeal, and ardor was the hallmark of youths such as Mayda and others whom I met. I saw much more of this zeal the next morning. I got up at four o'clock, and walked to Havana University from my hotel. I did not want to be late for the volunteer work on the state farm. I found that about twenty students had arrived before me. This kind of work had become a part of life in modern Cuba. Students and other young persons participated. It was supposed to be voluntary, but if you didn't show up you might regret it.

The early-comers were sitting on parapets or on benches dotting the campus, waiting for the trucks to take them to the farm. The enthusiasm and zeal of some were so pronounced as to be catching, but others looked half asleep. Some were decidedly grumpy. But those with zeal livened up the morning by singing revolutionary songs and shouting slogans. The moody weren't allowed to remain so for long. Soon they, too, joined in shouting the slogans. I couldn't understand all of these, but I was soon joined by Mayda, and she translated many of the slogans for me. There was a lean young man in spectacles who shouted: "Who comes?"

Two hundred voices, male and female, responded: "The university." From then on, the chanting went:
"Who are we?"

"The people."

"What are we?"

"Socialists."

"What will we be?"

"Communists."

I pitched in by making as much noise as possible. I found that I could shout as well as any of the young zealots, and I was not willing to be left out. Soon I got my reward. It was when a young man came up to me, asked me who I was, thanked me for coming that morning, and presented me with a small hammer and sickle. Dutifully I put it on the pocket of my shirt.

Soon our number began to swell. The students came in by the dozens, both men and women, all clad in pants and open-necked shirts. They were chatting excitedly—even animatedly—cracking jokes, chasing each other on the grass. Mayda arrived a little after I did.

Some young men pulled me aside and asked me what I thought of the revolution. I said it was great. I would have said more, but I was not allowed to, for from then on the conversation became very one-sided. The young man began telling me how good (and inevitable) Marxism is, and I realized that my role was just to listen. Apparently, they thought they were gaining a convert, someone who would go out of Cuba and carry the seeds of the revolution with him. I took care not to contradict the impression.

Other young men would stop by us, and I would be introduced to them. I would get a pat on the back for my "conversion," and be asked to stay longer.

It was that morning that I discovered that the best way to deal with the confusing talk of Communist revolutionaries is not to take it seriously. Just listen and laugh to yourself and you won't get tired no matter how much bilge is poured on. We waited for two hours for the trucks. It meant the waste of several hundred work hours, but that didn't seem to matter. Efficiency and dispatch are goals still to be achieved in Cuba. Even when the trucks, all old Russian troop carriers, arrived, there weren't enough of them. But we crammed ourselves into them, all standing. A few workers even perched themselves on the hood and the bumpers.

There was more chanting of slogans and then the trucks began to move.

"Where are we going?" I asked Mayda.

"I don't know," she replied.

"Aren't you told in advance?"

"Why should we be?"

We moved through the deserted streets of Havana. In the early morning quiet, everything seemed peaceful. The air was a bit nippy, but it had a dewy freshness in it. Soon we were in the country, and the roads became bumpy, but nobody seemed to mind. There were speeches and songs, the latter very off-beat. Someone might begin with: "I was hit in the face for I kissed a girl." But before the laughter ended and the singer could go on with the rest of the song, somebody else would barge in with an improvised line: "We were illiterate before; now we read, and today we go to cut fodder for our cattle." And all would take up the chorus.

I found that each truck had at least one young man who would begin a speech at the drop of a hat. The moment the singing ceased, he would take up a subject such as food production or militia duty and begin expounding the views of the government. Every talk included vituperative condemnation of "dollar diplomacy," or "capitalist blood-thirstiness," or "imperialism."

After an hour's drive, the trucks stopped in a small town for breakfast. We had to buy our own, such of it as was available. Coffee and hard rolls were the only things that could be had. A few of the students had brought their own food. Etiquette demanded that they share it with their comrades. Also available were large loaves of bread. Some students bought a loaf, ate bits of it, and saved the rest for lunch.

"Why doesn't the government provide breakfast?" I asked a student.

"Why should it?" he replied, giving me an odd look. "We are not charity cases."

An hour more of driving and we arrived at the huge Mayaquito farm, where fruit and sugarcane were grown and cattle and chickens raised. The girls, separated from the boys, were sent to rake leaves and pick tomatoes.

The boys were divided into groups for varying duties. My group was driven farther to a fifty-acre fodder field. Half of it had been cut by the regular hands. We were told to cut the remaining fodder and carry it to a corner of the field where a chopping machine had been set up. The actual cutting was assigned to about fifteen of us. The rest were to carry the cut fodder on their shoulders to a truck.

I was given a huge knife like the one I remembered seeing being wielded by the rebel Chinese in the movie *Fifty-five Days in Peking.* Somebody showed me—ever a city boy—how to use it. I was to grab with my left hand as many fodder shocks as I could and hack at them with the knife.

I can say truthfully that at first I enjoyed the work. It was refreshingly different from banging away at the keys of a typewriter. I thought I was doing a good job, too, but then a farmer arrived and told me that I was not hacking low enough. I corrected my mistake and kept hacking.

The day was extremely hot, the sun beat down fiercely, and very soon I tired. My pace slackened. A comrade next to me tried to cheer me up. He said Castro would be very pleased if he could see me, but the remark failed to spur me on.

Then a man on horseback brought water in dirty milk cans, which he left under a tree. All of us rushed to them, to drink from the rusty lids. This was repulsively unhygienic, especially since I saw that some of the men were coughing badly, but there weren't any glasses available. I wondered, too, why the water was not carried to the cutters in the field, instead of being left by the tree many yards away.

I went back to my cutting, but soon quit. I returned to the cans, drank more water, and sat down on a clump of trees to talk with some of the farmers.

Normally, when a foreigner is being shown around Cuba, he is taken only to the model state farms and shown the best aspects of them. But there are other farms that come nowhere close to the high standards of the model farms. Mayaquito was one of these. Castro claims that all state farms have newly built houses for the workers. That is true only for the model farms. For the others, it's only partially true. At Mayaquito, for instance, more than 75 percent of the houses were just old huts made of mud and boards with a thatched roof.

One farmer I talked with took me inside his hut. It was one of the most primitive I have seen. The floors were of beaten mud. There was no running water or electricity. Torn pieces of tarpaulin were hung on the doors. A piece of jute matting slung between two poles served as a cradle for the baby. The family slept on straw. There was only one bed, which was falling apart. Cooking was done on a mud stove. The out-house consisted of a hole dug in the ground. The mother was out working in some other part of the farm and had taken the baby with her. There were two other small children in the family. Barefooted, unwashed, they were dressed in torn pants and ragged undershirts. They played in the field, but kept coming back to the water cans.

And yet the farmer who owned this mud hut seemed happy. I asked him the reason. He said that he was a sugarcane cutter originally, and previously had had work only three months a year. The rest of the time he spent in Havana doing odd jobs when they were available. But now, on the state farm, he was assured of a job the year round. True, it didn't pay much—about four dollars a day—but he got his milk, coffee, and a few other things free. He said that he had been promised a house, but he did not know when the promise would be fulfilled.

I walked over to the chopping machine. It was American and was so old that it broke down every fifteen minutes or so. But somehow the Cubans kept it working. As the shocks were fed to it, it would chop them, and the pieces would fall out of a spout. A tractor kept them evenly spread. It, too, was American, but it had Russian tires. At one point the engine of the tractor broke down. A new engine was fitted to it, and I noticed that a wheel belt in it had been made in Czechoslovakia.

Molasses was brought in the drum of a water truck. It was poured into buckets made of oil canisters that had holes in the bottom, and through these holes it was poured over the fodder. While I was watching, one of the students produced from his wallet a picture of Castro doing volunteer work. I learned that such pictures were widely publicized.

By about eleven, most of the zeal with which the students had begun the day was gone, and their pace slackened. But I also noticed now that some of the students had been exhibiting only a phony zeal. They were the ones who were the first to get their clothes dirty, in order to pretend they had been working hard. Actually they had just loitered.

Quitting time was noon. No food of any kind was offered to us. We just climbed wearily into our trucks, picked up the girls, and headed back for Havana. There was no shouting of slogans on the return trip. Everyone was too tired.

Mayda had come on the same truck with me, and I was hoping that she would return with me. She had said that she would let me know then what time and where I was to pick her up that evening. When she failed to appear, I inquired about her and was told that she was in the truck behind mine.

On the return trip, I saw an example of the spirit of helpfulness toward each other among these Cuban youths. The wind blew the hat off the head of a girl in my truck. It was the only hat she had, and she was almost in tears as she saw it whisked to the road and roll toward the truck behind us. The occupants of the second truck saw it coming toward them, had the driver stop, and one of them jumped out and retrieved the hat. And I remember that, in the morning when we were waiting for the trucks, one of the students was doing his homework, and Mayda helped him draw a map of the Assyrian Empire.

The truck on which Mayda was supposed to be was late in coming. I waited for it, but when it arrived, Mayda was not in it. A girl I had seen with her during the day came over to me and said that Mayda had had to "go away," and would not be seeing me that evening.

9. For Shoes You Need a Permit

THE tall office building of INRA, the Cuban National Agriculture Institute, is located in Havana near Freedom Square. My visit to it led to an invitation to spend the night at the Pedrin Troya state farm, sixty-six miles from the capital.

I was driven to it in a Russian truck which had to make frequent stops to pick up supplies. I was told that the truck was about a year old, but through being used continuously, it had developed knocks in the engine. We were halfway to the farm when it began to rain. Water seeped through the roof onto the passengers. But the drive gave me an admirable opportunity to see much more of the country. We drove past about fifteen factories making such things as sheet glass, machine tools, and tin cans.

We arrived at the farm a little before sunset. The first thing I noticed was that the fence posts had been painted orange, which has almost become Cuba's national color. The farm spread over several hundred acres and grew mostly fruit. I was invited to visit the housing colony. It consisted of boxlike, two- or three-room structures for which no rent was charged. Upkeep, however, was the responsibility of the occupant family. Cubans are very fond of giving a name to their houses, no matter how humble they might be, and I found on the doorways nametags such as Villa Rosa, The Purple Flower, The Green Leaf.

The house I stayed in had one bedroom, a living-dining room, a bathroom, a kitchen, and a small storage space. There also was a porch. Four chairs, a table, a double bed and a shelf came with the house. The bathroom had both a tub and a shower. I slept on a camp bed in the storage space, and used folded towels for a pillow. My host family served me a dinner of rice, beans, and pork. The latter I refused.

There were 800 workers on the farm, and only about a quarter of them had houses in the colony. The rest lived in a nearby town. The colony also had a school, a library, a shopping center, and a recreation center. Mobile movies were shown once every fortnight.

I spent several hours sitting with a group of workers on a porch. The women and children had gone to see the movie. There was only one man who could speak English, and he was my interpreter. The group included a worker who the year before had been rewarded for over-fulfilling his quota by a free trip to Czechoslovakia. He talked endlessly of all the good things he had seen in that country and of how well he had been treated.

Food such as meat and milk were supplied free at the farm. Schooling, too, was free. The workers were paid an average wage of fifty cents an hour. They were encouraged to take part in party work and attend "assessment" meetings at which each worker's performance was judged openly.

There was no doubt that the workers on this farm were contented.

I visited two other state farms some distance from Havana. These were operated on a vast scale; I saw chickens and ducks by the million, cattle in tens of thousands, and sugar, coffee, and tobacco fields spreading as far as the eye could see.

But Cuban agricultural problems, I discovered, are far from being licked. In fact, they are getting worse. The soil is as fertile as before. Vegetation sprouts almost overnight, as it used to before the revolution. But gone are the days when food was plentiful and Cuban steaks were so cheap that they were flown to Miami to undercut American prices.

The main causes for the agricultural setback are mismanagement and inefficiency, both on a colossal scale. The government, in its early revolutionary zeal, thought that Marxism should be applied in managing agriculture in order to increase production and equalize distribution. But the human factor in agriculture was overlooked, and it was also forgotten that rules evolved for the nineteenth century do not alway fit mid-twentieth-century conditions.

It is true that before the revolution a large part of the land was held by a few absentee landlords who spent most of their time in the gaming casinos and playgrounds of France, Brazil, and the United States. Castro wasted no time in confiscating their farms. He also confiscated farms of those whom he considered lukewarm to the revolution.

All these farms were turned into collective farms on the Russian pattern and given to the revolutionary soldiers. It is no secret that the best jobs on the farms went to the best guerrilla fighters. But when these fighters laid aside their tommy guns and knives, it was found that they made poor farmers. They had no idea at all of how to go about the serious business of cultivating the land and producing a crop.

For this and other reasons the collective farms were a flop. A few years after the revolution they were turned into state farms, on which the farmers became employees. They are paid not in equal shares but in both cash and kind according to what they produce. Today about 42 percent of all farms are state-owned. The rest of the producing acreage, usually more isolated, still belongs to private owners, but they are required to sell 75 percent of their crops to the state at prices fixed by the government.

This causes much grumbling. The fear of confiscation hangs heavy, and there is no certainty that a cash compensation will be given. As a result, some landlords have been known to give assistance to the anti-Castro forces in the mountains. One foreign diplomat put the small landowner's grievance this way: "Suppose he spends one peso raising a chicken. The government buys it for two pesos, and sells it to the public for three pesos. Of course he feels cheated." This is the same thing that I noticed at the nationalized restaurants in Havana. Prices were phenomenally high, and I wondered who was getting the profit. I asked an INRA official about it, and was told that the profits were going to the people.

"But you don't have to eat at these restaurants," he added. "Nobody asks you to."

"It's not a question of being asked," I said. "It's a question of not having enough food on the ration card."

"Well, these things have to be tolerated. We are at war, you know. The early years of any revolution are apt to be hard, and you have to deny yourself a lot of things."

I changed the subject.

The government claims that it has given back to private owners more than 200 of the confiscated farms. This was done to prevent further deterioration in them. The fear that the government won't be able to manage the farms properly is what has put a stop for the time being to further take-overs. But nobody can say how long this will continue. Castro is pleged to Communism, and the feeling of the people is that it's only a matter of time before a complete take-over is executed.

It is therefore natural that private farm owners have become indifferent toward increasing production. A lassitude has set in, and the urge to work and give of one's best to the land has diminished. The general attitude is: "What's the use? Why should we produce more? The government will take it all away. We don't have anything left." And so production on private farms is lagging. The situation is further complicated by a lack of agricultural machinery and fertilizers. Such machinery as comes in from East European countries goes to the state farms. In many cases, the private owners have gone back to tilling the land with a hand plow. They once had tractors but they have broken down, and no spare parts are available. Once while I was in the country I stopped at a private farm. It looked dilapidated, run-down, neglected.

Efforts to galvanize production on these farms have not always succeeded. The government is constantly promising that the next crop raised will bring a higher price, but this promise and others like it are never kept. The treatment of private owners as pariahs and outcasts continues. Sincerity is lacking.

The revolutionary government's biggest mistake was its decision to diversify agriculture. It cut down on sugar acreage, because sugar smacked of "Yankee imperialism." The result was that a crop of only 3.8 million tons, the lowest output in Cuban history, was harvested in 1962. This was 1.8 million tons less than that harvested in 1960, and 3.2 million tons less than the record crop of 1952. The low yield caused a severe shortage of hard currency for the import of food, raw material, and equipment needed for the current programs. In the past, sugar provided 80 percent of the money the country needed for such imports.

The earlier emphasis on rapid industrialization also cut into agriculture, and just a few days before I arrived Castro issued a statement saying that agriculture, especially sugar production, would continue to be the mainstay of the Cuban economy for at least a decade more. I found on the farms I visited that the talk was once more about increasing sugar yield. At one farm, a slogan was posted: "Sugar is the base of our economy and development."

Officials I talked with told me they were expecting the arrival soon of 1500 mechanical cane-cutters and 3500 cane-lifters from the Soviet Union. They also said that army draftees would help harvest the corp. One official was certain that these draftees would be able to cut at least 225 million pounds of cane a day.

Other blunders in agriculture have been equally appalling. A diplomat told me that Castro ordered thousands of chickens for his country but forgot to order the proper kind of chicken feed. The result was that most of the chickens died. Hatching eggs that had been similarly imported were ruined because the incubator temperature had been kept at the wrong level.

I found that strong ordinances had been promulgated to prevent food speculation. One of these declared that anyone who bought more than twenty-five pounds of produce in a week, or who hauled food in a vehicle that did not belong to the state or a food producer, would be considered a speculator.

How have these economic catastrophes affected the nation's food supply and intake? When I was there, food rationing had been extended to 95 percent of everything edible. The supply of all food items was scarce beyond belief. After only two days in Cuba, I quit being particular about food. I ate, like everyone else, what I could get.

I was told that everything one might want to eat could be had with a ration card. That was the official line, and quite a few foreign visitors fall for it. The catch was in the meager quantity of each item supplied. For instance, chicken and eggs were on the ration card, but you got only one chicken and five eggs a month. Meat was on the card—six ounces a week. There was beer, too—one bottle a month if you were over fourteen.

Fresh milk was only for babies and persons who were ill or very old, and even then only by means of special permits, which were not easy to get. If you were sick, a doctor's recommendation was required. If you were old, you had to attach a copy of your birth certificate to your application. For the rest of the people, the ration was five very small tins of condensed milk every two weeks.

Such things as butter, cheese, jam, tea, steak, green vegetables— well, you just couldn't find them. Salt you could have; pepper, no. Margarine with a heavy lard content was supplied in place of butter. Even coffee was rationed. The day before I left, *El Mundo* carried a front-page item stating that for a few months the coffee quota was being cut from three ounces per month to an ounce and a half. "A few months?" one irate housewife said to me with contempt. "You can be sure the cut will be made permanent."

Bread was not rationed, but the quality was bad. It was always hard, and often stale, and I saw people with bad teeth soaking it in some liquid before eating it. Another item that was not rationed was locally produced fruit juice in tin cans. Imitation strawberry, mango, and banana were juices that were widely available.

There had been both Coca-Cola and Pepsi-Cola factories in Cuba before the revolution. They had been taken over by the new government, which lacked the formula for making these drinks; and so what passed for Coke was something that was sold in Coke bottles, looked like Coke, but tasted like a sugar-cane drink. Bottles were in short supply, and sometimes Coke was sold in old beer bottles. Everywhere in Havana I found Coke machines in their usual places. But they never worked and were gathering rust. Only once—at the government yacht club—did I find a machine that had not broken down.

The ration cards contained every food item, but there was no guarantee that the commitments would be met. In fact, they were seldom met. One week there would be a flood of avocados; the next, none at all. Government officials admitted that the distribution system needed improvement. There were many instances when a food item would arrive in Havana but would not be taken to the stores in time, and would rot. You could buy your rations only at a designated store; you could not go to another. If your store did not have some item or if that item had spoiled, you would have to do without it.

Technically, everyone was supposed to get things in equal quantity. In practice, this never worked. One person could get five eggs a month, another could get seven, and the third might have to be satisfied with only four. Havana residents got more food than Cubans in outlying cities. I learned that in Santa Clara the meat ration was one half that in Havana. But you could have enough of all foods if you were a soldier or a scholarship student. When the common people saw the soldiers lapping up the milk by the quart, they grumbled, sometimes loudly. You could also get additional supplies if you were a party member or had proper contacts.

A lot of the food came from the Red bloc, but since all Red countries were far away, the cost of bringing it in was high and the quantity was kept to the minimum. I was told that, recently, ducks had been imported from Red China and canned pork from the Soviet Union. In a hotel lobby, I met some Czechoslovakians, and was told that they were going to teach the Cubans how to prepare smoked meats. I had just been drinking Czech tomato juice, and I congratulated them on its good quality.

"How do you like our beer?" one of them asked in a harsh tone.

"Do you send beer, too?" I said.

"Of course," he replied heartily. "Our beer is the best in the world."

Cubans made their own beer, and it was fast taking the place of the famous Cuban rum. But it was not plentiful enough to meet the need, nor was it of a high quality. Czech beer, when it came, was always quickly sold out.

One night I happened to visit the Hotel Riviera, at which most government guests were put up. I wandered into a private dining room and found spread on several tables some of the most sumptuous food I have ever seen. I was told that it was for a "fraternal delegation" from Bulgaria. Even though the people didn't have enough, the government went to extravagant lengths to see that its foreign guests were well fed.

With me the food problem was aggravated because I eat no pork. I am not even allowed lard or margarine. At every place I went, the first question I asked was whether the food had any *puerco* in it. At every meal, I had difficulty in this respect, because pork was being very widely used in Cuba.

I went to the Julio Antonio Mella slaughterhouse, one of several in Havana, and a worker showed me around. He told me that the official policy was to develop the pig industry—meat for eating, and the skin for billfolds, ladies' purses, shoes, belts, and other articles.

The conclusion I reached was that although the Cubans weren't starving, they certainly weren't overfed. One diplomat told me that, under Castro, food consumption had declined 25 percent; that Cuba had dropped from third to seventh place in per-capita food intake in Latin America, and had fallen below the 2400-calories daily minimum established for Latin America. Truly, the capacity of the human body to sustain such punishment is phenomenal.

Besides a ration book for food, every Cuban was also issued an industrial rations book. This was because all manufactured goods of everyday use, from soap and toothpaste to shoes, were rationed too. In the book, a careful record was kept of all the goods you bought. For instance, if you bought a shirt, that would be recorded in the book. If you tried to buy a second shirt the same month, you would be refused. Only half-sleeved, open-necked bush shirts that hang out of the pants were available. All other kinds of shirts had gone out of fashion and were rare.

You needed permits to buy a full suit, towels, undershirts, socks, and shoes. I saw suits on display in shop windows, but there were no takers. Towels came only in one size. Small face towels or large bath towels couldn't be had. The soap ration was one cake a month a person. In Varadero, a town two hours by bus from Havana, I tried to buy a pair of shoes, and was asked for my permit. I said I was a tourist, and the manager got busy on the telephone. He was trying to contact someone in Havana to ask whether the shoes should be sold to me. After fifteen minutes he was still talking, and then he was called away. I decided to leave the shop. But I learned that before you could get a permit for shoes, you had to assure the authorities that your old shoes could be of no further service. No one was allowed to own more than one pair.

One young man told me that he hated bathrobes. I asked him the reason. He said: "Because that pig Batista wears them. Don't you read the papers?" I imagined that he had in mind a picture of a plump Batista wearing a dressing-gown and looking down upon a garden from the balcony of his house in Spain. I remembered thinking at the time that such pictures were published in the Cuban press to keep up the revolutionary fervor. Ties were no longer worn because they were considered a relic of the decadent bourgeois society that the revolution was supposed to have overthrown. The fact that Soviet Primer Nikita Khrushchev wore ties did not seem to register.

The scarcity of women's clothes was equally acute. Government stores had dresses on display, but again there weren't any buyers, and the samples had an old, shopworn look about them. A permit was required for a dress, too. Government magazines regularly published dress designs and sketches, but textiles, too, were rationed. Cuban women, once considered some of the best-dressed in the world, had become quite shabby.

All beauty parlors had been nationalized, and the government had reduced the price of a hairdo to sixty cents, but cosmetics were very scarce. One woman, who had friends in England, asked me whether on my way back I would ask one of them to send her a pink lipstick and an eyebrow pencil. At one store I found some nail polish on sale, but it was not selling well. One woman told me that it was hard to put on and to take off. One store was selling shampoo oil, but it, too, was of a low quality. Some stores had high-heeled shoes for women, but I learned that the government frowned upon such shoes as indicative of decadence and had stopped their manufacture.

Perhaps the biggest scarcity was that of nylons. I went to a show at the Hotel Nacional nightclub, and was given a table very near the stage. One dancer whirled close enough for me to observe that her nylons had long runs in them. Out in the streets, I saw no Cuban women wearing nylons. Rare also were girdles and brassieres. I was told that most women wore brassieres made at home from an old shirt.

The only well-dressed women I saw in Cuba were Russian. Their dresses were smart, they wore nylons, and their makeup was perfect. In fact they looked like good old bourgeois women from England and the United States and were extremely conspicuous. I observed the Cuban women casting covetous glances and I could tell that this display of ostentation by the Russian women was not creating a good effect.

One day, when I took my ball-point pen out to write something, a Cuban who was with me asked whether I would give it to him when I left. I promised I would, but a few days later, at lunch in the Hotel Habana Libre, I left the pen on the table. When I came back for it a few minutes later, it was gone. Señor Perruc of INIT, when he heard about it, presented me with a pencil. That was a sacrifice for him because pencils in Cuba were in short supply. Cuba had one pencil factory; nationalized, of course. Copybooks, pads, envelopes, in fact all stationery, were hard to get. I found students using the backs of propaganda pamphlets as note paper.

Toys for children were going out of fashion. They were rationed, too. A mother was allowed to buy only two toys for each child per year. The first could not cost more than three dollars, and the second less than that, according to the regulations of the Ministry of Interior Commerce. One rule stated that dolls could be purchased only for girls from one to twelve years of age. "Girls older than twelve should worry about their preliminary Marxist education," the government said. Bicycles and tricycles for children were scarce. Some had been imported from Czechoslovakia, but each family was allowed only one, no matter how many children it had. Emphasis was placed by the government on what it called "toys of an instructive nature," such as furniture kits, sewing and carpentry tools. But those I saw were all of inferior quality. Purchases could be made only at government distributing centers.

Store purchases were never put in brown paper bags. Paper napkins couldn't be had except at the best hotels. The toilet paper in use both at my cheap hotel and at the Habana Libre was of the same low quality.

And yet there was no shortage of paper for publishing thousands of low-priced books on Communism. Cuba imported paper, too, from behind the Iron Curtain.

When the government nationalized the hundreds of huge American department stores, it also confiscated warehouses that had more than a year's supply of goods. These goods had been used up long ago, and I would enter a block-long store and find the shelves almost empty. All such stores proudly carried a sign on the door saying that they now belonged to the people. I went to a Woolworth store. The display cases were empty, but the famous Woolworth price tags—the name of the company and the price in white italics on a red background —had not been removed. There still was a basement, but the goods there had not been reduced in price. Many stores had goods on only one of their several floors. The other floors were being used as offices.

One change made by Castro was in the store hours; they could be open only from late afternoon until nine in the evening. The reason given was that people were at work in the morning and the stores would have no buyers. But there was a shortage of buyers even when stores were open.

When non-American stores were nationalized, the owners in many cases were retained as managers. A detailed list was compiled of their stock, and they were made accountable for every item in the store. This was done to prevent the sale of goods in the black market. One result was that the former owners soon cared little about keeping the stores neat and tidy, or displaying the goods advantageously, or scrubbing the floors and windows. The situation became so bad that the government had to issue an ordinance making the managers liable for punishment if they continued to be slothful. The government also announced a system whereby each store would be checked periodically for neatness, the first ten in the city to be given awards. I found several stores displaying the sign that they had been picked as the neatest in Havana. The workers, in each case, were rewarded with either a week's holiday or two weeks' pay as bonus.

But these incentives were hardly a substitute for the personal-profit motive, and, apart from the award-winning stores, most continued to look dull, drab, and squalid. Neon signs were still there, but only a few were lit. The rest were either broken or there was no electric power available to light them. Dust had settled on them, and nobody bothered to clean them. Advertising of goods had, of course, been discontinued in Cuba. The newspapers and magazines carried no ads. "We are not out to make profit and to milk the people," one government official told me. "We are not capitalist profiteers," said another. Billboards from olden days were still there, but they were now used for displaying propaganda posters.

When I have the time, I like to window-shop. Twice I went window-shopping in Havana, but there was nothing to look at. At one store, when I lingered before the display window, the militiawoman who was guarding it became suspicious. She probably thought that I was a saboteur, that I was surveying the store to find a good place in which to plant a bomb. She cast a baleful look at me, and I moved away. Only in one store was I allowed to linger. It was located in the lobby of the Habana Libre, and was selling art objects that the Dutch government had unloaded on Cuba many years ago in exchange for some sugar. I spent an hour admiring the delicate artistry of miniature windmills and vases and glass tulips. Not one customer came into the shop during all this time. There was a woman minding the store, and she was glad of my company, although I could not talk with her because she did not know English. Floorwalkers in all stores had been displaced by militiamen, and the latter kept a sharp eye on everyone. I also like browsing in bookshops, but 90 percent of the books in every shop I visited were on Communism. Window-shopping, and real shopping, were dreary, and often pointless, in Communist Cuba, and I was repeatedly grateful for the fact that I was only a visitor.

T 10. How Much Pay Does Castro Get?

THE economic structure of Cuba today is remarkable for one reason—it operates without any statistics.

When Fidel Castro and the other leaders of the revolution speak about the "economic progress" made since 1959, they speak only in percentages and never give the base figures. They may claim, for instance, that the petroleum refineries are producing 100 percent more gasoline than last year, but they never tell you what the last year's figure was. On the rare occasions when they do, the figures sound so wildly unrealistic compared to the general economic condition of the country that you don't have to a be trained economist to know they are incorrect. But the ideal Communist is a person who believes everything the party or the state says and who never questions the truth or the authenticity of any statement. He is not supposed to think independently or to reason for himself. I found that Cuba was not short of people who had become or were fast becoming automatons.

One person, who claimed he was a government economist, told me that Cuba was producing more oranges than in 1953. I asked how he knew. He replied that the government said so. I asked whether he believed everything the government said. He answered that a "people's government" never lies.

"What if it should?" I persisted.

"It does not lie," he replied. He really believed it.

I checked at INRA and several other ministries with high-sounding names and tried to find out such things as import and export figures, the number of cattle in the country and other statistics. Everywhere I drew a blank, even on the most basic figures. But displayed at the entrance to most ministries were huge boards, which did give some figures. For instance, a board in front of the Ministry of Transport said that during the first six months of 1963, the Cuban Airline carried about 50,000 passengers, or 10,000 more than during the same period in 1962, and that this figure exceeded the planned increase by 10 percent. I went into the ministry to get some more information on the state of the Cuban Airline. There were no pamphlets or handouts available for the public. I was referred to the board. There was no way at all in which I could check whether these figures or any other figures were correct. Similar increases exceeding the planned quota were claimed by every department in every ministry. One got the impression that Cuba was moving ahead at a tremendous pace, and that it had licked the problem of human error and fallibility.

Revenue and expenditure figures were never given any publicity in Cuba. Few knew how much the country earned in 1962, or whether the 1962 earnings were higher or lower than the 1961 earnings. Few knew whether the government was running at a deficit, and if so, the extent of the deficit. Few knew the main items of expenditure or the allotments made for each ministry. I could guess vaguely that the government was spending more than half of all its earnings on defense. But nobody except perhaps Castro and his brother Raul, the minister of defense, knew exactly what was being spent on the three military services, and on such items as salaries, clothing, and food for the men and women in the armed forces.

This cloak of secrecy hung over all ministries. In a few cases it was only partially lifted. For instance, one could learn what was being spent on education, but again there was no way to check the claims. It might be argued that the defense figures were purposely kept secret, but I could find no explanation other than rank incompetence for the absence of figures not connected with strategy. For instance, I could not even find out what pay was given to the president of Cuba, to Castro, to the other ministers, or whether there was a pay scale for other government employees. A minor employee's salary most probably depends upon the good will of the officer immediately above him, who can recommend a raise or a cut in pay. The employee can't grumble; there is no one to whom he could complain.

In a Communist society this is the biggest advantage the government has—it is accountable to no one, and no one dares ask anything. Absent is the traditional parliament or congress controlling the pursestrings, demanding and minutely examining the budget, voting on each item separately, then voting on the budget as a whole, and holding the government responsible for every penny spent. In the Soviet Union and some other Communist countries there is at least a "rubber stamp" parliament, a body that does not really discuss the budget but merely gives consent to it. But in Cuba even such a false voting body was not to be found. The massive doors of the Capitol were shut when Castro marched into Havana as the conquering hero in 1958, and they have not been opened since.

But Castro has his own unique method of getting the "votes" of the people on a measure and giving them the feeling that their will is being exercised. He calls a huge public meeting. Upwards of 300,000 people show up. Castro makes a three-hour speech, tells them what new measures the government has decided upon, and asks them to give their consent by a show of hands. Since the crowd consists entirely of loyal party workers, students, and Young Communists, all hands are raised at once. If anyone should disagree, he has no chance to voice dissent. The penalty can be a thrashing by the crowd. The next day, the government papers carry the news that 99 percent of the people are behind the measures and voted yes on them.

I learned that one such meeting had been held, a few days before my arrival, at which the people had been asked to "pass some laws" providing funds for the purchase of more wheat from the Soviet Union. The measures were read to the crowd, and it roared yes to each one of them. This was how the people's "consent" was obtained on the nationalization of factories, farms, banks, hotels, houses—everything.

When the Fidelistas came to power, they began governing with the assumption that all previous economic practices were bad, smacked of imperialism, were designed to keep the Cuban down, and had only one aim—to make money for American investors and their cronies. Everything was to be altered.

It was not that Cuba lacked trained economists and business managers. It was just that the saner policies advocated by these men were rejected as decadent and not compatible with the spirit of revolution. Resentment aroused by the revolutionaries among the trained experts ran high. Almost 90 percent of Cuba's upper and middle managerial and technical personnel in every area of the economic life fled to Miami.

The pattern for these defections was set by several notable Cuban personalities. Chief among them was José Miró Cardona. He was once an ardent supporter of Castro. When the revolutionary forces came into power, Cardona was the man tapped for premier. When Castro himself took up the post, Cardona was appointed Cuban ambassador to Washington. But before he could leave Havana, Castro announced the confiscation of U.S. sugar mills. This was done in such an arbitrary manner that Cardona quit supporting Castro and sought refuge in the Argentine embassy. His loss deprived the country of one of its most noted legal minds and a man of great diplomatic competence.

I talked with about a dozen Cubans who were planning to leave Cuba, and most of them cited the example of Cardona. "We love Cuba," they kept telling me, "but we don't want it to become a province of the Soviet Union."

The jobs that had been held by the defectors were given to young men and women; strong, dedicated to the idea of revolution, starry-eyed, but unaware of the technicalities of running a government, factory, or office. They made mistake after mistake, and things went from bad to worse. One day I went to the National Bank of Cuba in Vedado to get my dollars exchanged into pesos. The first time I had gone there I had been helped by a young woman, Señorita Alicia Aiguiz. She knew the exchange process and it had taken her only five minutes to complete the details. The next time I went, she was absent. The woman who was working in her place did not know the process, and it took two hours to get the money exchanged. Señorita Aiguiz was apparently the only woman in that huge bank trained to do this work.

One Saturday I toured an ice factory in Havana. The twenty-four-year-old manager was doing a gallant job of running the factory, but even to my untrained eyes it was obvious that efficiency and optimum production were sadly lacking. On weekends, water was brought to the factory in trucks, because the taps didn't work. I saw one truck pull up to the factory. A pipe was attached to it to transfer the water to the containers in the freezing room. But this was done in such an inefficient manner that half the water was being spilled onto the street. It would not have taken much ingenuity to repair the leaks in the pipe or in the faucet of the truck, but nobody seemed to notice or care. I was told that the manager was in charge of four other such factories. This was because no one with even his limited know-how was available to share the burden.

The excessive use of slogans helps keep alive the revolutionary fervor. One day I expressed my view of them to an INRA official. "I think these slogans you use are for pigeons," I said. "They seem so childish, so sophomoric. If I were a Communist, I would not need them to do a good job."

"Ah, but you don't understand the Cuban mentality," the official replied. "If we don't keep goading our workers like this, they would go back to sleep. We have to keep needling them, reminding them that the work of the revolution is not finished. You may not need the slogans, but our workers do."

When I was in Havana, arrangements were in progress for an international conference on architecture. The Cuban government was doing a crash job of erecting a special pavilion for it on the opposite side of the street from the Habana Libre. Several times I stood and watched the workers. I found them inclined to do things at an infuriatingly slow pace. Although the work on the pavilion never ceased, night or day, the workers, at the slightest opportunity, tended to wander off to the nearest coffee stall. Or they would often just sit in a circle and laugh and chat.

On another occasion, I rode to the countryside in a government truck. I found my driver a jolly fellow. He was in no hurry, and twice he stopped and bought me coffee, all the time chatting gaily about the women he had known and the good times he had with them. He knew little English, but the way he expressed himself kept me laughing throughout the ride. I have never been to the Soviet Union or Red China, but I cannot imagine a worker from those countries behaving like that.

At one factory I learned something of the work incentives invented by the government. In the main office was a large blackboard with the names of four workers written on it. I was told that those workers were the top four in their performance during the past week. If a worker was able to get on the list six times in succession, he was sent on an all-expense-paid trip to Czechoslovakia or the Soviet Union, usually for two months. If he was on the list four times in succession, he was given a month's pay as bonus and two weeks at a government vacation resort. If he was on the list three times, he was given two weeks off to spend at the resort.

As far as political indoctrination is concerned, it is the duty of the foreman to take indifferent workers aside and talk with them about the glories of Communism. This is in addition to compulsory attendance

at political meetings. At one factory I saw the foreman taking the
charwoman aside for one of his chats. He bought her coffee, was polite
and condescending, but kept plugging away about how wonderful the
revolution was.

But the benefits to the workers of life under Communism are not
great. For instance, in Western society everywhere the 40-hour work
week has been prevalent for some time, and in many cases there is a
37- or even a 35-hour week. Cubans, too, had a 40-hour work week
before the revolution. Now, in the name of Communism and fatherland,
they are required to work a 45- or even a 50-hour week. True, health
care is free. It was free before. But today the standard of care is
lamentably low. I found one manager whose three-year-old daughter had
a disease of the spine, but there was not one hospital or doctor who
could treat her. Movies for the workers are free. But I discovered that
the movie houses do not have worthwhile or entertaining shows. Many
workers go to the movies because they have no other form of entertainment. Many never go.

I found that the salaries being drawn by the workers were inadequate. Before the revolution, Cuba had a per capita income of $334
a year. Only two Latin American countries, Venezuela and Costa Rica,
had higher incomes. Under Castro, the figure has slumped to an estimated $200 a year.

Salaries, instead of going up, have gone down. Before the revolution, wages were paid either on a time or a work basis. Under Castro,
the wages are paid on a piecework basis. A norm is set for each worker,
and if a worker fails to meet his quota, his salary is cut. If he surpasses
it, it is slightly increased. His quota is stiff: He is required to perform
one tenth more of the average work in one tenth less time if he is to
collect his basic salary. One percent of his salary is deducted for every
one percent of unfulfilled work. But if the quota is surpassed, the
reward consists of a one half percent salary increase for every extra one
percent of work.

The big catch in the plan is that the norm is set by the state. At
each project an account is taken of the amount of work each construction
unit performs; then the local leaders meet and set a minimum average
standard. The workers are consulted in the sense that they are asked
to endorse the decision. This they do with an obedience that can be
found only in Communist unions. If a worker dares to protest, a note

is made of his name, and the next day one of the labor leaders calls upon him and gives him a pep talk. At the next meeting, the worker stands up and confesses that he was in the wrong.

The wages for workers vary, but they are never more than $200 a month, because the government has passed an ordinance setting that limit. Before the revolution, the average wage of a sugarcane cutter was $3.15 a day. Now it is $1.98—if the worker meets his quota. Factory managers can get as high as $300 a month, and they are allowed to do such things as raising a pig and selling it in the open market. They rarely do such extra work, however.

On the average, 15 percent of the worker's salary is taken away as tax. The name given to this deduction is "voluntary contribution" for such things as industrialization and housing. The promise has also been made that some of it will go toward social security, but the government has allotted no funds for it.

Strict rules have been evolved to punish absenteeism or consistently low performance. The workers can be sent to jail for either, though the place to which they are sent is called a "correction camp." They can also be punished by a reduction in rank.

Workers no longer have the right to strike, or to change jobs. They are free to form a union, and several unions exist in Cuba, but the roles are considered different from those of unions in non-Communist countries. The official Marxist line is followed: Unions are to undermine a non-Communist regime, but when that regime is overthrown and a Communist regime established, the unions are expected to give it stabilization by supporting all its plans.

The unions in Cuba encourage their members to put in free hours of work, take pay reductions, and acquiesce to all government measures. The unions also conduct adult education classes. The weekly "reunion" meetings are held on Saturday afternoons. At these meetings, a stock is taken of each worker's performance; the good ones are praised and the bad ones are castigated. Attendance is compulsory.

Under Communism, the workers have gained in stature, but they are kept under iron control by the state and party, and the increase in stature is more showy than real. And as far as work benefits are concerned, they have diminished almost to the point where the worker can hardly be said to have any.

I 11. Ivan, the New Colonizer

SAW Russians everywhere in Cuba. They dominated the Cuban scene. In Havana they lived in hundreds of newly constructed houses in their own colonies; neat, exclusive colonies, barred to un-authorized persons. When there was a shortage of accommodations in these colonies, the Russians were put up at expensive hotels. In the lobbies of all good Havana hotels, it was possible any evening to run into Russian men and women sitting at the bars, chatting animatedly among themselves, laughing, joking, enjoying their newly acquired freedom and prestige in Castroland.

I saw the Russians in droves on the streets, traveling on country roads in air-conditioned buses, skin diving at beaches, ogling the show-girls at nightclubs, patronizing the expensive restaurants, where a corner was reserved for them every evening. One evening I tried to sit at one of their tables in the dining room of the Habana Libre Hotel, but was told to move. Fifteen minutes later, they began to come in. The food offered to them was exclusive; it was not on the general menu. Again and again I saw Russians receiving priority in everything. They never had to wait for cabs or for any service.

Russian airliners zoomed overhead in Cuba. Russian freighters rode the surf in Havana Bay. I saw fields being plowed by Russian tractors, cement being mixed in Russian mixers, and Russian trucks transporting workers and goods. I saw housewives making bread from Soviet flour, heating canned Soviet pork, serving Soviet tomato juice. I saw the grin of Nikita Khrushchev in millions of pictures, and several million more pictures showed him shaking hands with Fidel Castro. Printed passages from his speeches plastered the walls.

I saw young Cuban men and women fawning and gloating over their *Ruso* friends. I heard these youths shouting Soviet slogans, singing

Soviet songs, and I saw them proudly wearing a small hammer and sickle. Thousands of youths were studying in the Soviet Union; thousands more were preparing to leave for Moscow in the months ahead. Others dreamed hopefully that one day their chance, too, would come.

All told, the Soviet economic and political annexation of Cuba is so complete today that the island gives the appearance of being just an overseas territory of the Soviet Union, with Khrushchev as the sovereign and Castro as his doting viceroy. Soviet control is exercised through an estimated forty thousand "experts" and "technicians" spotted in key positions all over the island. In the name of "Communist internationalism," "proletarian unity," "Marxist brotherhood," and whatnot, the soul of Cuba is theirs today. When this is pointed out to Cuban officials, the usual answer is: "The Russians are helping us to socialize in record time. They are giving us the benefit of their vast experience in communism. We feel very obliged to them."

The obligation of the Castroites to the U.S.S.R. is not misplaced. The truth is that were it not for massive Soviet aid, Castro's regime would have collapsed long ago. One reliable estimate, made at the time I was in Cuba, was that the Soviet Union is spending $1 million a day on maintaining the regime. For 1962 the figure was higher. By one West German estimate, the Kremlin that year spent a total of $450 million on Cuba, apart from the military expenditures which could not be assessed.

Goods from the U.S.S.R. have to travel several seas and the Atlantic Ocean to reach Cuba. But Khrushchev is continuing his help in spite of it. When I was in Cuba, one Soviet ship or a ship chartered by the U.S.S.R. was arriving daily. I was told that one third of the Soviet Baltic Fleet had been devoted to the Cuban traffic. It was said that four more ships built in Finland just for this traffic would soon be ready. Pitching in to the best of their capacities were other East European countries, especially Czechoslovakia. All East European experts were collectively called Czechs.

Red bloc aid has been both in the form of goods and commodities and in cash allotments. It could not be ascertained how much was in the form of loans and how much in grants. I did learn that Castro was being forced to pay for some of this aid through the sale of Cuban sugar to the Soviet Union.

I wanted to know whether Castro had demanded any cash for the bases he had given the Soviet Union. "There is no question of any pay-ment to us for these bases," one official replied. "They are here for our protection. We are obliged to Nikita that he decided to build them on our territory."

Every government office I visited had a Soviet flag pinned to the wall, and a picture of Khrushchev grinning down, side by side with Castro's picture. I learned that Soviet "advisers" were attached to all ministries. They held no title. They kept in the background, but they were the ones who gave orders. In a way, this was essential if the minis-tries were to be kept functioning. Most officers who used to run these ministries fled Cuba when Castro took over. The youths, the ardent Cas-troites, did not have the technical training to take over their jobs. Those youths who knew anything were immediately promoted, and suddenly found themselves holding impressive titles and shouldering big respon-sibilities.

But the number of such youths was small, and Castro was forced to send an SOS to Moscow asking for office managers, superintendents, factory directors, statisticians, and experts in finance, commerce, educa-tion, health, and public works. Khrushchev was only too willing to oblige. He realized that such help would serve three purposes: it would greatly strengthen his hold over Cuba, enable him to mold the country in the form best suited to the interests of international Communism, and give him an opportunity to train a Russian cadre of civilian officers who might be called upon to perform similar duties in any other Latin American country that accepts Communism.

I learned that Castro sent his first call for help in this direction in 1960. It caught Khrushchev unprepared, because he did not have at his command any managerial help experienced in Latin American, espe-cially Cuban, affairs. But he did have some experts with at least some experience, and these were quickly dispatched. At the same time, a program was launched to train Russians in Cubanology. A survey of the kind of help needed revealed that Cuba required experts in all fields of endeavor. The Soviet government combed its provincial minis-tries and technical and business schools and got together a small army of civilian officers to work in Cuba.

In some fields, such as education and public health, it was possible to familiarize the men quickly with Cuban needs. In other fields, famil-iarization took a longer time. But as each group of experts finished its training, it was flown to Cuba without delay. Khrushchev was not willing to surrender this opportunity to take over a country without fighting.

The groups arrived to find a cracking economy, a disrupted governmental structure, and a country from which order had all but disappeared. Their job was to get the economy going, reorganize the various departments, create new ones, and, at the same time, to train young Cubans in the work that awaited them. They found that chaos had spread to even the provincial and local governments, and that reorganization was to be done at all levels. They also discovered that they had to be very subtle about it, because feelings of nationalism were strong, and although the revolutionary leaders were willing to accept help in reorganization, they insisted on laying down the overall policies.

When, in 1960, Castro decided to cut sugar acreage and diversify the economy, he did it over the strong objections of his Russian advisers. But things proceeded smoothly because Castro's anti-American posture was most pleasing to the Russians, and they went along with him even in policies which they thought were foolish and would not succeed. "There will be time to repent. Meanwhile, we must do everything to get him firmly in our camp." That, generally speaking, was their attitude toward these policies. They were right. Castro found himself depending more and more on the experts and the economic help he was getting from the Red bloc.

At the same time, the Soviet Union did everything to flatter Castro's ego. Soviet newspapers and magazines began to give a big play to news from Cuba, and the Russian experts inside Cuba were ordered to stay well in the background, do all the work, but give credit to the Cubans they were training and who nominally were the departmental heads. This policy paid off in rich dividends to the Russians. They found themselves in possession of an island with the potential of being the first Communist beachhead in Latin America. The Kremlin figured that no matter how expensive the project might prove, it was worth all the money needed, because it could be turned into an ideal base for subversion of the rest of Latin America.

The Russians found themselves holding in the palm of their hands the power to mold into their own image thousands of impressionable, emotional youngsters, the inheritors of tomorrow, the perfect material to become revolutionaries and carry the flame of revolution all over Latin America.

They found themselves controlling an island only ninety miles from the United States, and they were quick to realize the military possibilities inherent in such a control.

And so the Soviet Union began pouring money, goods, and experts into Cuba at an unprecedented pace. "The U.S.S.R. is the best friend of Latin America," I was told by a young Cuban official of the Foreign Ministry. "That country has given us more than one billion dollars. Just imagine, all that money to a country our size, when the Americans, through their Alliance for Progress, have promised only ten billion dollars for the whole of Latin America."

I pointed out that Soviet help had political motives, because Khrushchev, when he gave it, wanted only a beachhead. If, I asked, a nation of seven million people needed $1 billion to become Communist and barely exist, how much more money would a nation of fifteen or seventy million people need to go the same way?

"The Russians will not shirk their responsibilities," the official replied. I am not sure that the Russians would have liked this answer.

But in Cuba, at the time I was there, they were riding high. The Sovietization of the country was complete and absolute. The Russians had come in and conquered everything. Without firing a bullet, they had acquired possession and control of everything that was worthwhile to them.

Russian teaching experts set the curriculum for classes on all levels, from kindergarten to college; they judged the loyalty of the teachers and instructed them in how to conform with the Marxist philosophy of education. Russian managers directed the factories, controlled the output, decided on what was to be produced, what methods were to be used, how many men were to be employed, and how the manufactured goods were to be distributed. Russians decided on what new factories were to be set up, where they were to be located, and how large they were to be. Russian farm experts controlled the farming; the changeover from collective to state farms was done at their behest. They were the ones who sounded the alarm against the rapid nationalization of land. The reason was not that the Russians believe less in Communism. It was that they knew when a move would be practical, and they realized the need for curbing the wild-eyed idealism of their Cuban comrades.

In 1963 the Cubans were more willing to listen to these experts than they were in 1960. They were eager to wipe out the results of the blunders they had committed in the early stages of the revolution. They realized that when the Russians had anything to say, it was wise to listen to them, because the Russian advice was the product of the earlier experiences gained in the Soviet Union itself.

In commerce, the export quotas were set by the Russians, and they supervised the import policy of the nation. They ruled on the ships that were to be chartered. Because of their liaison with international shipping, they were sometimes able to get concession rates for the Cubans from Greek or Japanese shipowners.

In finance, the Russians decided on budget allotments, and coordinated the Cuban revenues with their own aid. They found the revolutionary leaders totally ignorant of such things as basic economic variables, overvaluation, multiple exchange rates, bimetalism, and the other myriad items in a modern economy.

The Russians found their task of managing the Cuban economy made infinitely hard by the tendency of Castro and the other leaders to appropriate funds without regard to the budget. There was a story going around that at one time Castro decided that a certain book by some East European Communist leader should be published. He personally made out a cash voucher for 25,000 pesos in the name of the National Publishing House. The Finance Ministry refused to honor it, because the allotments for the National Publishing House for that year had been used up. When Castro learned of this, he stormed into the Finance Ministry and stood over the top bosses until the money was found from other sources. The Russian experts fume and fret at these practices, but they have shown the patience of Job in meeting them. They draw the budget and pass it on to the Cuban officers, who make alterations in it, knock it completely out of shape, never release it, and claim the credit when, willy-nilly, things keep going.

The Cuban decision to take over the banks was made before the arrival of the Russian experts, but the organization of the Cuban National Bank was done with Russian help. It is Cuba's only central bank and commercial bank. I tried to find out its assets, but no reliable figures were available. I did learn that the Cubans were considering a proposal to tie its foreign activities with the Moscow Norodony Bank, which has branches in Paris, London, and Beirut.

In political organization, Castro's Cuba is one step ahead of the U.S.S.R. in that not even nominal elections are held in Cuba. But I learned that Castro was moving in the direction of forming just one political party—in the pattern of the Soviet Union. More of that later.

The organization of G-2 (the Cuban secret police), the Pioneers, the Young Communists, and the Committees for the Defense of the Revolution is all on the Soviet pattern.

The Russian role, however, also has caused discontent in Cuba. I was told that when the Russians first began arriving, Havana shops had not yet run out of American suits, shoes, and razor blades. They were quickly bought by the newcomers. The men went after the suits; the women made a beeline for dresses, handbags, and cosmetics. A typical Russian in Cuba is paid $1500 a month, half of it in dollars. The complaint was that this was contributing to Cuba's dollar shortage. Some Cubans also complained that the Russians did not suffer from food scarcities and that the government regularly gave them the things it held back from the people. At a pharmacy, I casually inquired about the drugs received as ransom for the Bay of Pigs prisoners. The clerk told me, just as casually, that most of the drugs were sent to the Soviet Union to pay for Soviet imports.

One thing going very much against the Russians is their refusal to fraternize with the Cubans. They mix with them only during work, then retire to their own groups. Nor do they invite Cubans to their homes; the only Cubans who can enter are servants. During my stay I met dozens of Russians. Never once did I see them in company with any Cuban, and for some reason their standoffish tendency is growing. Already they have earned the reputation of being snobs. One evening I saw a Russian get out of a cab in front of the Hotel Riviera. He was well-dressed—in clothes that fitted—and carried a camera; when he took out his wallet I saw that it was crammed with dollar bills. He paid the exact fare and walked away without tipping the driver, closing the door, or saying thank you. The look the driver gave him was a study in contempt.

A movie, *Tour Through Moscow*, was playing in Havana, and once I paused to watch the line of people before the ticket window. It was composed mostly of Castroite youths. A young girl was waiting on the curb. I asked her whether she had seen the movie. She twisted her lips, and with a snarl of disdain, said no. Then she spat, and walked away.

I also noticed little fraternization between the Russians and the technicians from East European countries. On beaches, the two groups never mixed or talked with each other. The few Red Chinese in Cuba lived entirely in a world apart. I was told that in Havana the diplomats of Red China and the U.S.S.R. weren't on speaking terms. Red Chinese technicians performed their jobs with discipline and restraint, never appeared on the streets, kept very much to themselves, and attempted to set an example of quiet, thoughtful, methodical work.

All these attitudes of their Communist brothers were strange to the friendly, easygoing Cubans. They refused to use the word *comrade*. They changed it to *compañero* for a man, and to *compañera* for a woman.

I gathered from talking with several Russians that they did not have much respect for the Cubans. It was the natural contempt that a giver has for a receiver whose needs are inexhaustible. Russian Communism has matured. Cuban Communism is still wild-eyed and brash. The Russians did not like the kind of zeal that manifested itself in loud slogans but little work. One afternoon, I saw a truckload of farm volunteers returning to Havana. They were shouting slogans at the top of their voices. A young Russian standing nearby wrinkled his brow and put his palms over his ears. "They do shout, don't they," I said, hoping he would understand. He did not know English, but he realized that I had noticed him cover his ears. At once he straightened his face, said "*Cuba si, yanqui no,*" and walked away.

I heard people talking about some drunken Russian soldiers who had raped a Cuban girl at a beach, but the incident was never reported in the papers, and there was no way of confirming it.

"Can it be true?" I asked a man who sat next to me at the coffee bar.

"It can be," he answered.

"If it is true, what do you think the government will do?"

"Nothing."

"Nothing?"

"Why should it? What's a woman's virtue compared to all the help we are getting from the Soviet Union?"

"You really believe that?"

"Why should I not believe that? We are taught to believe that. I believe."

I learned that the government had closed all Havana brothels except one in the old section of the town. It was reserved for the Russians. "I think Russian men like Cuban women," one young girl told me. I was told that the prostitutes had been driven off the streets and sent to the state farms. But I also learned that these women were regularly supplied to the Russian soldiers stationed in the interior of the country.

When I was in Varadero, an ice-cream vendor, who had visited

America, told me about three busloads of Russian soldiers who had come to the beach several days before. One part of the beach was fenced off for their use.

"Did they have their women with them?"

"They had women all right. But they were Cuban women," he replied.

"What do you think of that?"

"There is nothing to think."

"Do the soldiers come often?"

"Three or four times a month."

Everywhere I went I heard that Russian soldiers had visited the place at some time or other. But these soldiers were forbidden to mix with the people. They were kept well hidden. They were allowed into a town only in civilian clothes. In their camps they wore Cuban army uniforms, or just military uniforms with no national identification.

Everyone I talked with said that it was impossible to tell how many Russian soldiers and military technicians were in Cuba. One Western diplomat estimated the number at 13,000. That was surely the minimum; the number probably was much higher.

Everyone said that although the Russians might have removed the offensive missiles and the bombers that caused the crisis of October, 1962, some of the other sophisticated weapons installed by them were still in Cuba. The Russians continued to exercise control over these weapons, because they thought the Cubans too immature politically and inexperienced militarily to handle them.

The best estimate I could get was that the Soviet army in Cuba was divided into four armored units, each of battalion strength. Each was highly mobile and well equipped with T-54 tanks (the latest to come off the Soviet assembly lines), tactical rocket launchers, ground-to-ground missiles, and several kinds of antiaircraft weapons, including the gray, sharp-nosed SA-2 rocket.

According to this same estimate, the Russians had ringed Cuba with 24 antiaircraft rocket sites, had installed 144 launchers at these sites, and had stored 500 SA-2 rockets. These rockets have a range of 80,000 feet. In addition, the Russians were building about a dozen sites for coastal-defense missiles to supplement the conventional shore batteries.

Many Cubans pointed out to me with pride the fishing port the Russians were building some distance from Havana. But the gleam in the eyes of these Cubans, and the smirk on their faces, confirmed the fear of some neutral observers that that port would also be used as a base for Soviet submarines, as a place for refuelling and restocking them.

According to these observers, the Soviet Union was building a base for short-range coastal submarines in the area around Banes and the Bay of Nipe on the northern coast of Oriente province. The area was a Soviet military zone. Several Soviet ships brought cargo to it. It was announced that they brought only material for building houses, but the cargo could have been anything.

Cuba has hundreds of water-level caves bordering on the sea, and these were being enlarged and strengthened to serve as submarine pens. The naval potential of these caves was realized by the Russians several years ago, and they were first explored in November, 1961.

Soviet naval personnel was estimated by a Western diplomat to be about 2500, including the skippers of some of the patrol boats around Havana. Their presence frees some of Castro's forces for subversion in places such as Venezuela and elsewhere. They can be used any time to do away with Castro if he becomes troublesome to the Soviet Union, and if the Kremlin feels that it should install a leader more amenable to the overall Soviet strategy of world domination. Their presence considerably reduces the possibility of an internal uprising, and ensures that any invasion of Cuba will be very costly. Also, that Cuba cannot be reconquered merely by using conventional weapons. Russian troops stand also as a sort of reassurance to other Latin American nations that if any of them decides to accept Communism, the protection of the Soviet "shield" would be extended. Their presence, too, undoubtedly aids and abets the Red insurrectionists in Latin America.

12. The Gun-Toting Militia

PERHAPS the most dominant feature of Cuban life today is the presence of the militia everywhere. A foreign diplomat told me that there are tens of thousands of men and women who have been drafted into the militia, and who serve in it without any pay.

Wherever I went, I saw these hard-eyed, grim-faced, and scowling militia staring at me, watching my every move, defying me to do anything to hinder the progress of the revolution. I saw them on street corners, in front of all stores and most shops, in front of and inside all government buildings. They were at the doors, on the stairs, on every floor. They were also stationed on the roofs, to look down on the streets and fire in case of an insurrection. Every lobby in every hotel was guarded by them. They patrolled the beaches and the amusement parks. They were at bus stations, movie houses, theaters, nightclubs, schools, and restaurants.

All were armed with loaded rifles. Not everyone had a full cartridge belt, but all had at least six spare bullets. Some also had knives.

"But do you know how to use this rifle?" I asked a militiawoman in front of the office of the *Hoy* newspaper.

"Sure thing, *compañero*," she replied.

"Who taught you?"

"The government. Who else?"

"Do they train you in shooting before they assign you to guard duty?"

"Sure thing, *compañero*, or I would be a fool carrying a gun and not knowing how to use it."

"Are you a good shot?"

"Fairly so," she replied with a shrug of her shoulders.

"Will you give me a demonstration?"

"What?" she said in absolute disbelief. "I can't do that. I have to account for every bullet they give me."

"How many have you got?"

"One in the gun. Six in my pockets."

"Can I please handle your rifle?"

"No."

"Do you work anywhere?"

"My husband does."

"How many hours every day are you on duty?"

"Twelve hours a week. Sometimes less, sometimes more."

"Do you take your gun home with you?"

"No. We are not allowed to do that. At the end of the duty we have to deposit it at the office."

"What office?"

"You are too inquisitive. Who are you, anyway?"

I quickly changed the subject, but I did tell her who I was, and then I launched into a long statement of how impressed I was by the glories of the revolution, and that my curiosity was the result of admiration.

From another militia member I learned the next day that the rifles were deposited in the nearest office of the Committee for the Defense of the Revolution.

Each of the sections into which Havana has been divided has a unit of the committee. The unit keeps a record of all its militia and makes the assignments. Each unit, too, has been issued a roomful of rifles and cartridges. These are kept carefully locked. When a rifle is issued, the exact time, the name of the person to whom it is given, and its number are noted on a register. An entry is also made of the number of cartridges issued. If the militia member happens to use a cartridge, he is required to explain why, how, and on whom it was used. There have been cases when a member forgot to pull the safety catch and the rifle went off inadvertently.

I noticed that some of the rifles carried by the militia members were American Enfields, supplied to Cuba before the revolution. But one man let me handle his rifle, and I noticed that it had Russian writing on it and also a star inside a circle on the muzzle just on top of the trigger. From then on I kept my eyes open for this star on the rifles. I knew where to look for it, and I counted rifle after rifle that bore it.

All these rifles were .30-caliber and of the same design. They weren't automatic or semiautomatic. They were lever-action, single-shot, clip-loading weapons of the post–World War I years. All weighed the same, and weren't so heavy that they could not be handled by the women. I supposed they were discards from the Soviet arsenal.

I have noticed in all backward countries receiving Soviet arms that most supplies are of the older types. As newer weapons are invented, the older ones are given free by the Soviets to the emerging nations of today. These old arms would not be much use in a modern war, but in backward countries they can still cause havoc. Cuba was an example of this. It is true that the U.S.S.R. has supplied a lot of modern arms, too, but the conventional arms given to the Cubans in a far larger quantity are all of an older vintage.

Men and women of the militia wore uniforms of the same design— khaki or olive-green, cuffless pants, a full-sleeved shirt complete with epaulets of the same material, and heavy boots. Uniforms, like clothes for the scholarship students, came in three sizes: large, medium, and small. Medium-sized women, I was told, always wanted the small-sized uniform. This was evident in the fit of the trousers; several times I wondered how the women could run or even bend if they had to. Belts seldom came with the uniform. Most were homemade, of cloth with plastic buckles imported from Czechoslovakia. Everyone except unit commanders and other officers provided his own boots.

There were two types of militia: combat and guard. Combat members wore blue shirts to distinguish them from the rest. The age limit in the combat militia was thirty years; in the guard, fifty years.

Outside Havana there were twelve rifle ranges for training the militia. Training consisted of forty-eight hours spread over a week. After that, each member had to report for practice for several hours every two months. If the member was a student, he was excused from classes; if a worker, he was excused from his job.

My several personal contacts with the militia were both pleasant and unpleasant. One evening, in Almendares Park, I met a nineteen-year-old who was wearing the blue shirt of the combat militia. She knew English and told me that she lived with her mother. Her father, she said, had nineteen children born of four women, none of whom he had married.

She and I agreed that we would meet again the next evening at the same place. I was on time, but she was an hour late. This time, although she was wearing her uniform, she did not carry her gun. She was accompanied by a girl friend who had come along as a chaperon. She said she was sorry she was late and that she had to leave at once because she had forgotten she had to go for her weekly piano lesson. I did not mince my words in letting her know of my displeasure.

"I've heard much about the charm of Cuban women," I said. "Now I know all of it was a lie. You Cuban women have become so masculine," I said.

A flush of anger appeared on her face. "I know I should not have come at all," she said. "But times have changed. We can't always live in the past."

"I don't know what's happening," I said. "But for heaven's sake, don't quit being a woman."

"I am still a woman," she said.

"Look at your silly uniform," I said. "Don't you have a skirt you could have worn this evening? And look at your hair. It needs combing."

"I have come here straight from work."

I remember another encounter with the militia when I had been in Havana for three days, and had gone to Immigration to pick up my passport. That had taken the whole afternoon. There, too, the person who checked me and took down details about me was an English-speaking militiaman. He was the only man who noticed the entry in the passport stating that by profession I was a journalist.

"Ah-ha, a *podesta* from India," he said, with suspicion in his voice and eyes.

"No, a tourist," I said hastily.

"What is your newspaper?"

"I don't work for any. I hope to, one of these days."

"Then why this entry?"

"I am studying to be a journalist. Someday I hope to be one."

He did not pursue the subject, but gave back my passport and also issued me my exit permit two weeks hence.

Besides standing watch at vulnerable places, the guard militia performed police duty. Throughout my stay I saw few policemen. It's not that the police force had been abolished. It's just that its duties had been reduced and its number cut. When occasion demanded, the guard militia directed traffic, kept the crowd back, and guided children across the street. It also patrolled the streets at night, and in this way kept crime down. Its unit headquarters also acted as a lost-and-found department.

Women were summoned for duty only during the day and were assigned to such semi-important places as movie houses and theaters. Banks, the various ministry buildings, and shops selling industrial goods were always guarded by men. Each new housing colony in Havana was ordered to provide its own guard in addition to the militia assigned to it.

I was able to talk (casually, of course) with several combat militiamen. I learned that they were also taught street fighting.

"If invasion comes," one of them told me, "we will literally fight for every inch of Havana. We will fight from section to section, street to street, house to house. The Yankees will need a million men to comb us out."

Another militiaman was careless enough to tell me that detailed plans for street fighting were already in existence. "If an invasion comes, we will be ready for it. We won't panic. Each man will know where to go, where to station himself," he said. I asked what would happen if a large number of civilians emerged in the streets to go over to the side of the invaders. The man's face assumed a cruel look. "We will not hesitate to fire on such traitors," he said. He sounded as if he really meant it.

Another man told me that there was at least one militia member in each family, and that he would know how to keep the other family members from going over to the enemy.

"You fellows are separate from the regular army?" I asked, hoping that he would not get suspicious.

"We are. We are separate even from the workers' militia. We are the third, the civilian, line of defense," he replied.

The workers' militia (also called the workers' brigades) consisted of factory employees with good physiques. They were a paramilitary organization in that they worked in their factories for twenty days a month and spent the remaining ten days in military training. Some went for training ten days in a row; for others the period was staggered.

Their training consisted of more than street fighting. They were taught how to handle shore batteries, to act as tank maintenance crews, to dig trenches, set up road obstructions against an advancing army, fire from treetops and caves, destroy bridges to slow the enemy's advance, and to dislocate the railroad tracks. Their basic duties were to protect their factory and the area around it and to keep the factory working during attacks, but they were liable to be called to other fronts.

It is impossible to say precisely how many men and women are serving in the various militias, but an estimate would be 500,000.

Several reasons were advanced to me as to why the government was so keen on maintaining the militia.

First, it wants to guard against the possibility of sabotage by anti-Castro elements. There is no doubt that only severe military measures are keeping these elements from creating trouble. If the controls are relaxed, these elements could begin showing their hands through sabotage and terror. The militia comes in handy in keeping internal order. Castro took Cuba through the well-known Communist tactics of hit-and-run guerrilla attacks. He is fearful that his enemies might use the same tactics against him.

Second, the presence of the militia helps to keep the revolutionary atmosphere alive. The government, to justify its existence, is forced to present to the public causes, other than its own incompetence, for the acute shortage of food and consumer goods and the worsening of the economic situation. The best way to do that is to keep impressing upon the people that the Castro revolution still has a long way to go, and that hardships and sacrifices are still required.

Third, the fear of a second invasion hangs heavy upon Castro. There is no illusion that if it comes it will not be as ill-organized as the first invasion. The government actually expects that there will be an attack upon Havana by paratroopers, and the militia is trained in how to shoot them in the air before they hit ground. Several times I saw jaunty militiamen playfully aiming their rifles in the air at imaginary paratroopers.

When a visitor sees the militia for the first time, it is likely to scare him. But in the course of time I came to take its presence as nothing out of the ordinary. I, like the Cuban people, got used to it.

13. The Strongest Army in Latin America

I DID not know they were there until they raised their helmeted heads and the sun gleamed from their fixed bayonets.

I was riding in a bus just outside of Havana. We passed a field overgrown with shrubs. Nobody was in sight. Suddenly, heads began popping through the greenery, and I found myself looking at a Cuban army unit being trained in camouflage tactics. The soldiers, in light green uniforms with twigs sticking from their helmets, appeared tough, disciplined, and intent on doing a good job.

As I looked, somebody shouted a word of command, and all heads disappeared. Not even the keenest eye would have been able to discern that an army unit was hidden in the shrubbery.

Military activities like these were to be seen everywhere in Cuba. At seaside picnic spots, I saw green-painted tanks hidden at hundred-yard intervals under clumps of trees. Green tarpaulin had been spread over each tank to prevent detection from the air. The crews slept in the open, on camp beds, but kept their things in a green conical tent. There was always a guard to prevent unauthorized persons from approaching the tank.

One time, pretending that I had lost my way, I went up to the guard to ask for directions, and was able to sneak a glance into a tent. The first thing I noticed in it was the field telephone. A member of the crew sat beside it, reading a book. The telephone kept the crew in touch with other tank crews in the area. It was necessary to make possible concerted action.

I had been in Havana for only a few days when news arrived of a mercenary air raid upon Santa Clara, a town 186 miles east of Havana. The Havana papers carried the news under banner headlines, and I had *Hoy*'s account translated. It said that in the night two twin-engined bombers had flown over Santa Clara and dropped a few bombs, which hit several houses and killed or maimed a dozen persons.

The next day's papers carried several pages of photographs of the damage. Quite a few of the photographs were grisly, and I was surprised that they did not cause much excitement among the people, although I noticed that the pictures were clipped and pinned to the bulletin boards in most government offices, hotel lobbies, and at street corners. I attributed this lack of excitement to the fact that he Cubans had been living in a near-war atmosphere for five years, and raids and bombings had lost their novelty for them.

I was told that the Santa Clara raid was the fourth within the past month. First a sugar mill in Camagüey was strafed and bombed by a plane that had no markings on it. Three nights later, another unidentified plane appeared over the coastal town of Casilda. Its lights were out and its engine had been cut. I was told that it threw yellow flares, and in their light launched three rockets at an oil-storage tank. It also blew up a railroad car. The third raid was by exile commandos. They arrived in two landing crafts, sailed up the Santa Lucia estuary and fired bazookas at the Patrice Lumumba metal-processing plant. They fought a running battle with Cuban guards and managed to escape in their crafts.

I tried to assess the importance of these raids being made by exile groups operating out of Guatemala and the more than seven hundred islands of the Bahamas. I concluded that although the raids were causing some damage to the Cuban economy, they had, in general, only a nuisance value, and could not appreciably alter the political situation.

This conclusion was the result of my impression that the Cuban army was the strongest in Latin America and was continually gaining in strength—in arms, training, and the myriad other things required by a modern fighting force. Nobody knew definitely how many men were in the Cuban army, but observers on the spot, which included several Western diplomats, were of the opinion that Castro had a hard core of about 200,000 battle-ready combat troops to defend his regime. Some observers thought that the figure was much higher, but even if we go by the first estimate, it makes the Cuban army the largest in any country south of the Rio Grande. And this is so in spite of the fact that Cuba has an area of only 44,000 square miles and a population of about 7,000,000. Brazil, with an area almost as large as the United States, and a population of about 75,000,000, has an army of 85,000. Such low figures are true of other Latin American nations: Mexico, 51,000; Argentina, 90,000; Venezuela, 15,000.

But some observers said that the structure of the Cuban army was loose, and Castro had yet to iron out several organizational problems of major dimensions. One was the creation of a unified command which could guide unified resistance by the various units—the infantry, field artillery, shore battery, and others. At the time I was in Cuba the situation was a jumble; in case of a major assault on the island, the infantry would be fighting according to one plan, the field artillery according to another, and the tank units according to a third.

Cuba is so small and narrow that what is known as fighting in depth is impossible within its boundaries. There are no vast, open spaces such as in Russia, and large-scale maneuvers spread over a vast territory are out of the question. It is impossible to launch against it a violent, surprise offensive by massed air force and mechanized ground force, working in coordination, and to exploit the mobility of the latter to the full. Both offense and defense have to take into consideration the fact that much of the terrain is extremely mountainous and that there are extensive areas in which it is impossible for a modern army to operate. Also to be taken into account is the fact that, while the sea is a natural barrier against invasion, the Cuban coastline presents a hundred points at which a strike could be made.

Until the revolution, Cuba had never had any occasion to organize a modern fighting force. The sea protected it from invasion by unfriendly countries in Latin America, and although Cuba declared war on Germany during World War II, no Cuban contingent of any size was sent to the European front. In fact, Cuban participation in the world conflict was limited to allowing the United States to build the $8 million air base and air training center of San Antonio de los Baños outside Havana. The need for this base arose in 1942 when German submarines began sinking Allied vessels in the Caribbean. To keep peace inside Cuba, the various dictators were satisfied with some ragtag infantry units, a limited supply of modern U.S. arms, a few modern airplanes for show purposes, and a few patrol boats.

When Castro came to power, he began a pell-mell increase in the army. He recruited thousands of men, armed them with modern and semimodern weapons from the Soviet bloc, and never gave a thought to the precise and detailed tactical requirements for defending the island.

It is reported that the first round of massive military assistance from the Soviet bloc, delivered between the fall of 1960 and late summer of 1961, consisted of: 50 to 100 MIG jet fighters, 150 to 200 medium and heavy tanks, 50 to 100 assault guns, 500 to 1000 pieces of field artillery, 500 mortars, 200,000 small arms, 4000 trucks and other vehicles. Also supplied were such items as helicopters, piston-engine trainers, and small single-engine transports. To train the Cubans in the use of these arms came a horde of Russian military technicians. (Russian combat units were to follow later.) And so the army kept growing, the arsenals kept mounting—the Cubans apparently under the belief that the bigger the two, the safer would be the country.

Preliminary reorganization of the army included the creation of three groups—Western, Central, and Eastern. Each group was divided into armies, divisions, brigades. But the big catch was that this reorganization never went beyond the paper stage—the idea of an army was so new to the Cubans, they didn't have trained generals to give practical shape to the plans.

The lack of the conventional rank structure continues to be a frustrating problem. Castro, when he was fighting Batista, had only an army of guerrillas. A commander on the spot could call himself a general, a major, or even a field marshal—but that didn't amount to much. Rank was not conferred upon a man by his seniors; seniority and experience were not required for it.

As Castro's victories mounted, his guerrilla bands grew into the militia, the home guard, composed of fanatics but still paramilitary in content and with little formal organization. When Batista was defeated, Castro did not inherit any military organization worth the name. There were a number of officers who had been trained at West Point, but they were either executed by the new regime or else they had fled to Miami.

But as the privates began to multiply and Soviet technicians began coming in, the need arose to instill a better order into the ranks. Soviet technicians, I was informed, were appalled at the lack of military knowledge of their new friends.

Much of this lack has to do with the Cuban temperament, which is not warriorlike. The Russians found that the Cubans would start something new with tremendous zeal, but that very soon their ardor would wane.

I heard many stories about the encounter between the Russians and the Cubans. The Russian instructors once wanted to know whether there were any training manuals in the Cuban army. A few were produced, but the Russians found them so inadequate that they decided to use the Russian army manuals. Some of these were hurriedly translated into Spanish and run off the presses. One chapter in a manual had to do with saluting regulations. The Russians found it difficult to teach the Cubans the proper rigidity of the body in saluting. The erstwhile guerrillas thought saluting a waste of time. They had been taught that everyone was equal: they saw no point in a private saluting his officer nor in an officer's receiving special consideration in the matter of transportation, lodging, and food.

On several occasions when a Cuban officer tried to impress his men with his newly acquired rank, he was hooted and jeered for it. As for the Russians—they went pink with anger. In their own country this would have led to court-martial, but that was impossible in Cuba.

There was confusion galore over how a guard of honor was to be mounted. The Russian regulations prescribe that as the man who is being honored walks down the line of soldiers, each soldier turns his head toward him. But the Cubans could not understand the reason behind such turning of heads. Some would turn their heads and some would not. The rule was finally dropped.

The Russians complained, justifiably, that the Cubans did not take good care of their equipment, especially their trucks. One reason advanced to me as to why the Russian trucks broke down after a few months was that they were not suited to the Cuban climate. This was somewhat true, but the main reason was that the Cubans did a very poor maintenance job on them. I had occasion to ride in several of these Russian trucks. Not one ran smoothly; something was wrong with every one of them. Havana was full of truck dumps, where vehicles lay by the hundreds, rusting in the sun and the rain.

One morning I happened to be on the lawn behind the Hotel Nacional. It is an elevated piece of ground and commands an excellent view of Havana Bay. But one portion of the lawn had been fenced off, and inside the fence a shore battery had been bolted to the ground. I walked to the fence. A guard challenged me, and I stopped. I told him I had lost my way. As we talked, I got an opportunity to see the battery at close range. I saw the familiar Russian lettering on it, but I also saw that there was rust on the carriage and on a compass used for aiming. It obviously needed a thorough cleaning.

I pointed this out to the guard and told him peremptorily to clean the battery. He was taken aback by my words. He replied that he did not have any cleaning fluid. I said he should get some. He answered that he did not know where to go for it. "It is not my work to rub guns. I watch, not clean," he added, and that ended the argument.

The approach of the average Cuban to soldiering remains casual, and the Russians find this extremely exasperating. When a Russian officer barks a command, he expects his men to obey on the double, but the Cubans just won't do that.

One story circulating through Havana concerned a Russian officer who directed his Cuban orderly to bring the staff car to his house at 5:00 A.M. The orderly brought the car at 5:05.

"You are late! Why?" shouted the Russian.

"I am late by only five minutes," protested the orderly.

"*Why* are you late?"

"I was polishing my boots. You told me that a soldier should wear shiny boots."

"Why didn't you polish them before going to bed?"

"I was too *tired!*"

Another story concerned the wife of a Russian officer. Her husband's Cuban orderly fell in love with her. He tried every ruse to manage a meeting with her, but every time he failed, because the officer worked him very hard. One day during parade he threw himself on the ground and pretended he had fainted. He was carried to the hospital. The officer's wife did volunteer work there, and during one of her rounds he was able to see her. He took her hand in his, and said: "I love you, *compañera.* I love you very much."

"Don't be silly," she replied. "You cannot shoot well, and I cannot love a man who cannot shoot well."

Thereafter, the man began going to the firing range every day to practice. One day he spotted his officer through the range-finder and put a bullet through him, as if by accident. The woman, according to the story, married him.

There was also the tale of a Cuban guerrilla fighter who was sent to Russia for military training. In Moscow, he went to the Bolshoi Ballet and was introduced to a pretty ballerina. The girl was much impressed, and thought he should take lessons in ballet. He quit the army, joined a ballet school, and very soon he had learned all the steps. One day he was asked to dance the role of a prince in some performance.

"I can't be a prince," he said. "I'm a Cuban."

"You are in a ballet group, and you follow orders here," he was told.

"I don't follow orders! I'm a Cuban," he replied.

"But don't you like this nice, silk costume you will wear?"

"I can't wear silk. I'm a Cuban."

So on the dialogue went. I heard several versions of the story, and in each the Cuban was offered good things, but turned everything down by saying that he was a Cuban and could not have it.

"Well, what *do* you want?" he was finally asked.

"I want to go home and be a guerrilla fighter with Fidel," he replied.

I heard several stories, too, that were obscene, not only in subject matter but also in the way they were told. Most were inventions but all pointed up the nonmilitant nature of the average Cuban.

However, very soon I realized that in spite of their easygoing attitude toward soldiering, the Cubans, through rigorous and harsh training, can sometimes be made very amenable to military discipline. They can be taught to be alert, punctual, precise, single-minded, unwavering. I realized this when I visited the military establishment at the Morro Castle, and was almost arrested for prowling through the pillboxes.

14. *Inside a Castro Fortress*

THE sentry who signaled my cab to stop was barely seventeen. He was too small for the khaki uniform he wore and too weak for the semiautomatic rifle he carried. The uniform sagged on his body, and he sagged under the weight of the rifle. His voice was boyish as he asked the cab driver where the hell he was taking me. I could not suppress a smile at his attempt to be stern; it was so ridiculous. But he had the badge of authority, and the cab driver had no alternative but to submit to being questioned.

I had had him drive me from downtown Havana and up the steep road to Morro Castle, a late-sixteenth-century structure built by the Spaniards to meet an expected assault by Sir Francis Drake. Castro has turned the blockhouses, vaults, and dungeon of the castle into a camp for his army. On the pretense of studying the castle's architecture, I tried to get a look at the camp. In spite of the heat, I had dressed myself in my Indian clothes to ward off suspicion. My cab was stopped far from the outer enclosure of the castle. About fifty soldiers were living nearby in small, makeshift buildings.

The cab driver told the sentry that he did not know anything about me, and that all questions were to be directed to me. The sentry did not know English. I said to him the single word *turista* and explained in broken Spanish that I wanted to get into the castle. He asked me through the cab driver to produce some identification. I gave him my passport. He disappeared with it into one of the buildings. For ten minutes we waited, and still he did not return. The cab driver developed cold feet. He had me pay the fare and drove off. I sat down on a boulder and took a good look around.

All about me were mud pillboxes and dugouts, evenly spaced in the open ground. Some of the dugouts were covered with boards or palm matting held down on the edges by bricks; others were open to the sky. Some were empty, but others contained high-caliber machine guns, their mouths sticking out from slits. There were also some abandoned trenches, but they were being used as field latrines.

There weren't many men around, and I was considering walking up to one of the pillboxes when the sentry reappeared, followed by two other soldiers. One of them knew English, and began asking me questions about who I was, whether I had a permit to enter the castle, and whether I was carrying a camera. I took care to remain calm and appear casual. My clothing was a big help in dispelling suspicion, and I answered all the questions in as agreeable a manner as possible.

"Why do you want to see the castle?" I was asked.

"Because I also am a student of architecture," I lied.

"But there is nothing special in this castle."

"It is a Cuban castle, and that makes it special."

"It is forbidden to civilians."

"But I am not a civilian. I am a tourist."

This preposterous answer made the soldier laugh. He translated it for his comrades, and they all laughed.

"Are you a guest of the government?" he wanted to know.

"I am my own guest, and a guest of the Cuban people."

"Do you belong to the Communist party in India?"

"I do."

"Where is your card?"

"I left it in my hotel."

"Why didn't you come here with someone from the government?"

"Why? Aren't you in the government?"

This kind of talk continued for about fifteen minutes. The man took down some particulars about me, went in to consult with someone, and allowed me to enter the castle on the condition that I take no pictures. He said also that a soldier would accompany me during my tour and I would not be allowed to stay by myself anywhere for any length of time. He made another phone call, and a young soldier with his sleeves rolled up arrived to be my companion. I was disappointed when I found that he could not speak English, since I might have been able to get valuable information from him.

I found that the castle moat was still there. That is, it had not been filled up. Filling it would have been a formidable task, because it was at least twenty-five feet deep, though it contained only a few inches of water. The castle drawbridge was down. Some grass had grown where it touched the ground, and from this I gathered that it had been put down permanently. However, the pulleys and chains used to lift it were still in working order. The drawbridge was broad enough and strong enough to let a ten-wheel truck or tank pass over it. Beyond the bridge was an iron portcullis. It was down, but there was a doorbell attached to it. My guide rang it, and someone inside the castle set into motion the mechanism for lifting the portcullis. It was brought down when we had passed through it. Beyond it was a long, open alleyway of sorts. On my left was a low parapet overlooking uptown Havana, and on my right a fifty-foot wall belonging to the castle proper.

We walked up the alleyway until the wall ended. We turned right and came upon an open gateway where several armed guards were stationed. One of them sat at a rickety desk writing in a thick register. It was here that I was searched for a revolver and a camera. (My feeling was that I should have been searched before I passed through the portcullis.) I was then allowed to proceed.

My guard and I spent about forty-five minutes going through the castle. Only twice was I allowed to stop. The first time was when we went up a small tower and the guard pointed out the view of Havana. The second time was when we came to the dungeon in which Batista used to imprison his foes. It was also the place where the Spaniards incarcerated the famous Cuban patriot and freedom fighter, José Martí. The desk he used, the bed on which he slept, and the lamp by which he used to write were still there.

The rest of the time we were just walking, going from one part of the castle to another. We went through several long tunnels, passed under half a dozen vaults, climbed up and down several ramps, tramped through the halls and the stables. By slowing my walk several times and once bending down to tie my shoelaces, I was able to get a better idea of the kind of military base the castle had been turned into. I also saw the nucleus—the first faint beginnings—of a modern army.

I found that most of the rooms and the halls had been turned into barracks, with rows of double-decker iron cots. The soldiers were out drilling, but I was surprised that the beds had not been made up. In other armies I have known, it is incumbent on a soldier to make his bed before he starts the day. But discipline in the Cuban army apparently did not include such a regulation.

From a balcony, I looked down into a courtyard and found that military trucks had been parked in it. To the back of each truck had been hooked a howitzer, ready for transfer at a moment's notice to any place on the island. There must have been fifty of these howitzers. I had no way of judging their caliber, but it is probable that they were 75-mm, best suited for mountain fighting. The holds of these trucks were covered with tarpaulin, but one had its tarpaulin off, and I saw that it carried several neatly packaged crates of ammunition.

In another part of the courtyard, under an awning, I saw about two dozen heavy mortars. And in a small hall that we walked through were stacked about two hundred light mortars. They were the kind that are easy to disassemble and can be carried by foot soldiers over short distances.

I found the castle well equipped for air defense. I counted three antiaircraft guns, one the kind that is mounted on a platform. It had a height-finder and a computer attached to it. Also stacked in the castle were about a dozen mobile low-caliber antiaircraft guns, the type that are used for troop support in battle areas and for protecting convoys from strafing.

The ramble through the castle brought me to a cluster of tanks. I counted twelve of them. Two were American, no doubt inherited from Batista; the rest were Russian. Five of the Russian tanks were the old low-silhouette KV tanks, weighing fifty-two tons and carrying 76-mm guns. The letters KV stood for Kliment Voroshilov, former president of the Soviet Union. Since he fell into disgrace under Nikita Khrushchev, I wondered what the new name of the tank was, but I got no opportunity to ask. The remaining five tanks were of an improved design and of a later vintage, but apart from discerning that they were new, I could not find out anything about them.

I walked past the big communications center in the castle. It was locked, and although the windows were open they had iron bars fitted in them. By looking through those windows, I was able to see facilities for communication both by radio and wireless telegraphy. There were some fifteen men, fiddling with dials. One wall had an apparatus with blinking lights. I would have liked to stay, if only for a few minutes, but my guard would not let me.

He drew my attention to a ten-foot cannon that was pointing toward the sea. It was an interesting piese—but it was three hundred years old.

Stacked near it were five cannonballs. My guide lifted one up to demonstrate his strength. I took it from him, but it was so heavy that I could not hold it.

Another room farther on was occupied by a man who was pointed out to me as an expert in doing a quick repair job on boots, belts, and holsters. My guard decided to introduce me to him and took me into the room, but when he sought to open a conversation, the fellow rudely brushed us aside. He said something which I took to mean that he was very busy, which he was, indeed. Piled on a large table and on the floor were dozens of boots and leather articles. He had no helper, no mechanized sewing awl, not one item of modern shoe-repairing machinery. He was using old-fashioned tools, but he was getting the work done.

In another room sat three tailors with old sewing machines, repairing uniforms and canvas kit bags. (I found out later that soldiers have to provide their own underwear.) The commissary served three good meals a day, which included meat, milk, and vegetables, plus an occasional cigar. The service was in battered zinc trays, but they were kept clean. I learned these additional facts when I was discussing Morro Castle with the military attaché at a Western embassy. At the end of the tour I tipped my guide three dollars, which made him very happy, but I noticed that he glanced to his right and left to make sure that nobody was looking before he accepted the money. He showed me out of the castle, and I went down the road, looking for a cab.

When I found one, the driver, instead of taking me downtown, took me to a building at some distance from the castle. Soldiers surrounded me, and I was asked bluntly: "We are glad you are visiting our country, but what were you doing in Morro Castle?"

"It's a famous castle. I wanted to study the architecture," I replied.

I realized that if I was not careful, I would be arrested. The man who had asked me the question had a very threatening look on his face. He asked me to identify myself. I stuck to my original story—that I was a tourist, an admirer of Fidel Castro, and so forth.

"Well, what did you see in Morro Castle?" my interrogator wanted to know.

"Oh, I was much impressed by the way it was built. There are castles like it in my country, and I was comparing your castle with our castles," I said nonchalantly.

"What else did you see?"

"I saw old cannons and new cannons, and I saw soldiers. I'm glad you're putting the castle to some use. Nobody lives in our castles, nothing is done with them, and that's bad."

And so the interrogation continued; at times I thought it would never end. My attitude throughout was conciliatory, beaming, fawning. I refused to be provoked. I refused to get panicky. I remembered everything I had read about how to stand pressure. I didn't put up a wise-guy show. I took care not to appear "smart." I projected a picture of myself as a rather unobservant, easygoing visitor. I did not overdo my pro-Castroism. I lied, of course, in most of my answers; lied unthinkingly, automatically. I had no alternative. Someone took notes of what I was saying. My address was taken, but luckily I was not asked to sign anything, and after thirty minutes I was allowed to leave.

The cab driver who had picked me up was nowhere in sight. I realized that he had seen me, a stranger, coming out of Morro Castle, and driven me to the military building on his own initiative, as a way of demonstrating his revolutionary zeal. But this was not surprising.

Morro Castle was the only military establishment into which I was able to talk my way. I have said earlier that I saw in it the first faint beginnings of a modern military organization. I meant that it had everything an army requires to be called modern; things such as light and medium artillery, antiaircraft tanks, signal facilities, service units. True, I saw no presence of an engineer combat battalion, nor of a reconnaissance company, but I was convinced that some start had been made in these fields too.

Creating an army is one thing, maintaining it is another, and keeping it supplied with and trained in the use of modern weapons, a third. Castro had to start from the very beginning. Never in history was Cuba a military power. Never were its people militant. Never were they called upon to give up their indolent life and learn how to use a rifle.

Castro had a formidable task before him. I think he has done a remarkable job in that direction. To me the wonder lay in the fact that he was able to get the whole business of military organization off the ground in the first place, and to keep up the momentum. His gains outnumbered by far the glaringly evident deficiencies.

During my stay I had occasion to discuss Castro's problems in military tactics and strategy with several knowledgeable persons. All agreed that the problems were stupendous but that Castro seemed fully aware of them and was on his way to solving them.

It was pointed out to me that he has to guard against four eventualities: a second attack by the exiles; a direct assault by the U.S., both by way of the sea and by airborne troops; an internal uprising; and haphazard internal sabotage, such as sniper attacks and dynamiting of bridges and roads.

The Cubans agreed that the Bay of Pigs invasion was an ill-planned, badly executed venture. One of the reasons it failed was that the exiles had no air cover. Cuban military planners are now fully aware that a second attack, if it comes, would be entirely different and would not have the deficiencies that the first one had. A second invasion definitely would have an air cover. Castro, therefore, is increasing his air power, and, I was told, has ringed the entire island with conventional anti-aircraft batteries.

His basic tactical problems are those that arise from Cuba's being an island. This is both a blessing and a curse. It is a blessing because the sea stretches around Cuba like a giant moat, and any invading force would have to provide itself with a large and varied number of sea craft, not only to get into Cuba and carry the weapons but also to keep its supply lines open. Exile units have been reported to be going through training in Guatemala, but that country is five hundred miles away, and a strong armada would be required to transport troops from there to Cuba. The Bahama Islands are nearer, but they are British-owned, and the British navy is cracking down on exile boats operating out of them.

The fact that Cuba is an island is a curse to the Castro military planners because it gives them a long coastline to guard. It is a coast-line that has a hundred landing places. It is impossible to guard every one of them. That would take an army at least ten times bigger than the one Castro now has. Consequently, he has been forced to keep his army in a high state of mobility. If an invasion comes, the units in the immediate vicinity would have to hold out for some time until reinforcements could reach them. Cuba has good roads, built mostly before the revolution, but logistics would still present a problem. Transporting an army with its equipment, getting it to its destination fast, and seeing to it that its combat effectiveness is not impaired, is no easy thing.

The first reinforcements would naturally come from the nearest de-fensive points. But this would weaken these latter points, and the Cuban nightmare is: What if the assault is made not at one point, but at several? The situation is further complicated by the possibility that the assaults could come simultaneously, or they could be evenly or unevenly spaced over a week or ten days. This raises the need for having troops in reserve. All armies have reserves, but the important thing is their effectiveness.

It is fairly obvious that new invasions of Cuba would not involve a war of position. The situation would be such that the lines of battle would be continually changing, and the area encompassed by them would be shifting.

If Castro has a strategist of the Von Moltke or the Kemal Atatürk caliber, I have not heard of him. Really great military minds are rare. I mean the kind of minds that are flexible, can keep track of every possibility, make use of all available means, exploit every weakness of the enemy, be quick-thinking and ready with a new plan at a moment's notice should the first plan fail; and know how to adopt a strategy of tactical withdrawal or of fighting for every foot of ground according to the need of the hour. If Castro has military thinkers of this caliber, they are well hidden from the public. His brother, Raul Castro, vice-premier, minister of defense and commander-in-chief of the armed forces, is the only known figure.

As far as a direct U.S. assault is concerned, Castro is aware that he would not be able to stand up against it for any length of time. He knows that once the attack commences, Washington will not hesitate to use all its armed might, because victory will be for the U.S. a matter of prestige in Asia, Africa, Europe, and, closer to home, in Latin America.

Castro's safeguards against such an attack are:

1. The presence of Soviet troops in Cuba with the accompanying certainty that these troops would be drawn into the fighting, and create the possibility of Soviet-American clashes in other areas around the world.

2. The assurance given by the late President Kennedy that the U.S. will not attack Cuba unless provoked to do so—by, for instance, an attack by the Cubans on Guantanamo. Castro has taken pains, in spite of his blusterings, not to provoke the U.S. in any such manner.

But the threat of an internal uprising is very real to Castro. Although the chances for such an uprising are not imminent, Castro is in no position to let down his guard. He knows that in case of an uprising he might have to call upon the Soviet troops for aid. This can result in American intervention, because America has made it clear that it will not tolerate in Cuba a Hungarian-like situation in which a genuine revolt of the people was put down with the aid of Soviet troops.

Furthermore, such an uprising would place the Soviet troops in Cuba in a very difficult position, and I attributed the preponderance of the militia to Castro's precautionary measures in this direction. He does not want an uprising, but if there is one, he wants to be able to crush it quickly and keep it from spreading. The longer it lasts the shakier his regime would become. It would cut through his economic plans and expose his weakness as few things could.

As far as internal acts of sabotage are concerned, they have been going on for some time. But these acts, plus the occasional aerial attacks by the exile groups, are not of decisive importance. Their long-term benefit is that they retard the consolidation of the Castro regime and perpetuate the atmosphere of crisis inside Cuba. But their continuance also provides Castro with a justification for the scarcities and a reason for him to call upon his followers to make more sacrifices.

Yet another inkling I got of Castro's considerable strength was when an employee of the Ministry of Foreign Affairs proudly showed me the picture of his airman brother, the pilot of a Mach-3 airplane. This employee was just a minor clerk. He attached himself to me one evening, and we spent several hours visiting the bars. I don't drink, but I bought him all the drinks he wanted. He thought he had found a sucker, and I kept up the illusion.

"Where did your brother get his training?" I asked.

"Raul sent him to Russia. He was there for six months," he replied.

"Where is he now?"

"Somewhere in Cuba. I don't know where. He is not allowed to tell."

"What kind of plane does he fly?"

"Oh, every kind. But now he flies a Mach-3. You know, the kind that goes three times the speed of sound."

"Is he the chief pilot?"

"Not yet. But he will be. Very soon. All his heart is in flying."

"Who is the chief pilot in his crew?"

"It used to be a Russian major. Now I think it's a Cuban. We have good pilots, you know. Very good and brave ones."

Cuban purchase of Russian military planes began in early 1961. It is true that at the time of the Bay of Pigs invasion, Castro had no worthwhile air strength. But immediately afterward he received twenty-six MIG jets from Russia.

Castro did not have pilots of his own. In the initial stages, these planes had Russian crews, but a program was launched to train Cuban crews. In all haste, promising young men were sent to Russian air academies and put through a crash training program on the officer level.

The first jets supplied were of the Korean War period. Primarily defensive fighter planes, they carried rapid-firing cannons, but their destructiveness was capable of being increased considerably with rockets and napalm bombs. It was reported that these jets were received in crates and assembled at the San Antonio de los Baños air base outside Havana. The Russian assembly crews instructed the Cubans in maintenance problems, set up repair depots, organized the storage of spare parts, and the construction of underground fuel tanks.

The organization of the Cuban air force was done rapidly, but at the time of the missile crisis in October, 1962, it was far from having achieved combat viability. An American U-2 reconnaissance plane was actually shot down on Cuban soil during the crisis, but probably the crew that fired that killing rocket was Russian, though credit for it was claimed by the Cubans. In fact, at the time of the crisis, the giant offensive bombers in Cuba were all under Russian control and being flown by elite Russian pilots. The bombers are said to have since been withdrawn, but the Cuban air force is in possession of an advanced type of MIG fighter. One Western diplomat estimated that Castro had one hundred of them, and that more than a third were late-model MIG-21's, capable of carrying A-bombs at a speed of one thousand miles an hour.

The Soviet Union has also supplied a large number of smaller aircraft for observation purposes. At the time of the Bay of Pigs invasion, the Cubans already had some of these, and they were effectively used to determine the disposition of the exile forces. When I was in Cuba they were being increasingly used for short flights over the sea around the island to track U.S. Navy vessels, and to get their exact type and course.

I also saw a large number of helicopters from the Soviet Union. They were being used for patrol duties over Havana. Several times during my drives to the country, I saw helicopters hovering over my bus. I was told that Castro wanted more of them, for use in carrying riot troops to pockets of insurrection in the interior. I could not ascertain whether Russian supplies have included transport planes and troop carriers. The guess was that some transport planes have been supplied, but they are small and their tactical usefulness is doubtful because of the biggest problem that besets the Cuban army—lack of coordination among the various units.

All observers agreed that the Cuban air force had not reached the stage of being organized into groups and wings. The closest unit of organization was the squadron. But even the squadrons were incapable of being distinguished as fighter, bomber, or observation units, nor was there any provision for the division of a squadron into flights. The consensus was that each squadron combined in varying degrees all the functions of war aviation. There was no specialization.

I was told that the foundation had been laid in Cuba for a national air academy. There were several government flying schools before the revolution. Castro combined these and improved their standards of training. Basic training in flying now can be had at this school. For specialized training in aerial warfare, the students are sent to Russia.

It is impossible for civilians to learn to fly. There were many flying clubs before the revolution, and they are still there, but they don't have any training aircraft. Immediately after the revolution their planes were expropriated, and all persons holding pilot's licenses were ordered to report for some form of aerial duty. Most of them fled to Miami.

Cuba does not have a navy in the modern sense of the word, but what there is of it has an infinite capacity for mischief. The country does not have any destroyers, cruisers, or submarines. But it does have a very large number of frigate-type patrol gunboats that can be put to various uses. I learned that in the first flush of revolution Castro insisted that Russia should supply him with minelayers. He planned to lay a network of mines in Cuban waters, and was dissuaded from it only when it was impressed upon him that the mines would be a hazard to Russian commercial vessels coming to Cuba.

The main vessel in the Cuban navy is the Lambda-7. Often posing as fishing boats, the Lambdas patrol the Cuban shores and transport men and arms for insurrection activities to other countries of Latin America.

Cuba has five shipyards, the largest being the Chulliam, on the Almendares River in Havana province. Lambdas are being built there at a very fast pace under Soviet guidance and with Soviet equipment. Each Lambda has a fuel capacity of fifteen tons, and a crew of twelve. It has a cruising radius of 3600 miles, and is well provided with such things as radar, sonar, and radiotelephones. It also has several types of firing equipment, including two ship-to-ship missiles with a range of ten to fifteen nautical miles.

Another type of vessel in use is the ETA-25 boat. It has a smaller range, but it makes very little noise as it prowls through the sea in search of exile commando boats or of boats carrying escapees from Cuba.

One diplomatic guess put the number of all these boats at two hundred. But it could be considerably more. It certainly is increasing. I was told that the captains of quite a few of these boats were Russian; if they did not know Spanish, they gave orders through an interpreter.

A naval school has been established by Castro in the town of Cienfuegos. It is called the Victoria de Playa Girón naval school. The name celebrates the victory at the Bay of Pigs in 1961. Twice in Havana I ran across cadets from this school, wearing the familiar white navy uniform. I tried to get into conversation with them, but they wouldn't stop to talk.

Before the revolution, coastal trade in Cuba was plentiful. There is not much of it now, but the small craft formerly used for carrying goods are now being repaired, and their number has been increased. Castro plans to use them for transporting men and equipment from one Cuban port to another in case the land routes are severed by counter-revolutionaries. For this purpose he is being supplied with Soviet landing barges, diesels of shallow draft. He has also been given a number of Soviet boats of the LST type, and he intends to use them as repair shops for his Lambdas.

During the time I was in Cuba, I saw that Havana harbor was not as busy a place as it used to be. Most ships coming to it were from the Red bloc. Cargoes were unloaded rapidly, and ships were on their way back to Russia in a matter of days. The S.S. *Yuri Gagarin* docked on September 2, a day after my arrival, and had left by September 6. I found Havana harbor well provided with tugboats, floating docks, and oil storage and gasoline barges.

15. The Betrayal of a Revolution

AN anti-Castro Cuban told me that the best way for the Voice of America to discredit Fidel Castro before the Cuban people was to begin broadcasting the speeches he made before coming to power.

In those speeches, Castro was idealistic—even utopian, quixotic. He made many extravagant promises. He held out the hope of an era of reform and progress; an era in which there would be no dictatorships, and in which the common man would really come into his own, be free from tyranny and exploitation, and have all the freedoms the human soul craves.

Never once did Castro sound like a Communist. Never did he say that he was one. Never was he taken to be anything except a reformer on a Latin American pattern of Thomas Jefferson, Sir Robert Peel, and Theodore Roosevelt.

Castro's previous life had made him the ideal of the masses. As the fearless lawyer who defended without fee the victims of the Batista tyranny, he had the people behind him. The rest of the world pondered the cruelties of Batista, contrasted them with the activities of the heroic lawyer, and saw in the young revolutionary a new Robin Hood, a Cuban d'Artagnan, born to lead his people to democracy and prosperity.

The joke was as complete as it had been when the world thought that the Reds in China were only land reformers. The general belief was that the Chinese character would never accept the Communist militancy. Everyone thought that peace-loving Buddhism and indolent Confucianism were so much a part of their way of life that the Chinese would never go to the extremes advanced by Karl Marx. Events in China since 1948, when the Reds took over, have proved how wrong the world was.

I was working in Washington in 1959 when Castro had just seized power. The capital did not lack trusting people who thought that Communism with a Latin beat just would not swing. They pointed out that the Cubans were too gay and lazy to become Reds, and that Cuban Communism at best would be half-baked compared to the dedicated version behind the Iron Curtain. These people said that Castro had his own party, the 26th of July Movement, which was separate from the Cuban Communist party, and that in allying with it, he was using the Communists only to advance his aims.

Castro is still not a member of the Cuban Communist party, but the question can well be asked whether, in the early stages of the revolution, he was using the Communists or the Communists were using him. His aims and the aims of the Reds were the same and still are the same. These were to get rid of Batista, nationalize all private property, seize all American and foreign capital, and lead the island into the world Communist bloc. The fact that his party and the Communist party had different labels didn't mean a thing when it came to the execution of these policies on which both agreed. There was full and complete agreement on principles. If there were any differences, these were only on methods. In any case, the differences were minor. The two parties have since coalesced, and organizational differences between the two exist only on paper. The differences in method still don't amount to much.

Cuba had a very democratic and liberal constitution, formulated in 1940. It provided for social security, minimum wages, and reforms of various kinds. But dark clouds began to gather over the country when Fulgencio Batista took over the presidency in 1952 as the result of an army *coup d'état*. It was when Batista suspended the constitution that Castro organized an armed rebellion in the mountains of Camagüey province. In this, he and his party were joined by the Popular Socialist party (the Communist party) and a smaller group known as the 13th of March party.

It was Castro's party, however, that was active in the forefront. It was his party that carried out a wide-ranging program of sabotage and kidnaping, did most of the fighting, and made the most sacrifices. The national elections were scheduled for June 1, 1958. The Castro terror was such that the Cuban Congress declared a national emergency, gave extraordinary powers to Batista, and postponed the voting.

But these steps could not kill the rebellion. Castro was now receiving clandestine arms shipments from Iron Curtain nations. The rebellion, previously limited to guerrilla warfare, now changed to pitched battles. On New Year's Day, 1959, Batista fled the country, and soon after that

Castro entered Havana to the thunderous cheers of the multitude, almost as if he were a Roman hero, like Lucius Brutus, entering Rome after having driven out a tyrant.

But what did he do the moment the power was his?

One tyrant had been tumbled, and Castro took over the vacant chair —not to fulfill his earlier promises but to launch a new form of tyranny through subtlety, stealth, guile, deceit, and bombast.

He did not show his hand at once. At first, all his actions were very proper and correct. He conferred the presidency upon a respected nationalist, Dr. Manuel Urrutia, who was known to be a foe of Communism. Dr. Urrutia was persuaded, or cajoled to go along with Castro's actions, and to back them with the authority of his name and reputation, because of the extraordinary situation in the island. There was no denying that things were in disruption, and Castro argued that in order to restore stability strong measures were necessary. He personally took over as premier on February 16, and announced the promulgation of a vague and obscure document called the Fundamental Laws.

The document was based on the 1940 constitution, but it carried modifications for rule by a *de facto* government. A promise was made that the document would be repealed as soon as the situation became normal, at which time national elections would be held. The elections were promised for an early date.

Castro flew to Venezuela and grandly prophesied that all Latin America was ripe for revolution. Later in the year, he managed to contrive an invitation to Washington. President Dwight D. Eisenhower refused to see him, but he had long talks with Secretary of State Christian Herter and many Congressional leaders. He made it clear that he wanted American economic aid, but he refused to commit himself to democracy. He was asked whether he planned to be neutral in the struggle between the East and the West. His evasive answer was that Cuba was too poor, did not have an army worth the name, and that it did not really matter what side it took. His strategy was to cast upon the United States the onus for refusing the aid, and find a justification for a break with the West and his plans for nationalization of property in Cuba.

No Communist could have carried out this strategy better. Castro returned home, and his first action was the promulgation of an agrarian reform law limiting individual holdings to one thousand acres and restricting ownership to Cubans. The immediate result of the decree was that it stripped American-owned sugar mills in Cuba of all their plantations. The U.S. protested the act. It led to a split in Castro's cabinet, and five of its members resigned, but Castro refused to revoke the law.

President Urrutia now began to get a faint inkling of the course his premier was planning to pursue. He came out in opposition to all such actions. Castro retaliated by resigning the premiership. His purpose was to find a reason for his mobs to take to the streets and hold wild demonstrations against Urrutia. This the mobs did, and did it so well that Urrutia, feeling harassed and checkmated, was compelled to resign and leave the country. Castro returned to power, and installed one of his henchmen, Osvaldo Dorticos Torrado, as the president.

The arbitrary seizure of both farm and nonfarm properties was now stepped up. Through forced lending to the government, new and heavier taxes, exchange control, changes in the civil law, and revision of fiscal legislation, Castro took steps toward Marxism like any other good Communist anywhere. The Cuban labor federation withdrew from the Inter-American Regional Organization of Labor, because the latter was anti-Communist. In its place, Castro instigated the founding of the Latin American Confederation of Revolutionary Workers.

He also acquired control of the professional bodies of lawyers, accountants, engineers, doctors, journalists, writers, and others by having his followers or agents inside each group move for the expulsion of the nonconforming elements. "We need a strong government. We need Castro. It's our national duty to support Castro," was the theme of these followers. Everywhere they won, because they could make the most noise and were organized.

The year 1960 saw nationalization carried to its extreme limits. The giant net of expropriation fell over the land, over all sugar plantations and mills, mining and petroleum enterprises, power plants, telephone companies, airlines, shipping companies, land transportation concerns, commercial houses, banks (except two Canadian banks which were later sold to Cuba), and urban property. All these and more became state property. No Communist could have done it better.

The year 1960 also saw the signing of trade and aid agreements with the Soviet Union and other Red countries. The U.S.S.R. contracted to buy Cuban sugar and provide Cuba with $100 million credit for machinery. The U.S. kept lodging protest after protest with Havana, but to no avail. The diplomatic war between the two was growing in intensity, and there seemed to be no way of stopping it.

When America quit buying Cuban sugar and tobacco, Castro complained that his island was being subjected to economic strangulation. He posed before the world as a victim of "dollar diplomacy," and presented himself as just an innocent nationalist whose only aim was to bring "freedom and dignity and pride" to his small nation.

In mid-1961 he thought himself strong enough and sufficiently entrenched to discard his mask and proclaim officially that Cuba would be a Marxist state. He made the declaration after the May Day parade, and also confessed that since his student days he had been a devotee of Communism. He thereby completed his betrayal of the revolution. There would be no turning back for him now. The Red bloc was already calling him a savior of the Cuban people. It now began pouring aid into Cuba to make it impregnable to assaults.

But with his mask off and the last pretense of loyalty to democratic traditions removed, Castro launched into the other phases of creating a Marxist society. Elections were postponed indefinitely. His cabinet made a habit of exceeding the limits placed upon its actions by the Fundamental Laws. The judiciary was purged. The remaining private and social clubs were confiscated. The workers were deprived of the right to strike, their income was reduced by "voluntary" deductions from their pay checks, and new paper currency was issued without gold reserves to back it. Castro did all this, but continued to refuse to join the Communist party.

The strategy he adopted toward local Communists was unique. He took care, while doing all their work, not to lose to them his upper hand in the affairs of the country. Some observers have presented Castro and the men closest to him primarily as radical nationalists, with only a thin and unsure coating of the discipline of Marxism spread over them. I studied this suggestion closely. It is true that many Fidelistas I talked with assured me that they were not Communists. I found that they did not have much respect for the local Reds. Their antipathy toward them was based on the charge that these Reds did not bear their full share of the fighting against Batista. "They hid under the bed while we were meeting the bullets," was the way one Fidelista expressed his feelings.

The cue for this attitude is provided by Castro himself. He is on record as having gone out of his way on several occasions to subject the Reds to scathing criticism. He continues to do that. He thinks they are "dogmatists," and "unproductive theoreticians, incapable of solving personal problems."

The Fidelistas are fond of quoting the quarrel between Castro and Aníbal Escalante, the noted Cuban Communist. Early in 1962, Castro caught him involved in political machinations to establish his personal ascendancy. Castro lost no time in cutting him down to size. He publicly accused him of sectarianism, and on March 26, 1962, spoke about it: "We are convinced that comrade Escalante . . . followed a non-Marxist policy, followed a policy which departed from Leninist norms . . . and that he tried to organize an apparatus to pursue personal ends." The rest of the speech was very moving and argumentative, but it would be folly to look upon it as embodying disagreement with Marxism or a willingness to lessen its rigidity. It was, rather, a speech of personal gripe against a Red leader who wanted more power than Castro would like him to possess. My impression was that Castro wanted total Communism, but wanted the credit for himself. He was unwilling to share it with the local Reds.

Those who listen to his long-winded speeches, his harangues, are often led to believe that he is not a man of depth. Nothing could be more wrong. The man has a brain. He can think, and he can aim his thinking at the years ahead rather than let it be bogged down in the years that have passed. One result of his personal hold has been that he is able to make his followers accept contradiction in thought and action. "You say you are not Communists," I said to the Fidelistas who had claimed they weren't, "but you are following a leadership that wants to establish Communism. Aren't you being self-contradictory?" These men, I am sure, realized that they were being just that, but they had no answer to give me.

One reason the orthodox Red leadership in Cuba has been unable to assert itself is that it doubts that it can run Cuba without Castro. The Cuban Reds are staunchly in Moscow's camp, and Moscow and they realize that if Castro is not allowed to have his way, he might very well turn to the Red Chinese. And that's something that Moscow does not want at any price. The Kremlin is as fearful of losing Cuba to Red China as it is of losing it to democracy.

When I was in Cuba there was an official party, called the Institution of Revolutionary Organizations, commonly referred to as the ORI. It was an amalgam of the Popular Socialist party, the 13th of March party, and Castro's own 26th of July Movement with Castro's party having the upper hand.

But the foundation of a new party, the United Party of the Socialist Revolution, had already been laid. It was the result of a realization by the Fidelistas and the orthodox Reds of their interdependence. They needed each other—the Fidelistas needed the Reds to project more successfully their ideals and methods of organization, and the Communists needed Castro for mass-supported enthusiasm.

The new party had been given a broader base, and about 15,000 members had been recruited. Castro was already being referred to as the First Secretary. I was told that the party did not accept for membership just any Cuban who could pay the dues. Selection was made on the basis of five qualifications:

1. The candidate must be an A-grade worker, and have been the "best worker of the month" in his group at least once.

2. He must belong to one of the defense organizations, such as the militia or the reserves.

3. He must be a confirmed atheist.

4. He must have a good record of voluntary work, both in his regular employment and outside.

5. He must be occupied in some form of self-improvement, such as night education classes.

I have earlier mentioned the way a Young Communist is selected. The selection procedure for a UPSR member is the same. If a worker, through consistent good work, comes to the attention of his fellow-workers, it is likely that at a reunion meeting his name would be put forward for membership of the party. If so, his entire past life is subjected to a microscopic examination by the other workers. They examine all his attributes, behavior, attitudes, blemishes. At one such meeting a candidate was rejected because he had once refused to work in the rain. A second was set aside because he was found trying to get two dolls at the same time for his daughter.

If a candidate emerges unscathed from this kind of treatment, his name is put to a vote. If 70 percent of the workers vote for him, he is recommended for membership to the party high command, which alone has the power to decide finally. It conducts its own investigation of the worthiness of the applicant.

The goal was to have 60,000 members in the party, recruited from factories, farms and offices. I could not ascertain whether soldiers, too, could belong to the party, but I doubt that they are excluded.

A party member receives special privileges—such as priority in the distribution of scarce goods, in getting train reservations, and in numerous other ways. He automatically becomes a man of influence in his community, and, on the basis of his membership card, he can approach men in the highest echelon for something he might want done.

The national committee of the ORI also became the national committee of the new party. It has twenty-five members—thirteen from the 26th of July Movement, eleven from the Popular Socialist party, and one from the 13th of March Party. On the national level the party is responsible for the direction of policy, but on the local level it promotes the policy's development and progress without interfering with local administration.

16. Training Camp for Subversion

IN Havana, young men from at least fifty underdeveloped nations in Asia, Africa, and Latin America are undergoing training from Russian and Czech experts in how to spread Communism through subversion. I met and talked with and heard about quite a number of these wild-eyed, fire-breathing youths.

There was Enrique, aged twenty-four, from Colombia. He was in Havana ostensibly to study engineering. But in actual practice he was being taught how to organize and launch a Red revolution in his country. Probably not this year, maybe not even the next; but sometime during this decade you may well hear of Enrique's leading a guerrilla band against the government in the mountains and forests of Colombia and winning his way to success or dying in the attempt. There is no turning back, no middle course, for men such as Enrique.

How was I able to learn about him? Oddly enough, through his sweetheart, Miss Gloria Sanderson of Canada. This was how it came about.

In Havana I was eager to meet some English-speaking man or woman from the West with whom I could relax and chat. I asked the tourist office whether it had some such visitor on its list. Gloria's name was given to me, and I was told she was staying in Room 321 at the Hotel Flamingo in uptown Havana. I called her on the phone, but she was out. I left my name, and an hour later she returned my call. I said that I had recently come from Canada and would be going there again. I told her I would be very happy to carry any message she might have for her family, and I asked her whether she would have supper with me. She said no, but said she would be available for a chat at six o'clock that evening.

She came down to the lounge to talk with me. She was a wan, pale girl of nineteen, tall and very thin. She had a beautiful face, and long russet hair, but dull eyes. I talked with her for two hours, but I did not enjoy the meeting.

She told me that when she was sixteen, her parents were divorced, and that her mother soon remarried. Gloria found it impossible to get along with her stepfather. She moved out of her mother's house, quit school, and got a job at a bank. Her father was sending her an allowance, and she found economic independence quite pleasing. Toronto had a rich social life to offer, and she took full advantage of it. Between then and the time I met her, she had been engaged twice, but each time the engagement had been broken. In January, 1963, she went to Jamaica for a vacation, and there met Enrique, who had been on that island since the previous October, trying to find a boat to take him to Cuba. He had been given a scholarship to the University of Havana, and was confident that he would be able to hitch a ride on some small boat plying the narrow neck of water separating Jamaica from Cuba.

He would have succeeded but for the blockade of Cuba by United States vessels in October, 1962. He was forced to prolong his stay in Jamaica. Gloria told me that she met him one evening on the beach. She immediately took a liking to him, and he liked her. They began to meet frequently, and their feeling for each other soon changed to love. At the end of the vacation, Gloria had to fly back to Toronto. When the two parted, it was with a solemn promise that they would keep in touch by letter.

In February, Enrique found a boat to Cuba. Gloria wrote to him and he responded with an equally passionate letter. When I met her, she had come all the way from Toronto to see him.

"Are you engaged?" I asked.

"More or less," she replied.

"Do you plan to marry Enrique?"

"Maybe."

"Has he asked?"

"No."

"Do you see any future with him?"

"I don't know."

"What does he plan to do when he returns to Colombia?"

"Why, he will be a revolutionary, of course."

"Would you like to be the wife or girl friend of a revolutionary and be hunted from cave to cave, not knowing what will happen tomorrow?"

"Why not?"

"Are you a Communist?"

"No."

"Will you give up being a Canadian?"

"Yes, if Enrique wants me to."

"I don't think he will. He will probably want you to return to Toronto and organize Red cells."

"How do you know?"

"Because in a Communist society the only use for love is to further the interests of the party."

When she did not reply to this, I asked her whether she saw Enrique often.

"He is very busy, but he comes whenever he can for a few hours," she replied.

"Did he know you were coming?"

"Yes."

"Was he at the airport?"

"No. But I don't mind. He is a busy person."

I felt sorry for Gloria, sorry about her thinking, sorry about her hollow-eyed, sunken-cheeked haggardness.

"When did you eat last?" I asked.

"I had a fish sandwich for breakfast."

"Any lunch?"

"No."

I renewed my invitation to supper. She refused again, because she was expecting Enrique in a few hours.

Gloria had been in Havana only five days, but had already lost several pounds. I asked her how she liked Cuban coffee. She said she had brought a jar of instant coffee with her and was existing mostly on that and on crackers. Had she seen Havana? She replied that she had to be in her room all the time, because Enrique was likely to drop in at any hour of the day or night, depending on his other activities. She admitted that she let Enrique spend nights with her in her hotel room. She also began criticizing the free-enterprise system and everything the free world stands for. She was using the familiar Red clichés, and I doubt that she understood what they meant. To me she appeared to be a girl in some sort of trance.

But I let her talk. She gave me her mother's address, and asked me to tell her that she was all right. She also told me a lot about Enrique and his colleagues. She said that there were thirty young men from Colombia studying in Havana. Tuition and living were free for all of them. They received some instruction in a profession, but they were mainly taught how to spread the seeds of revolution on returning to their own country. I tried to prolong my stay, hoping to be able to meet Enrique, but fifteen minutes before he was due, Gloria hurried me away.

During the following days, however, I had occasion to meet young men like Enrique from Jamaica, British Guiana, Ecuador, Peru, Morocco, Ghana. I also met one student from Red China. I lost no opportunity to get them talking. In other parts of the world I have found that a hard-core, dyed-in-the-wool Communist is usually very secretive concerning his activities. But the fledglings I talked with in Cuba had not yet reached that high state of sophistication. I posed as one of them, as a revolutionary from India, and they opened their hearts to me.

My biggest shock came when a student from British Guiana turned to me and asked me in all innocence, "When do you think India will be free?"

"But we are free, and have been free for fourteen years," I replied.

"No, man, not *that* kind of free."

Then I caught on. He meant when would India be a Communist state. "It won't be long, comrade," I responded. "We're working on it. By the end of this decade, maybe."

I found that to these young men no country in the world is "free" until it is a Communist state. The cue for this mode of thinking lies in a slogan widely painted all over Havana: "Cuba—the only free country in the Western Hemisphere."

To one student from Jamaica, I happened to mention casually that I was present at the Independence Day celebrations of his country in Washington, D.C., the previous year. He shot me a look that said, "Jerk." He said that Jamaica would be free only when it went Red.

There was one fire-breathing bore from Georgetown, British Guiana, who, if you asked him where he came from, always replied that he came from "Latin America." He never said that he was from Georgetown. We met several times, and one day I asked him for an explanation.

"You know, comrade," he replied, "all Latin America is one country, just as all Africa is one country. The political divisions you see in these continents are the work of dirty European colonialists and dirty

Yankees. One day all of Latin America will unite into one country and all of Africa will unite in the same way."

"You are right, comrade," I replied. "I agree with you one hundred percent. That will surely happen." He was talking in all seriousness, and I was astonished at his naiveté.

One of the most popular books with these young men was a manual on guerrilla warfare written by Industries Minister Ernesto Che Guevara. It bore striking resemblance to a manual on the same topic written by Red Chinese leader Mao Tse-tung. Also being widely read when I arrived was a Guevara article advocating the overthrow of non-Communist governments through bloody revolutions. The article took the Red Chinese line that Communism can be spread only through war. Most of the foreign students I met seemed to know the article by heart, and were very fond of quoting from it; to them, every line was incontrovertible.

One afternoon I arrived at a dormitory with some Cuban students. A Red Chinese student was standing guard at the gate. I was introduced to him, and the moment he learned that I was from India, without even so much as saying hello he began accusing India of having launched a war of aggression against his country. He didn't need a cue; he just lunged right into it in language that was impolite and indecent. He might have been an Army sergeant, and I a private caught stealing bread from the mess.

"Why don't you withdraw your troops?" he shouted at me. "You have become a Yankee slave. You are rubbing your nose on the ground before Kennedy for more arms. You want to conquer China. The mill-owners in Bombay rule India. You are a slave of them . . . "

This outburst continued for about two minutes. I took it in my stride, as something not worth bothering about. Frankly, I found it amusing. But it embarrassed my Cuban hosts, who tried to lead me away. But then a student from British Guiana intervened and asked me: "Why doesn't Nehru leave Chinese territory?"

"We did not start the war," I replied.

"You did," the Guianan said.

This pleased the Chinese immensely, and he said to him, "Ask this man what percentage of the Indian population is literate."

I said that about 25 percent could read and write.

"Only twenty-five percent," exclaimed the Guianan. "You say you have been free for fourteen years, and still not everyone has been educated. Here is Cuba, free for only four years, and everyone is literate."

He was referring to a program of mass literacy launched by the government in 1961. I thought that the Guianan was exaggerating its results.

"Oh, in *that* way, everyone in India can read and write," I said. "I thought you meant really literate."

He did not understand me, but the impression I got was that these non-Cuban students were out-Castroing Castro in their zeal. A close study revealed that their training in Cuba included such things as how to organize Communist cells, how to go underground when danger threatened, how to recruit new members and test their loyalty, how to make Molotov cocktails and plastic bombs, how to burn government buildings and raid banks for funds.

The curriculum also taught them how to kidnap opponents, hold their relatives as hostages, burn bridges, dynamite the roads, uproot railroad tracks, steal arms from government arsenals, and secretly import arms from other countries.

The students told me all this. But whenever I asked whether there was a special school where these things were taught, I did not get a direct answer. They hedged, and procrastinated, winking at each other and smiling.

I asked one of them: "What do you do in capitalist countries in which the standard of living is improving and the grounds for spreading Communism are becoming vague?"

"In such countries," he replied, "the real Communists just go underground, or they set up a front and use it as a cover."

Another student, who was from Ecuador, said that no matter what improvements were made in the capitalistic system, it just "has to go." There was no room for compromise, he asserted.

I managed to glean some more information by pretending that I had information of my own to impart. One night I said to some Guianans: "Do you know the best way to beat off an attacking police party?"

"What?" they asked eagerly.

"Well, chili is very common in India. You get yourself a supply of it, mix it with boiling water, and use small sprinklers to shoot the water at the police. It can burn fearfully," I said.

"Why, that's very good," one of them said, and he went on to tell me how to make plastic bombs.

Another bit of information I freely gave was: "If you want a fellow to buckle down to you, find out how he can be hit the hardest and attack him in that way. For instance, if he is very fond of his wife, tell him that if he doesn't do what you want him to do, his wife will be hurt. You first have to know what he is really fond of—his wife, children, father—and hit him through that fondness. That's where he is most vulnerable."

"You are very soft-hearted," the Guianan student replied. "I would just kill the fellow. That would be a lesson to others and they would come to our side. Look how much time and effort you would save. I have no inclination toward any mercy. We can't afford to be soft. Strength is the only thing I can understand."

The students talked in terms of plans and counterplans, of who was to be set up as the leader, and who had the capacity and the potential to lead. A lot of things they said were just talk, but there was substance, too, in their chatter, and to me it was often chilling. There appeared to be nothing haphazard about the plans. At times they appeared not fully drawn and a bit farfetched, but even so they had an element of great danger in them for the free world.

The impression I got was that a formal school for teaching subversion to these young men does really exist somewhere in Cuba. One rumor had it that it was located in the Sierra Maestra, but there was no way by which I could confirm it. My impression was that not all foreign students are assigned to it. They are first given a sound grounding in basic Communism and taught elementary methods of spreading confusion and chaos. My feeling was that most of them would be sent back to operate as advanced fellow-travelers, while the actual work of spreading terror and guiding its course would be reserved for the elite among the students (and all may not be students), who are given instruction by Russian and Czech experts hidden from the public eye.

I have visited college campuses in a great many countries and have listened to almost every kind of campus talk. But the campus talk at Havana University was entirely different. The foreign students there seemed to be straining at the leash, wildly eager, to go back to their countries and launch "the revolution."

The best estimate I could get of the number of such students from

Latin American countries was 2000; and from Africa, several hundred. There were also some from France.

I was urged by a few to prolong my stay in Cuba and to apply for the status of a scholarship student. "We have no one from India. We must have someone from India, too," these young zealots said. I made inquiries at Havana University, asking whether it would accept me. The officials I talked with said that they would be willing to consider my case. They even appeared vaguely eager to have me. An undercover agent would have jumped at the chance, but I was a reporter, and my first duty was to get a story.

On several occasions I called Gloria Sanderson to ask to see her a second time. I wanted her to introduce me to Enrique, but she put me off every time. She always had an excuse, and at times sounded brusque. I think Enrique had chided her for telling me about him, and he probably had even forbidden her to see me again.

The Canadian embassy officials were worried about her. They told me that her father had written to the embassy, asking them to keep an eye on her. But they did not know what to do. The last time I talked with her on the phone she said she had gotten a visa to Mexico, and was planning to stay there and work until Enrique sent for her. She said that his training was almost over and in a few months he would be returning to Colombia. I asked her why she didn't prolong her stay in Cuba until then. She replied that Enrique had asked her not to, because he was going into the interior of the country for specialized training and it would be impossible for him to see her.

She left for Mexico City two days before I flew out of Cuba, and I don't know where she is now.

17. The Gusano Menace
—Anti-Castroism

IN Spanish, the word *gusano* means "worm." Fidel Castro uses it to describe everyone who is against him. But the amazing thing is that the anti-Castro people, instead of becoming angry about it, have taken it on as their official name. Today, when one *gusano* meets another *gusano*, the two identify themselves to each other by wiggling their fingers to imitate the wiggling of a worm.

One afternoon I was going up in the hotel elevator to my room on the fourth floor. Two other men were aboard. As I watched, one of them began wiggling the index finger of his right hand. The second man replied by wiggling his own finger. This surprised me, but before I could ask anything, the two got off on the third floor. I saw the same signal being exchanged between two men in the Almendares Park. This time I went up to them and asked what they were doing. They glared at me, said nothing, and lost themselves in the crowd. It was only much later that a Cuban explained the sign to me. I asked whether there were many *gusanos* in Cuba. He said that their number was substantial.

They aren't organized. Their opposition does not show much. They are guarded in their speech. The extent of their dislike of Castro varies. Some hate him passionately, some just dislike him, some are indifferent. My first talk with an anti-Castro girl was at Varadero beach.

I had been in Havana only a few days when I visited the beach. It is two hours by bus from the capital and is one of the best beaches in the world. The sea is warm and shallow, and its floor is extremely smooth. The beach stretches for several miles and is lined with hundreds of houses. The owners of many of them have fled. These houses were taken over by the government, and workers on holiday stay in them now.

I have rarely had a more enjoyable time than the morning I spent at Varadero. I plunged into the sea, let the water lap against my chest, then floated in the waves with my eyes closed. After my swim I was lying on the sand absorbing the warm Cuban sun, when a lovely girl wearing a two-piece bathing suit came toward me. She was slender and made a pretty sight with the breeze playing against her long black hair.

I lost no time in getting up and asking her whether she could speak English. She said yes. I introduced myself, stressed the point that I was a newcomer, and asked her whether she would take the trouble of showing me around. She replied that she was on her way to join her parents, but that she would not mind taking a dip with me. I asked her if she would teach me how to do a backstroke. She agreed to do so.

I found her a good teacher and she found me a quick learner. When we paused to rest, at least a hundred yards from the shore, I asked her what she did for a living. She gave me her name and said she was a teacher. She told me the name of a town in Camagüey province where her home was. She said she was eighteen and was in Varadero with her family for vacation. I asked her what she thought of the Castro regime. The vituperatives poured out in a flood.

"You should be careful," I pointed out. "Somebody could catch you talking like this, and then you would be in trouble."

"Who would catch me here?" she answered. "That's why I brought you here—so that we couldn't be overheard."

"Oh, so you came to talk, not to teach me swimming," I said.

"You don't need to be taught. You already know the backstroke," she replied, smiling.

I asked her whether she found it easy to be a teacher. She said that the teaching part was not hard, but the regime was always testing her political reliability, forcing her to say things she did not believe in. I asked whether one had to be a Communist to become a teacher. She said that one need not actually belong to the party, but that one was expected to go along with the party line. The Teacher's Union, she said, was dominated by persons loyal to the revolution.

"So, if you disagree with something, what do you do?" I asked.

"We just don't say anything."

"What if you did say something?"

"We would lose our jobs, or be thrown into jail, or given some inferior job."

"Would it reflect on your family?"

"It could."

"How?"

"My father would come to be known as the father of a traitor, and that's not good in Cuba today. They would accuse him of not bringing me up well."

I asked whether there were others in her family who thought the same way. She said her father agreed with her but that he was too old to care. Her brother, too, had the same opinions, but he was only sixteen and unable to do anything. I asked whether there were many people in her province who were anti-Castro. Yes, there were, but they were disorganized, confused, and scattered.

I made a date to meet this charming and voluble young teacher at a restaurant later in the afternoon, but she didn't show up. The impression I got after talking with others like her was that the anti-Castro people are drawn mainly from among those who had belonged to the upper and middle classes of society before Castro seized power; those who used to benefit from the $50 million annual American tourist trade; those who have been to the United States and have a clear idea of the benefits of democracy; those who have come to realize that Castro has sold the Cuban revolution to the Soviet Union, and that when the Cuban rank and file supported Castro against Batista, it only exchanged one dictator for another.

Then there are those whose relatives have been able to escape from Cuba and find refuge in the U.S. and elsewhere. It is estimated that 500,000 Cubans so far have fled the country. For a while some were able to send food parcels to those back home. But after Hurricane Flora, Castro decreed that all such parcels would be confiscated. This did not make the would-be beneficiaries happy. Even before the hurricane those who used to receive such parcels were looked upon with suspicion. And finally there are those who have begun to "crack" under the scarcities, the regimentation, and the militancy of the Cuban regime.

Observers I spoke with agreed that in a free election Castro would lose by a wide margin. But the chances of overthrowing him through democratic means are nil. This leaves the dissenters with only one course: to initiate widespread sabotage and prepare for an internal uprising.

Five years after the revolution, complete peace continues to elude the island. The first uprising against Castro was in August, 1959. It was put down. Through the rest of that year, there were sporadic uprisings in Pinar del Río, the westernmost province in Cuba, as well as in the central provinces. Castro's drumhead war courts executed more than a thousand of these counterrevolutionaries.

In 1960 counterrevolutionary movements were reported from central and eastern Cuba, where acts of sabotage occurred all through the autumn. Important Fidelistas were assassinated, and neither side showed mercy in executing prisoners.

In 1961 some 1500 rebels were reported to be operating in the Sierra de Escambray, a mountainous area in south-central Cuba, and Castro had to send 10,000 militiamen to destroy them. The rebels put up a fight, but soon realized that they were outnumbered, and dispersed. In 1961 there were also several clandestine organizations operating in the cities, carrying out widespread sabotage. There were repeated cases of bombs being thrown into a government office, or of a state-owned store's being put to fire. There is no doubt that had the Bay of Pigs invasion not failed, and had the invaders put up a lengthier fight, these saboteurs would have been able to give valuable support to them. But the failure of the invasion clipped their wings. Their number was reduced, and those who were not arrested and who did not lay down their arms found it expedient to curtail their activities.

During 1962, the year of the missile crisis, rebel activities were reported from both Pinar del Río and Sierra de Escambray. The year was also noted for the widespread rumor that Castro had been put aside by the orthodox Communists, or that he had taken refuge in the Mexican embassy. The reason for the rumor was the elevation of two top Reds to important posts in the country. Juan Marinello, a former head of the Cuban Communist party, was made rector of the University of Havana. The post has much power and prestige. In addition, Carlos Rafael Rodriguez, editor of the Communist newspaper *Hoy*, was made the director of the Institute of National Agrarian Reform. The rumor about Castro did much to hearten the rebels, but it did not spark a general uprising. Soon it was proved wrong.

In June, 1963, one reliable report stated that Castro had disarmed several of his militia units in Pinar del Río, because of the suspicion that they were secretly helping the rebels by passing arms to them and slowing down the government's counteroffensive. The report was that in every encounter with the rebels, the militia units let them escape. There also were reports of commando landings from Central America, bringing in arms for the guerrillas.

These reports apparently had some foundation, because later in the month Castro went on the air and declared that his army was launching a final sweep against the guerrillas. He said: "They who believed that imperialism would arrive to impose its rule have been abandoned to their fate by this imperialism. The enemy has been reduced by 50 percent, and the imperialist attempt to infiltrate counterrevolutionaries and arms and to assassinate teachers, peasants, and workers is approaching its last days. Not a single band, not a single bandit will remain." Later reports indicated that his army had only partly succeeded in curtailing the guerrillas.

Early in September, 1963, came the news that twenty-five anti-Castro underground groups had formed a "National Government in Arms" in the Sierra de Escambray. But observers told me that the report meant at best the establishment of some sort of coordination between the groups. There was no way to check the report fully. It could possibly have been a canard.

I found Havana an ideal place for rumors and tales of inconsistency and uncertainty in all fields of government activity. This is always the case in every country where discontent is rife and where a controlled press presents only one side of the picture. One rumor going around the embassies was that some officers of the Cuban air force had revolted because they did not like to be bossed by the Russians. The story was that some of those officers had been arrested but had escaped and joined the rebels. Another rumor was that the army was removing the women and children from some villages in Sierra de Escambray, and that it planned to destroy everything usable because the villages were being used as hideouts by the rebels. A third rumor claimed that the bomber attack on Santa Clara had actually been made by government planes posing as rebel planes, and that the object was to excite enthusiasm.

"Why don't we hear of an exile plane's being shot down?" one Cuban asked. "We hear of these raids, and we are told that our air force is very strong, and that we have lots of rockets, but why aren't these rockets ever put to use?"

The man who asked this was obviously getting tired of the scarcities in Cuba. I learned that men like him, although not engaged in an open rebellion, freely engaged in petty sabotage: foot-dragging on the job, deliberate misplacing of files and materials, putting roaches and flies in soft drinks made and bottled in government factories, and hiding razor blades in soap. These are the persons who are known to listen to U.S. radio stations in Florida and Alabama. The U.S. broadcasts are usually jammed, but on some mornings it is possible to get Miami or even New Orleans and listen to the latest American songs.

Although there are thousands of Cubans inside Cuba who have become disillusioned with Castro and who are very much against him, and although the militant foes of Castro have not been fully suppressed, the chances of an internal uprising against him on a large scale are slim. There are several reasons for it:

First, there is no single Cuban leader, inside the country or living in exile, with reputation and personality enough to rally the many diverse anti-Castro groups scattered throughout the land. The rebels just don't have any energetic or colorful leadership of the Castro brand.

Second, I failed to detect any effective liaison between the anti-Castro elements inside Cuba and the exiles. All incoming and outgoing mail is carefully censored. The exiles are afraid to write to their relatives back home for fear of incriminating them; and the relatives won't write for fear of being suspected of having anti-state interests. The government, if it wants to, can twist the most innocent of letters to mean something entirely different. One man gave me the address of his mother and brother living in exile in Orange, California, and begged me to write to them from Canada and tell them that his wife was going to have a second baby. There were several other Cubans who gave me such addresses and asked me to write, because they themselves were afraid to do so.

Third, the Castro militia is so strong that an uprising would have to be on a very large scale to succeed. Minor uprisings could be crushed easily by the militia, plus the army, plus, if need be, the Russian soldiers. True, there are elements within the militia that might go over to the rebels in case of an uprising, but the number of such men is not big enough to have any decisive effect over the outcome.

Fourth, Castro hopes to make big dents in the economic blockade of Cuba by the U.S., and thereby alleviate some of the hardships and scarcities. I heard much talk of trade prospects with Europe and Japan. The hope was high that more and more countries would defy the U.S. embargo.

Fifth, the Cuban secret service, the G-2, is so strong and well organized that in case of an uprising or invasion it can round up within hours those it fears would not stand by the government. This was effectively proved at the time of the Bay of Pigs invasion in 1961 and the missile crisis in 1962. Several diplomats told me that when the news arrived of an exile landing, the G-2 agents went into action all over Havana and in other cities, and in no time at all were able to put into confinement all civilians with anti-state tendencies. The main prison in Havana has a big ditch around it. Thousands of the captured civilians were pushed into it, and guards with machine guns posted over their heads. In that ditch they remained during the twenty-four hours the invasion lasted. They were fed nothing. And while the fighting was in progress, members of the Young Communist party and other youth organizations were out in the streets making a hideous din in support of the government. "Come on, we are ready for you," they went about shouting and screaming, proving once more that sometimes making a lot of noise can be as effective as using bullets. The anti-Castro elements had no chance at all to reveal themselves or do anything to support the invasion. They were outmaneuvered, outclassed, checkmated. The story was the same at the time of the missile crisis. Youths took to the streets, shouting defiance at the *yanquis,* and making it impossible for the enemies of Castro to show their heads.

All this means that the G-2 is very well organized in matters of internal security. It has complete dossiers on every person of any consequence in the country. Its powers are immense. Few know where its offices are, or the exact nature of its organizational structure. It can arrest anyone at any time without a warrant. There is no habeas corpus procedure, and once a person is behind bars he can be there indefinitely. G-2 has full powers to torture and kill. With G-2, there is no such thing as an appeal to a court or a release order issued by a judge. In fact, the G-2 is not even bound to tell the relatives of an imprisoned person where he has been taken. It is not bound to tell anyone, except the men at the very top, anything. It can expropriate any property, break any rules, go to any lengths; it is answerable to no one. It really is a government within a government.

Who is the G-2 head? Nobody knows. There may be one man at the top, or perhaps several; nobody knows for sure. But I did learn that its organization owes a lot to expert help from the Soviet Union. Several hundred agents of the Soviet secret service were called in, and it is to their direction that the G-2 owes its efficiency.

Closely allied to the G-2 are the committees for the defense of the revolution. Their work is another factor preventing an anti-Castro uprising. Havana and the other cities have been divided into sections, each with its own defense committee, whose office is usually located in an expropriated house or empty store. The functions of a defense committee are varied. Some are quite admirable. For example, it sees to it that if cholera shots are being given, every person gets one. It sees to it that rationed food is distributed as evenly as possible, and that every family gets water when the water trucks come in the morning. It checks on reports of high-handedness by petty government officers. It sees to it that all children in the area go to school, that crime is prevented, and that squabbles between neighbors are avoided.

But the committee also keeps a list of all men and women capable of militia duty, and sees to it that all are enrolled and do their share of the watching. The committee is in charge of the rifles the militiamen in its area use. It is responsible for holding regular public meetings at which fire-breathing speakers harangue the populace on the glories of the revolution and the Yankee menace to Cuba. It is the job of the committee to ensure that everyone in its area is properly indoctrinated and that there is no backsliding.

Such a meeting normally begins at eight in the evening, in any open space. If none is available, a street is fenced off for the purpose. The committee sees to it that everyone comes. The meeting lasts three hours, sometimes more. Loudspeakers are used for all the speeches. I remember two nights when I could not sleep because of the din from a meeting near my hotel. One night I attended a meeting. I marveled at the speakers, who, drenched in perspiration, would not cease speaking until their voices gave out. There was applause at proper intervals, but I had the feeling that quite a number of times it was automatic or forced. Seldom was it spontaneous. Podium décor included several large placards showing Uncle Sam being kicked in the pants by a muscular Cuban warrior.

Another function of a defense committee is that it encourages "little brother" organizations, composed mostly of young people. Their job is to keep an eye on and report all suspicious activities within a house, block of apartments, school, office, or street. There was a case of which the Fidelistas were very proud, in which a boy reported his parents for counterrevolutionary talk with the neighbors. The family was summoned by the authorities for chastisement, and the boy was reprimanded for failing to teach Marxism to his parents.

This collective form of vigilance, which includes telephone-tapping, constant public warnings against counterrevolution, and coast-to-coast papering of inspirational posters, completes the sacrifice of privacy in the name of the revolution. It serves its purpose of hampering an uprising, but adversely affects the nerves. For instance, in Varadero, when I was waiting for a bus, the sky suddenly became cloudy and there was a peal of thunder. A young man I was sitting with jumped to his feet, thinking that Varadero had been bombed by an exile plane. Several days earlier a few bombs actually had fallen on nearby San Cristóbal and had caused quite a scare. The man threw me a nasty look, as if I had had something to do with it all. I had to put on my best smile and appear as innocent as I could to allay his suspicions.

Anti-Castro elements inside Cuba find it disheartening that no new invasion of the island by the exile groups in Florida and Central America appears to be on the horizon. At the time of the Bay of Pigs invasion they had placed great faith in the brave pronouncements of the exile leaders in Miami. They were sure of all-out help by the U.S. But their hopes in all these directions were shattered. The exile leaders continue making the same pronouncements. The rebels hear reports of commando training in Guatemala and Nicaragua. Occasionally, they get a few caches of arms. Occasionally, an exile plane drops a few bombs on some Cuban city. But the news fails to cause any stir or create excitement among the anti-Castro people.

"These liberation leaders sound like that old Chinaman—what's his name?—Chiang Kai-shek," one Cuban said to me bitterly. "He, too, keeps dreaming of returning to the mainland. But he is growing old. In fact, he is old. And his army is growing old. Who do you think he is trying to fool?"

I found that the tendency was growing among the rebels to give up thoughts of a struggle. The spirit of rebellion was dying out in them. It was seeping away because of the lack of decisive action and the shattering of the hope that Castro would not last more than a few years.

An outcome of this feeling was the growth of the idea of joining the Fidelistas. It was a simple case of "if you can't lick 'em, join 'em." I met one factory manager who did not have a trace of bitterness toward the West. If he was a Communist, he was very lukewarm about it. Two years earlier he would have joined an uprising, but now he seemed resigned to living under Communism.

"I am twenty-eight," he said. "My whole life is before me. A year ago I married. Now I have one daugther. I don't want to leave Cuba. I love my land. The government has given me a good job. You say Communism is bad. I say, so what? Even if it is bad, there is nothing

I can do about it. I am going to make the best of things as they are."

His attitude reflected that of the thousands of young men and women in their late twenties or early thirties, who have no alternative. I met a large number of youths who had embraced Communism because it was Cuba's "law of the land," but who did not really believe it, and did not really know what it was. I spoke with a young couple I met in a restaurant and asked what they thought of Castro. They had praise for him. But when I asked questions on Communism, they knew almost nothing of the ideology.

Time is on Castro's side in the sense that the longer he stays in power the more solid his regime becomes. The more difficult, too, will be an uprising or invasion, the more time he will have to correct the mistakes of the past, and through clever maneuvering, to make headway in diplomacy in the non-Communist world.

In this race for time, the youths now in their teens are with Castro all the way. Their indoctrination is complete. They don't know anything but Communism and have no other values to judge it by. They are being rapidly trained to take up the technical jobs left vacant by the flight of the older technicians. In another five years they will be ready.

Their presence is yet another factor preventing an uprising. When Castro talks to them, he speaks as if they have already taken over. Castro is not yet forty and he tells them that his revolution, the armed revolution, is over, and that the torch has already been passed from his generation to theirs. "It's for you that I freed Cuba, It's yours. Take it," he says, and they roar in applause. When they are grown, in a few more years, the possibility of an uprising will be reduced to zero. It will cease to exist as it has ceased to exist in the Soviet Union.

The older generation alive today, deprived of leadership and cohesion, does not seem to possess the will to keep its children from going Castro's way. Those over fifty look upon these activities of their children with an indulgent eye. No matter how much they may dislike the activities, there is nothing they can do to block the process, so they just flow heedlessly, negligently, with the tide. A weary despair has taken hold of them, a despair born of the realization of their approaching old age. And old age, everywhere, usually blunts the will to action.

18. "Of Course We Have Books on Anti-Communism"

I WAS visiting the Havana Public Library near Revolutionary Square. Built in 1956, it is housed in a beautiful building of marble and stone.

I asked an English-speaking clerk behind the counter: "I suppose that now you must have a large collection of books on Communism. How about books opposing Communism?"

His cool answer to me was: "Of course we have books on anti-Communism, but they're hard to find. Nobody reads them anymore. They're just taking up valuable space."

I spent several hours at the library, trying to find out what it had and did not have. I inquired whether it still had the Bible and books on the Bible. The clerk assured me that the Bible was there. He took me to a section in the basement which had books in general demand. But the Bible was not on the shelf where it was supposed to be. I was assured that it had been checked out. I wanted the clerk to verify that, but he refused.

The catalog, however, showed several books on theology. I picked one out at random. It was brought to me, but the woman who brought it held it between her thumb and forefinger almost as if she would rather not touch it. The book needed a new binding, and the feeling I got was that very soon it would be discarded and destroyed. The catalog showed that a Spanish translation of the Holy Koran was still in the library. I checked on *Science and Health,* the standard book of Christian Science. It was not there. There were fewer than a dozen books on Judaism.

Available in plenty were Spanish translations of books by Charles Dickens. I asked the clerk why this was so. He said that Dickens paints a wonderful picture of the disintegrating capitalistic society and that it was appropriate that the Cuban people get to know all about it. I pointed out that Dickens wrote in the past century, and said that the England of today is vastly different. He said that I was wrong, that no improvement should be expected in any society that preaches the exploitation of the many by a few.

One section of the main reading room had been partitioned off; it contained books in Russian. The library offered free courses in the Russian language, and this section was much in use by wide-eyed intellectuals who thought that books imported from Russia were the thing to read. There was also an English section which contained some old editions of the *Encyclopaedia Britannica* and a few other general reference books. The *Britannica Year Books* weren't there. There was a large Rand McNally *Atlas*. I idly flipped through it, and was amused to find that somebody had drawn a hammer and sickle across the map of the United States.

A recent addition to the library was a large chess room. I was told that on Wednesday evenings it was opened to teen-agers who wanted to learn to play the game.

I wanted to find out what Western newspapers and magazines were in the library. The catalog showed every major American, British, French, and Spanish periodical. But the latest copy of *The New York Times* was more than five months old. Other periodicals such as *The Christian Science Monitor*, the *New York Herald Tribune*, *The Reader's Digest*, and *Time* magazine weren't available. There was a two-month-old copy of the London *Times*, but no copies of any French newspaper. However, the library had not been purged of the bound volumes of pre-1958 American magazines.

I checked on Spanish-language newspapers from other countries— such famous ones as *La Prensa, La Nacion, El Nacional*, and *ABC, YA*, and *El Alcazar*. None was there. *Pravda* and *Izvestia?* Yes, files of these two papers were kept up to date.

The library had framed copies of famous works of art on display, and these could be borrowed for hanging in the home. This was the only place in Cuba where I did not see pictures of the revolutionary leaders on the walls, and it was a relief to see no slogans displayed anywhere.

The last books I checked in the catalog were *Dr. Zhivago* and *1984*. Both were there, but the clerk was already becoming suspicious at my incessant questioning, and I did not ask that they be brought to me.

Printing of books, newspapers, and magazines now is done entirely by the government. There are no private printing companies or publications. All printing is done through the Editorial Nacional de Cuba, the national publishing house founded in 1960. It began by producing a large number of Russian translations, but recently there have been many reprints of Spanish classics. One that I found being sold widely was *Don Quixote de la Mancha* by Cervantes. It was on cheap paper, cheaply bound, and priced at one peso. The flyleaf proclaimed that 100,000 copies had been published.

The publishing house takes great pride in a series which it calls *Obra Revolucionaria*. It reproduces the speeches and lectures of Cuban leaders. The series being sold when I was in Havana was numbered 103. On sale also was a small book in English, called *The Banana Empire*. It described in the usual Communist phrases the dependence of Central American countries on their banana crop and its sale in the U.S. The United Fruit Company came in for its usual share of slander and disparagement.

On the back of the book were facts and figures about the activities of the publishing house. I copied them down. It was claimed that the house had ninety-five printing shops throughout Cuba; that they employed 6,217 workers, and that so far 480 books and booklets had been published, with a total printing of 68,535,208 copies—about ten copies per capita.

The statement on the publishing house ended with the words: "Its creation was highly beneficial for the printers—many part-time workers now have steady jobs earning greater salaries; former news venders have become book binders, and all have the greatest facilities for learning and becoming useful. All work with joy and enthusiasm, because they know that each page printed is a victory against lies and ignorance." I was to read these same words in other places and in several magazines.

I spent many hours on several days touring the bookshops in Havana. Of course, all bookshops have been nationalized. Window displays left much to be desired. The biggest bookshop in the capital probably is the one attached to the Habana Libre Hotel. Fidel Castro has a habit of visiting it about once a month. He spends some time in browsing and in chatting with the people in the shop. There was another big bookshop in front of the capitol, near my hotel, but most of the time it was closed.

The books on sale included such works as *The Hidden History of the Korean War, Note from the Gallows, The Fundamentals of Socialism in Cuba, The Oil Empire, Fundamentals of Marxism and Leninism, Huckleberry Finn,* and *Course for Workers.* I was surprised to see *Huckleberry Finn.* I checked on the publication year. It was 1959. In some bookshops I spotted works by Ernest Hemingway and Mark Twain, but they were in a very limited number.

Also on sale were works by American Communists. Books by other foreign Communist figures such as Julius Fucik, Georges Politzer, and Otto Kuusinen were available in cheap editions.

In no bookshop anywhere in Havana was a Bible to be had. I inquired at shop after shop, but to no avail.

I also walked into several secondhand bookshops. These, surprisingly, had not been purged. At the University of Havana bookshop, an old copy of Dale Carnegie's *How to Win Friends and Influence People* was available. Cheap detective novels and girlie magazines are no longer published in Cuba. Old ones are still available but only in small bookstalls outside Havana. I came out of Cuba with a cheaply printed collection of some mushy songs, but there was no title page to it and it was impossible to ascertain when it was published. It may well have been a collection put out for soldiers.

The national publishing house is making a regular practice of pirating textbooks. I visited a hospital and found that the interns were using a pirated edition of *La Prensa Médica Mexicana* by Dr. José Laguna, professor of biochemistry at the National University of Mexico. The title page gave credit only to the Cuban publishing house.

Much poetry is published in Cuba. Of course, none of it is counter-revolutionary, but some is decidedly noncommittal. I had a few poems translated, and found none with any appeal.

My visit to the offices of *La Tarde* and *Revolución* was interesting in the sense that it gave me an opportunity to learn something about newspaper practices in a Communist country. Both newspapers are housed in one building and are printed on the same presses—recently imported from East Germany. *Revolución* is supposed to be Fidel Castro's pet. It was founded personally by him, and he continues to take personal interest in its running. When I walked into the building, I was stopped by the militiaman guarding it. He had to get clearance from someone in the newsroom before letting me in.

In the newsroom I was presented to city editor (or town editor, as he is called) Armando Valdes. I told him that I was planning to be-come a newspaperman, and that I would like him to tell me something about his paper. The first item he showed me, with a great deal of pride, was the pneumatic-tube system used to carry copy to the com-posing room. He thought it would be something new for me, and I did not let him think otherwise.

"Do you publish crime stories?" I asked.

"We have no crime in Cuba," he said solemnly.

"I see that you don't carry any advertisements. Where does your revenue come from?"

"Advertisements are the product of the capitalistic system. In a newspaper, they are a waste of time and effort and space. Everything is owned by the people, and people can't compete against people. So there is no need for advertisements."

"But you do carry announcements from various ministries. Do you get paid for them?"

"Sometimes, yes; sometimes, no. But that's unimportant."

I asked him what his main news sources were. He replied that he had forty-three reporters on the staff, and that the paper subscribed to the Cuban *La Prensa* news agency and to UPI. The Havana UPI bureau has dwindled in size considerably, but it still manages to click out all the stories that the news service makes available to its clients elsewhere.

"Do you use a lot of UPI stories?" I asked.

"No, only a few. The service is not reliable. How can we know it is telling the truth?" he answered.

The newsroom had a total of nine desks. I asked where all of his forty-three reporters sat. He said that they were out, and came in only when they had a story. He said that his paper had a daily circulation of 83,000 copies, and that *La Tarde,* the other paper in the building, was larger.

In *La Tarde's* office, I was introduced to one of its English-speak-ing employees. The first question I asked him was how many copies the paper printed. He said its circulation was 25,000. Señor Valdes was still with me. I saw his face blanch, but pretended not to notice it.

I was taken to the world room of *La Tarde.* There I saw a huge radio-monitoring device spread over an entire wall. I learned that the paper monitored newscasts from all over the world, especially from Moscow and other East European capitals, and used them in its columns. It was one good way—in fact, the only way—to get the news from those capitals quickly.

I learned that when Fidel Castro was in the Soviet Union earlier in the year, the monitoring device kept operating twenty-four hours a day, and in this way everything said about him was received instantaneously by the paper. The complete coverage of his visit in the Cuban papers was the result of following this method. I asked whether any of these papers had a correspondent in Moscow. I was told that only *Hoy* had a man in the Russian capital, but that he sent mostly feature stories and did not bother with topical news. I wanted to know whether there were Soviet correspondents in Cuba. I was told that there were several from the U.S.S.R. and the other East European countries.

Broadcasts by the Cuban radio also are extensively used by the newspapers. The radio is state-owned, and a lot of its broadcasts have to do with the activities of the government and with the pronouncements of its leaders. Sometimes *La Tarde* does not send its reporters to cover events, but relies mostly on the radio, and since the radio carries only what the government allows to be put on the air, the paper does not feel obliged to challenge the relays. It copies them without asking any questions. The attitude of the editors was that they would just be wasting time in sending their own men, and they insisted that they did not have enough manpower to duplicate reporting.

I asked who decided what was to go into the paper. I was told that all decisions in this respect were made by a board of directors. It meets daily and decides on the items to be run. It has a large amount of freedom in the matter, but it is obliged to follow a few policy guidelines laid down by Castro and others. If the board does not agree with something done by Castro, it is not allowed to write an editorial criticizing him. It cannot demand openly that a certain minister resign because he is inefficient. It cannot suggest a policy on trade. It cannot offer its own opinions on industrialization, agriculture, or foreign policy.

Nor is it allowed to criticize the Soviet Union. It is obliged to take the part of the Soviets in every encounter with the free world. But in the matter of the Sino-Soviet conflict its policy is to stay neutral. If a Russian soldier in Cuba goes on a drinking spree and is involved in a fist fight, the papers are not to carry the story.

Cuba is receiving arms from both the Soviet Union and Czechoslovakia. If the board thinks that the Czech rifles are not very good, it cannot express its opinion in the paper. In fact, it cannot assign any of its reporters even to look into the matter. It just has to endorse what Minister of Defense Raul Castro has to say.

What we know as investigative reporting cannot be found in Cuban papers. There are never any exposés, and the picture of Cuba that the papers are obliged to project is one in which everything is always fine and dandy.

They are not allowed to do feature stories highlighting poverty or shortages. If the government reduces the quota for eggs, the papers are expected to go along with the decision. If a certain road has too many holes in it, the papers cannot publish a picture of those holes. If there is cruelty in a prison, the papers cannot "blast the story sky-high," as we say here. If the government does not publish the budget, the papers cannot demand its release. Human interest stories are carefully avoided. In the U.S., if a cow sat on a railroad track and stopped a train, the chances are that its picture would be in all the papers. But this can never happen in Cuba.

Also carefully avoided are profile stories. In England, every newspaper reader knows how many children and grandchildren Sir Winston Churchill has, what Harold Macmillan's favorite food is, and what Sir Alec Douglas-Home does for recreation. But similar details about Castro and the other Cuban leaders are never published in the Cuban press. People know in a vague sort of way that Castro was once married, and they know he has a son, but that's about all.

The papers, however, are expected to extol every virtue of the government, minimize its faults, and justify all its actions. For instance, if the government cuts down the coffee quota, the papers declare that the cut is only temporary and that it will soon be restored. They follow this up with a long account that the U.S. blockade of Cuba is being increased, and that the time for making sacrifices is not yet ended.

The papers sometimes indulge in criticism. But it is always done in soft tones. The controversy is usually over whether a government department should follow a strictly Marxist line in a certain matter or dilute Marxism to suit the particular needs of Cuba. The biggest paper in Havana is *Hoy*. It often happens that *Hoy* takes one position and *Revolución* advocates something else. There was once a controversy between the two papers on whether the government should import only Russian and East European films, or whether it would be all right for it to import films from non-Communist countries as well. *Hoy* took the position that non-Communist cultural influences should not be allowed to permeate Cuba through films. *Revolución* thought that as long as any film or book did not specifically oppose Communism, it was all right to import it.

Card-playing is frowned upon, and no paper carries a bridge column. Comics as we know them in the U.S. are out. Before the revolution, they were supplied by U.S. syndicates, but not now, and there are no local artists producing them. On occasion some drawings do appear, but they are mostly propaganda efforts and have no real narrative or entertainment value.

The papers are not allowed to publish news of any economic gains in the free world. In fact, the only news from the non-Communist world that the papers can carry without fear of penalty is news that puts the free world in a bad light.

"What is your policy on the news of racial riots in America?" I asked one of the editors.

"We believe that full publicity should be given to the brutalities against the Negroes in Birmingham and Atlanta," he replied.

"But how about efforts by the Federal government in Washington to combat the situation?" I asked.

"The Federal government is doing nothing to combat the situation. It just makes a show of concern for the Negroes, but takes no action. We can't tell our people a lie. We can't be fooled," he replied.

On the other hand, the newspapers are expected to give full publicity to events in the Communist world. Most of the items used are culled from *Pravda*. If a new factory is opened in Russia, the news is sure to be carried in Cuban papers.

The papers are priced at five or ten cents. On weekdays, they have six or eight pages. On Sundays, a four-page feature supplement is included. Seldom is any use made of color.

For several days I had the headlines and a few of the stories translated. They made very dull reading; nothing but activities of the government or events in the Soviet bloc. Not once did I learn what was happening elsewhere. I had the feeling that if an earthquake demolished my home town of Lucknow, India, I would not hear of it unless the Soviet Union sent a few bottles of medicine for the victims. Then the Cuban press would blazon the act as one of the greatest acts of mercy in history.

Except for those in Havana, there are few Cuban newspapers worthy of the name. Since the distances are not great, the distribution of Havana papers elsewhere poses no problem.

I could not escape the feeling that so far as news gathering and news projection were concerned, the various editors and reporters had a very easy time. *El Mundo* is the fourth daily newspaper in Havana. There is never any competition among the four papers. They don't care who gets the news first, who writes it best, or who sells the most copies. They compete neither for circulation nor for revenues, since all costs are met by government subsidies. They compete only in their efforts to stay in the good graces of the government.

The government also publishes several magazines, the best being *Bohemia*. In the library I browsed through one of its issues. It had 106 pages, and there were more than a dozen pictures of Castro in it. Then there is a magazine for women, full of designs for clothes. A third magazine is meant for the militia. It contains stories on what to do in case of an air attack, how to track down infiltrators, and so on.

There is the Writers and Arists Union to stimulate the arts as well as keep them on the right ideological lines. Its president is Nicolás Guillen, whose works have a wide vogue in the Communist world.

The Red countries supply Cuba with many magazines. From the Soviet Union come the *Literatura Soviética*, the *Unión Soviética, La Mujer Soviética*, and others. There are separate magazines coming from Czechoslovakia, Bulgaria, and Red China. The last country sends magazines in English too, but these are for sale only at the big hotels where the foreigners stay.

19. Religion amid Atheism

ONE evening I saw a very unusual sight in Havana. I was walking down Velazco Street, and happened to look into a shoe shop. On a bracket on the wall was a small statue of the Virgin Mary, and around its neck, hanging from a thread, was a small hammer and sickle.

I had never seen such a combination of religion and atheism. As I stood in the doorway, gazing at the statue, a man behind the counter pointed at it, and said: "Ah-ha! That's how we like our Virgin Mary to be—a good Communist."

This confusion over religion, over what to believe and what not to believe, is a prominent feature in revolutionary Cuba. The government is telling the people to give up religion. But force of habit and some lingering, faint cognition of God seems to be compelling them not to do so. The policy of the state is to discourage, and eventually kill, all belief in God. The state thinks that if a man buys a Bible he is wasting his money, and if he reads it, and goes to religious services, he is wasting time that could have been spent in "constructive" activities.

All publishing is in the hands of the government, and so no Bibles have been published since the revolution. One Western diplomat told me that the Bible Society in his country sent two thousand Bibles to Cuba for free distribution, but the consignment was confiscated by the government and reduced to pulp. Other books on religion, such as *The Confessions of St. Augustine,* and *City of God,* are also unavailable.

Havana, and in fact the whole country, is plastered with the old Marxist slogan: "Religion is the opiate of the people." Even in remote villages, I saw this sign painted on the walls of mud houses. It is printed on the backs of bus tickets, too.

The Cubans are taught that the idea that there is a God was invented by ancient leaders as a psychological weapon to control the people. The Cubans are told that these leaders tricked the people by posing as representatives of an all-powerful being which they presented as hidden but real. God, says the state, exists only in the imagination, and His actuality is unverifiable.

The state stresses that the one aim of a church, any church, is to enslave the masses—keep them from working, take away their money, make sure that they remain docile and unquestioning, and dangle before them, as a reward for all this, the promise of a heaven that does not exist, and frighten them into submission with thoughts of a hell that is also nonexistent. One of Nikita Khrushchev's sayings crops up often in conversation with the Fidelistas. It is: "The church promises you a reward in some other world at some other time. I promise you a good life in this world and now."

The Fidelistas never cease harping that before the revolution the Cuban church was an enthusiastic supporter of Fulgencio Batista. This was true because Bastista used to make big contributions in money and land to the church. Whenever he attended services, the Cuban papers played up the story and published pictures of him being blessed by the padre, singing the hymns, kneeling before the altar. His reasons were political. He wanted the church in his corner because of its hold upon the people. The church fell for the ruse, and supported him even when his dictatorship was at its ignoble worst and the loot of public money by crafty officials was at its maximum. "You were duped," shout the Fidelistas now to the people. "Your precious church let you down. It tricked you." The church, stymied, has no answer to give. It realizes that most of the charges are true.

But as always happens in such cases, the distinction between religion and the misuse of religion is lost, and it is Christ who has to take the blame for the errors of the clergy. Castro's real war is not against the latter. He knows that the clergy without Christ are lost. His aim is to wean the people away from Christ.

This aim is being pursued in a very cunning manner. I wanted to know whether theology was taught at Havana University. One student said yes, and that he was studying it. I carefully scrutinized the course he was taking. It was perfectly clear that its purpose was to make him better equipped to be anti-God. It included selections from the Bible. But only those stories had been selected that were calculated to make the book appear ridiculous. Included in the course were stories of how the daughters of Lot slept with their father after the destruction of

Sodom and Gomorrah; the way David loved Bathsheba; and how Jonah lived in the belly of a whale. The Laws of Moses, the Psalms, the Proverbs, and Ecclesiastes weren't included. The Ten Commandments were being taught, but in a manner calculated to destroy their effectiveness. A Marxist commentary had been affixed to each. The command to observe the Sabbath had not been removed, but it was specifically stated that in revolutionary Cuba there is so much work to be done that the command cannot be observed, and so should be rejected as obsolete. The command to honor one's parents had been endorsed only partially. The commentary made it clear that if the parents are counterrevolutionaries, it is the duty of the children to turn them in, and that parental love should not be allowed to retard the course of the revolution.

The command "Thou shalt not covet thy neighbor's house" was also included, but with the provision that if the neighbor has two or three houses he has to be deprived of all but one. In mentioning the command "Thou shalt not kill," it was clearly stated that the rule did not mean that the enemies of the state should be spared liquidation.

The biblical God was presented as a being that sanctioned killing and plunder. Widely quoted were extracts such as "The Lord is a man of war" from Exodus XV, but the goodness, mercy, compassion, or justness of God weren't mentioned.

The same kind of clever editing had been done with the New Testament. The story of Christ's birth was presented as an example of the unscientific basis of religion. The Beatitudes and the Sermon on the Mount were included, but with the kind of interpretation that had been given to the Commandments. Following the injunction of Christ that one should be kind in heart and turn the other cheek if slapped, the commentator asked the question: "Does this mean that we should not be content with the Yankees possessing Guantánamo, but also turn over other parts of the country to them?"

Much play was made of Christ's saying: "Render therefore unto Caesar the things which be Caesar's, and unto God the things which be God's." The commentator's advice was that religion should not be allowed to interfere with the interests of the state, and that the latter should come first in all situations.

Christ's injunction that God should be loved with all of one's being and that one should love one's neighbor as oneself, drew the comment: "Does this mean that we should begin loving our neighbor, the United

States, and turn over our state to the clergy's pet, Fulgencio Batista?"

The passage in Acts which says that the early apostles lived together and held all things in common, was played up very well; but St. Paul was depicted as an adventurer in religion and politics, and as the model for the heroes in cheap American novels.

Of various antireligious displays in Havana, two come to mind.

The dining room at Hotel Habana Libre displays a drawing of a thin farmer being whipped by a fat landowner. A priest with a crucifix, instead of trying to stop the whipping, is telling the farmer not to scream.

I learned that the government issued a decree in 1961 forbidding anyone under eighteen from taking an active part in church affairs. The young people I met either did not believe in God or their conception of God was the distorted Marxist version. They were made to realize that if they wanted to progress in their jobs, they had to be atheists. Membership in the various Red organizations, the first step to advancement, was clearly dependent on the applicant's disbelieving in God.

Before the revolution, the predominant religion in Cuba was Catholicism. Castro's offensive against the Roman Catholic Church began in 1960, when he violently attacked Archbishop Evelio Díaz of Havana for taking a stand against Communism.

The Cuban dictator said that the prelate was a stooge of the Spanish and Belgian priests, who had been in Cuba since before the revolution. He announced that these priests would soon be expelled. He also threatened confiscation of church property.

The axe fell in February, 1961, when President Osvaldo Dorticos charged the Roman Catholic schools in Cuba with teaching counter-revolutionary precepts. This was the prelude to the nationalization of these schools. That was done forthwith; all church property was confiscated, 110 priests were expelled, and 400 priests left voluntarily or were recalled by their superiors.

These measures were, of course, opposed by the Vatican, and in January, 1962, it announced Castro's excommunication. Cuban papers carried the news under banner headlines, and sarcastically suggested that Batista should be made a cardinal. But the papal nuncio, Monsignor Cesar Zacchi, was not withdrawn, and he continued to reside in Havana.

The church's power, however, has been broken. The reason it survives at all is that it has entered into the same sort of unofficial bargain with the government as it has in the Soviet Union and other Iron Curtain countries: the bishops, in return for being allowed to exist, have ceased issuing pastorals against Communism. Today there are 2 archbishops, 4 bishops, 200 priests, 50 brothers, and 180 nuns in Cuba, most of them residing in Havana. They lead a very withdrawn existence, and the impression I got was that they have adopted a do-nothing, sit-tight policy. Instead of planning for the future, they are waiting to see what happens.

One Sunday I went to the Jesús de Miramar church in Havana. With its imposing murals and carved altar, it is a beautiful example of Roman architecture. It was less than half full. Most of the worshipers were middle-aged or old. Some had brought along young children, and I was told that after the service, catechism lessons would be given in the church proper. But everything was very subdued and mechanical. There was no spirit or enthusiasm in anything. A sermon was delivered, but it lasted only three minutes. A few hymns were sung, but only a handful of persons raised their voices. I was told that no social or cultural activity was planned after the service. A few families stayed for catechism. The rest quietly went away.

It was worse in the interior. I went to the big church in Varadero one Sunday at about noon. It was locked. I pressed the rectory bell, but nobody answered. There was a sign saying that if there was no response, the caller was to go to the door at the back. I went, and found that the door had been bricked up.

The official church paper, *La Quinzena,* in Havana, had ceased publication even before Castro could order its suspension. The church in Havana had no extra Bibles. In fact, it had no literature at all to give away, except 10,000 copies of Pope John's *Pacem in Terris,* received from Spain. These had not been confiscated, because the encyclical had been praised even by Khrushchev—and that decided Cuba's policy toward it.

The small Protestant communities, including Baptists, continue to exist, but they are small to the point of being unnoticeable. Twice I went to a Christian Science Reading Room, but found it closed both times. The government's crackdown on evangelists and on such sects as the Jehovah's Witnesses has been complete since evangelists were preaching the primacy of the Word of God and the other sect wanted the Sabbath observed fully.

But these measures, although they have caused a diminution in religious fervor, have been unable to stamp out belief in God. Many people who outwardly conform to the fashion of the day—atheism— still pray in secret. I visited the apartment of a young couple. The husband was employed by the Ministry of Industries—Ernesto Che Guevara's ministry—where it would have been bad for him to let his colleagues know about his faith. But he and his wife had erected a makeshift altar in their bedroom, and told me that they prayed every night. One woman, an employee of the tourist department, told me while she was my guest at dinner, that she still believed in God. "I am fed up with the Cuban church," she said, "because of the way it sided with Batista, but I pray at home every morning." I asked her why she prayed. She said that she found it very soothing and comforting.

The newspaper *La Tarde* in Havana is devoted to atheism, but when I visited its composing room I found that the workers had put up a statue of the Madonna on the wall. On another occasion I was riding a bus back to Havana. We passed a cemetery, and every woman aboard made the sign of the cross and the men took off their hats. Statues of the Crucifixion and the Resurrection are prominently displayed at bus sta- tions and in private homes, and Madonna medallions are still worn by most persons. I visited a family at a state farm. The house had four bedrooms, and at the head of each bed there hung a statue of some saint. One new housing project also included a small, modernistic chapel, built at the insistence of the workers.

The feast days of the various saints are still observed, and they are occasions for dancing and merrymaking. Quite a few of the saints were new to me. I tried to learn something about them, but nobody knew who they were. It didn't matter—the feasting was the thing that counted.

The feast day of La Caridad occurred during my stay in Havana. It was the occasion for a party in an apartment across the street from my hotel. Around eleven o'clock at night, everyone paused for a brief service and prayed for success in his job and for good health. After- ward, there was dancing and loud music and much rejoicing. It did not end until 2:00 A.M. I learned that such parties were held all over town that night. Hard liquor was scarce, only a limited quantity of beer was served, and there were few things to eat, but that did not prevent the Cubans from having a good time. Before the revolution, sending of greeting cards was very common, but the custom is gone now. The government printing presses print no greeting cards.

Oddly enough, one sees Madonnas and rosaries being sold in government shops. It is not that the government wants to sell these things. It is just that the shops selling them are nationalized and the government feels it has to get rid of the stock. But it has found that Madonnas, being much in demand, bring in good money, and it has permitted local craftsmen to keep on making them. Cubans complain that the Madonnas now being made don't have the finish and the beauty of the old, and they are also priced higher.

Church weddings are still in fashion, but bridal gowns are usually homemade. In all of Havana I saw only one store selling them, and the prices were extremely high. The government does not encourage such luxuries. Marriage applications are filed before a court, and the court's consent has to be obtained for a marriage to become legal. The church ceremony is not necessary, but the Cubans, if only because of the festivity involved, still prefer it. The practice of taking children for baptism continues. Services for the dead are still held, but occasions were mounting when a man was buried or cremated without a service. The requiem mass has been simplified. Funeral homes are now government property. Usually the service is held in a small attached chapel, and it lasts only a few minutes.

In considering religion, one must remember that the Cubans never were a very religious people. The population includes a large number of Negroes of African descent. Their ancestors added weird jungle rites to Christian worship, and identified voodoo gods with the saints. The result was the emergence of saints who went about carrying a sword in one hand and the severed head of an enemy in the other. Such tableaux can be seen all over the country. These rites are being encouraged by the government, too—in the name of a folk art revival.

Will religion survive in Cuba if Communism is not overthrown? I doubt it. The younger generation is being brought up on atheism. Religion is not taught; there are no books available on the subject, and it is not mentioned on the radio. True, some younger people, under the influence of their parents, know something about it, but their number is not great. The result will be that when the older generation that has known God eventually dies out, religion will die with it. To kill religion, outright persecution is not necessary. Just keep the younger people away from it, and time will see to it that it perishes.

20. Love in Cuba

THE time was ten at night, and the weather was nice; a perfect evening for a walk down Maceo Avenue fronting Havana Bay. A stone parapet had been built to keep the sea out. It was broad enough to sit on, and at that hour it was occupied by dozens of dallying couples who were out to have a spot of fun, to enjoy the breeze, and watch the waves breaking against the shore.

The revolution notwithstanding, Cubans continue to be romantic. Courting couples can be seen by the hundreds any evening in most Havana parks and at the beaches. Almendares Park, built after the revolution, is famous for the opportunities it provides for open-air dalliance. Its benches, lining a canal, are the anchor points of these couples. A big boat cruises down the canal, and a couple can take a trip on it for two dollars. Nobody will pay any attention to what they do. Or they can rent a boat of their own and paddle it to some lonely spot where the chances of being disturbed are nil.

It is common for office girls, if somebody produces a song book, to cluster around a table and burst into song. Sometimes, even the boss does not mind. He looks the other way, keeps time by clapping, or leaves the room.

Two singers, Mucho Corazón and Idalberto Delgado, are the Eddie Fisher and Bing Crosby of modern Cuba. Corazón is of Spanish-African descent. His mustache gives him the appearance of a villain, but he has the kindliest, saddest smile of any man I know. Delgado is noted for his serious mien. Miguel De Gonzalo is popular for his harp-playing, and Carlos Orihuela is a crooner with the face of a Spanish ranch owner. Another upcoming singer is Carlos G. Pérez, a baritone whose golden voice, dark eyes, and flashing smile thrill many a Cuban maiden and throw her into fits of shrieking and swooning.

Among the girl singers, Miriam Acevedo, Judith Velasco, Rosarito Moreno, and Pucha Rippers are the most popular. Miriam is also famous for her blonde hair with bangs and a puffed crown. Judith and Rosarito have busts like Jayne Mansfield's, and pictures of them wearing bikinis are much in demand. Judith has sultry eyes and "so invitational lips," as one Cuban put it. The fourth, Pucha, is extremely vivacious, and this quality is reflected in her singing. Another group of singers, the Trio Los Rodrigos, also makes nightly appearances at the cabarets, and sings popular love songs to the accompaniment of guitars and maracas.

One popular song, *Let Me Believe*, runs as follows:

Let me believe, my love,
I need to believe in you,
I need to know what was wrong;
That all is good again.

Let me believe, my love,
It's so easy to make me believe.
Give me back the faith I had in you.
For without it, I don't want to live.

Kiss me, kiss me, and make me want you,
Make me live again.
And say sweetly you didn't mean to speak harshly.

Let me believe, my sweet,
Lie to me, if you wish.
And, in the end, if you know I want to believe in you,
Let me believe.

The freest places for lovemaking are of course the nightclubs. There are about fifteen of them. Gambling has been banned at all. Liquor can be had only with difficulty. Pickups aren't available in profusion, but the nightclubs continue to be places where one can relax and have amorous adventures.

Not far from Hotel Habana Libre is the Club Sherazad. It rarely opens before nine in the evening. But things begin to be lively around eleven. The use of neon signs is restricted because of the power shortage, but this club has a large one. The door is black, and painted on it are a date tree and a woman with a veil on her face. The rest of her body is practically nude. This door opens into a large closet, which is the hat-check room. A brass, intricately carved chandelier hangs from the ceiling. It has eight sockets but only two bulbs, and only one of those is lit. It is green.

Through another door one enters a large hall, very dimly lit. A bar is at the far end, with some men sitting at it. Nearby is the dance floor and the band platform, but no band is playing. The rest of the hall is furnished with divans lining the opposite walls. A low partition is around each. On these divans, you will see couples engaged in necking, petting, and sometimes intercourse. But nobody is fully undressed. The charge for the use of a divan is five dollars, collected at the bar.

At such nightclubs, it is easier if you take a woman of your own. However, if you don't have one, it is possible that one will come up to you. But that won't happen right away. You will have to sit at the bar and order drinks, and pretend that you're lonely by staring at the pinups and gulping down such liquor as you can get. All the time, the bartender will be watching you. Give him thirty minutes. If at the end of that time his judgment is that you aren't putting on an act, he will make a sign to an attendant, who will disappear behind a curtain, and fifteen minutes later a woman will emerge and sit down beside you.

She won't look in your direction. She won't be the first to open the conversation. She will order a drink, which may or may not be alcoholic. In the dark, you don't even get to see her face. When the bartender brings the drink, that's your cue to cut in. You do that by offering to pay for the drink. The girl will put up a show that she wants to pay herself, but you persist, and in the end she will appear to have been persuaded by you. Don't try to entice her to the divan at once. That won't work. She is afraid of you. You could be anyone. You go about it gradually. You will have to buy her more drinks and talk to her in a low whisper. You will have to dip into your wallet; twenty dollars is a fair amount. You pay in advance, and take your chance that after accepting the money she won't disappear behind the curtain and leave you flat. But if you hold out the prospect of more money, she won't.

She will be on the divan with you for about an hour. Afterward, you pay her ten dollars more, kiss her good-bye, and go your way. She will tell you her name, but it won't be the right one. If you meet her the next day, you won't be able to recognize her. Like you, she could be anyone.

Another club I visited, the Club 23, at 156 Twenty-third Street, is the same kind of place as the Club Sherazad. Its first floor has a restaurant. The other portion is in the basement. But this club does not have any divans. Once you have got a girl, you are expected to take her to your own place.

Castro is supposed to have driven the prostitutes off the streets. His theory is that street women used to thrive in prerevolutionary Cuba because of American tourists and unemployment caused by the United States control of the Cuban economy. The most famous fleshpot in Havana of earlier years was the Mambo Bar. Castro nationalized it. It is now a workers' cafeteria and is called "Restaurant Prague." But in spite of all of Castro's measures, streetwalkers and call girls continue to do business, plying another of the few forms of free enterprise to be found on the island.

Besides the fifteen nightclubs mentioned earlier, there are innumerable cheaper places in downtown Havana where a woman can be had for ten dollars or less. And she does not make the stipulation, "Only one time, señor." All clubs inevitably have pictures of Castro on their walls, but I was amused to see that at one of the cheaper bars, the scribbles on the men's room walls were not the usual obscenities but revolutionary slogans, straight out of the pages of Carlos Marx.

One diplomat, a young bachelor, told me: "If these Cubans spend in studying economics only half the time they spend in bed, Cuba can become one of the most prosperous countries in Latin America." But the truth is that, with liquor hard to get, with the movies showing only uninteresting propaganda pictures from behind the Iron Curtain, indiscriminate lovemaking is about the only form of relaxation, the only release from tension, left to the Cubans—and to foreigners who visit Cuba.

One Cuban told me that prostitution has gone underground, but that it is more prevalent than before because of low incomes. Another Cuban said that the birth of illegitimate babies has gone up because contraceptives are now hard to get, and that all the new progeny are being called "Fidelista babies." The Cuban explained: "Were it not for the economic measures of Fidel, the birth of these babies would not have been possible, and so we name them after him."

My diplomat friend said that housewives whose husbands are on military duty and away from home, salesgirls, and office girls are often found engaging in prostitution on the side. During the day they are respectably managing files, or selling things; after dinner they go to their second jobs. "But once an office girl has been in your apartment," my friend continued, "she keeps calling you, under the impression that she has established some sort of permanent claim on you."

At the better hotels, it is possible to get pickups in the lobbies. Toward evening girls come and sit there, and all you have to do is to sit next to one, open conversation with her on some pretext, and then invite her to have a drink with you.

Although these big hotels have been nationalized, the government is interested in keeping their nightclubs going. The costs have been cut everywhere. The best show is at the Hotel Riviera. Here you pay seven dollars for food and drinks. Other quality shows are at the Nacional, Capri, and Habana Libre. Here the charges are lower. The shows are sometimes very entertaining. There is good singing and dancing. A show very popular when I was in Havana was one in which a girl pretended she was a bull and a man played the part of a bullfighter. Other girls posed as bull-goaders. The "fighting" always brought the house down.

These shows, however, operate on a low budget. It is quite usual to see a chorine go through her steps in ragged mesh hose or soiled costume. For the men in the audience, there are no dress restrictions. Factory workers come in open-neck bush shirts. These shows also have proved to be a big hit with Russian and East European audiences, who appear never to have seen anything like them.

Before and after the shows, many of the show girls loiter in the hotel lobby. They are dressed in very, very tight slacks and tight blouses —the usual sign of availability. But if you want a rendezvous with them, you'd better have a lot of money.

Across the street from the Habana Libre, there's a radio station. In the basement of the building, there's a big restaurant and bar, and it was pointed out to me as the place that homosexuals frequented.

I had been told to look for that famous thirst-quenching place, Sloppy Joe's. It's still there. Pictures of international celebrities such as Frank Sinatra, Mickey Rooney, Clark Gable, and other Hollywood stars who made it famous still line the walls, but the place was almost deserted when I visited it. The only clients were a few Cubans sitting disconsolately around a table. I was told that the bar was still under private management, but that its previous income of $1000 a day had dropped to $20. I also went looking for the old Floridita bar, a favorite of Ernest Hemingway. It still stands at 557 Obispo Street, but the large mirror behind the mahogany bar made famous by Hemingway has been replaced by a garish fresco of Castro and his guerrilla warriors all set for an attack. Hemingway's bust is there, but it has been pushed to one side, near some propaganda posters.

The only drinks easily available in Havana are throat-searing rum, cheap Cuban gin, and brandy. The rum highballs have been dubbed *mataratas* or "rat-killers." One tall Cuban drink, long a favorite with East Europeans, is the famous mixture of rum and cola, the Cuba libre. But the wits call it a *mentirita*, or "little lie." Good drinks can now be had only at the embassies or at parties given by the government for visiting dignitaries.

Some Western clubs still operate. One is the American Club on Martí Prado. It's allowed to run because most of its members now are British or Canadian. But J. Niven Alleyn, the only American in Havana, is a member. There is also the Rovers Club near the airport. It once was British. Portraits of the royal family still hang in the lounge, though most of the members now are Cuban. The only remaining golf course in Havana belongs to this club. Lastly, there is La Torre, the diplomatic corps club, in the Fosca building facing the sea. But it's very expensive. Good drinks are available—at ten times the price they would be in New York.

The Habana Libre, the former Havana Hilton, now is a sad sight. Built of chrome, marble, and glass, this blue-and-white building once was a showplace in the city, but now it is running to seed. Of its many entrance doors, only one is open. The others are locked all the time. Originally, the door opened under the pressure of your feet on the threshold; now you have to push. The glass dome in the lobby has many of its panels cracked. The lobby fountain plays only now and then. "We have no water to waste," a waiter told me. The Committee for the Defense of the Revolution and the tourist department have their offices in the lobby. The shopping arcades, decorated with the inevitable slogans, don't have anything to sell. There is one shop selling expensive art objects from North Vietnam and Holland.

I managed to look inside a third-floor room, and saw that the plaster was peeling, the carpet was stained, and the sheets were mended. There was dust under the bed and the mirrors needed polishing. I learned that all but a few of the vacuum cleaners had broken down, and replacements weren't available. The air-conditioning plant did not work all the time. Lines of washing fluttered from many balconies, and I saw that one man had turned his balcony into a kitchen by installing a portable stove. The main restaurant, as in most Havana hotels, is seldom open. All meals are served in the cafeteria, decorated with pictures of farmers being whipped to death by the bourgeois. There is never any menu; the waiter wheels around a cart on which are displayed specimen plates of the day's three dishes. There is bean soup every day, and rice is the only vegetable.

This decay is the most prominent characteristic of modern Havana. The city that once was one of the world's gayest, most wide-open playgrounds, and a matchless blend of Miami Beach, Las Vegas, and the French Riviera is, under the revolution, dull, drab, boring. During the first years of Communism there was a frantic spree of building. Housing colonies for the workers, schools, and a few hospitals were erected. But the spree tapered off in 1962, and had all but ended when I was in Havana. Nothing was being constructed but a few government buildings, and old buildings weren't being repaired. Plastering, painting, fixing—all these things needed doing, but there was no material for such projects.

Elevators don't work, telephones don't operate. You put in your money, and it's gone. Telephone books are rare. When you find one it is several years old, and half the numbers in it are wrong. They belong to people who have fled.

On every other street corner there is a broken-down and abandoned car. The posters and the militia, the antiaircraft guns and the shore batteries, the searchlights sweeping the sky at night, and soldiers being transported in carriers—all these things give Havana the appearance of a city under siege.

But a very commendable thing about it is that crime seems nonexistent. One reason is that the punishment is very strict. A pickpocket does not have his hand chopped off, as happens in Saudi Arabia, but he can be sent to jail for thirty years. And a robber can get life imprisonment, or be shot. I wandered through the city at all hours of the night, and not once did I fear that I would be held up. I always carried all my money with me because I didn't want to leave it in the hotel. My pockets were never picked, not even when I was walking through the densest crowd.

However, the black market flourishes, and on it one can get anything from girls to auto parts; from penicillin to champagne or nylons.

A fifth of American whisky can fetch forty dollars. There are stringent laws against such selling, and occasionally someone is caught and sentenced to hard labor. But the practice is so widespread that the government usually looks the other way. Families are allowed to keep chickens, but are forbidden to sell eggs in the open market. They don't mind; they get more money selling them secretly.

INIT, the tourist department, is efficiently run, but the tours it arranges are expensive. The price quoted for a day's outing at Varadero beach was thirty dollars. I did it on my own for seven dollars. It is possible to rent ten-year-old Cadillacs for twelve dollars an hour.

I saw visitors in Havana from at least twenty countries, not including the Iron Curtain countries. Japanese were much in evidence because of trade prospects with Cuba. There were a lot of Arabs from Algeria and Egypt. I was introduced to a student from Morocco. He was pointed out to me as a "devil with women." I also met Mrs. Rachel Baruch from Israel. Her husband was teaching physics at Havana University. It was she who presented me with a tube of American toothpaste. She invited me to her apartment at 511 Eighth Street, for which her husband was paying 10 percent of his salary. She had a maid for thirty dollars a month plus meals, and was very happy with her stay in Cuba.

A pleasant experience for me was a visit to the National Museum. It was closed, but when I told the curator that I would be leaving Havana the next day, he arranged a special tour for me. The girl who was assigned to take me around was fun to be with, and not without a sense of humor. We came to an old Italian painting of some building in Venice. The initials INIT were on it. She said: "This was our INIT office in the fifteenth century."

21. The Transportation Muddle

THE inscription on my bus ticket that I am saving as a souvenir from Havana reads in translation: "We shall show America and the world that we not only can destroy imperialists and counter-revolutionaries with arms but also with economy, production, and work—Commander Raul Castro." Below that are the words: "COUNTRY OR DEATH."

No bus rider in Cuba has the time to read such inscriptions, because he is so hemmed in by the other passengers that he can't do anything except to sit and stare and breathe as regularly as he can—and hope that when the bus stops at his disembarkation point, the thirty-second stopping time will be enough for him to shoulder and push and apologize his way to the street. The stop bells in most buses don't work. The ropes are gone. You can holler for the bus to stop, and if you are in the back, the chances are that the passengers in front will take up your cry and carry it to the driver.

Bus rides are a nightmare in Havana. This is because the number of buses in service is small compared to the need, and they are all very dilapidated. The demand upon them is all the greater because taxis, too, are breaking down, replacements aren't arriving, and few private cars are in operation.

The sale to Cuba of 300 British city and interurban buses will ease the situation, but not to an appreciable degree. Cuba needs at least a couple of thousand new buses and several thousand tons of spare parts. It also needs mechanics, because a large number of mechanics have fled Cuba since the revolution, and there aren't many people available who understand how a motor works and what should be done to prolong its life.

Before the revolution, Cuba had 4459 public buses, 2400 of them operating in Havana. All were American. When Cuba quarreled with the United States, buses ceased coming. The import of taxis, cars, and spare parts was also ended. Soon the spare parts in stock were used up. One by one, vehicles in use began going out of service. An attempt to improvise spare parts was hardly sufficient. Junk-yard scraps were fitted into the buses as much as possible, and some buses were cannibalized to keep others running. But still their number kept going down, and when I was in Havana there were just 700 buses in operation, and only about half of them working full time. The rest would be driven a few hours and taken back to the garage.

One morning I took a bus from my hotel to the INIT office. It conked out after about a mile. For ten minutes the driver tinkered with the motor, but he could not get it running again. One of the passengers said he knew something about repairs, but he, too, was unable to do anything with the engine. Other buses were driving past us; their drivers would slow down and jeer at us. Our driver put through a call for a replacement, and was told that none was available. The passengers were asked to find some other means of transportation. The next morning, when I passed the spot, the bus was still there.

It's a common sight in Havana to come across a bus or car mounted on four gasoline drums and a mechanic working under it and depriving it of every nut and bolt. Small foundries try to manufacture various parts according to the specifications of the old. Sometimes this method succeeds, sometimes it doesn't; and even when it does, the improvised parts don't last long.

The government, hoping to save money, imported some bus engines from the Soviet Union, and had them fitted to American buses. But those engines had a cooling system that could not be adapted to Cuba's hot climate, and the breakdown was frequent. The government found that it was losing rather than saving money.

Some spare parts were coming in from Canada and Mexico. But in January, 1960, a government decree banned the importation of all rolling stock and parts. The result was that their prices zoomed. A fan belt, priced at $2.50, now began selling for $12.00. The price of a spark plug jumped from $0.80 to $3.00 and the cost of an electric coil for the dynamo rose from $6.00 to $35.00. People were putting their names on a waiting list for batteries. Since government requests had priority, the common people found themselves waiting for months without success. The black-market price of a battery rose to $100 without any service guarantee.

Every bus ride was the utmost in discomfort, but, people took the overcrowding in good humor. Somebody would say something in Spanish, and those near him would begin laughing and pass his words on to the others. Every time this occurred, I took care to have someone translate for me. The following are some of the comments I picked up:

"Don't crush me. I am already crushed."

"You see, we stick together."

"We are all one—don't fall."

"It's good exercise, anyway."

"*Señorita,* I want to be close to you. My wish is being fulfilled."

"*Señorita,* now no one can say that we are separate."

"Onward! Let's move forward in a group!"

"It pays not to be fat."

Another happy factor was that everyone was so courteous—at least to me. When they saw a foreigner in their midst, they would make room. Even when I was boarding, people would break the queue for me, and those inside would pull me in. I did not know my way around, but people took time to explain the directions to me. One morning the person sitting next to me insisted on paying my fare. "You see, we are not bad people," he said. "Please go back thinking well of us."

The effervescent Cuban character also showed whenever the progress of a bus was stopped by a car coming from either the left or the right. Almost all the passengers would join the driver of the bus in shouting imprecations to the driver of the car.

I must also take my hat off to the Cuban women. No matter how large the crowd, they were never deterred. They would just push their way in. This led to some odd situations, but the women were very good-natured about it.

Each bus has a conductor in addition to the driver. The conductor issued the tickets. Because of the overcrowding, the driver can't do that. No uniforms are issued to the personnel of the city bus system. At country bus stops, I noticed a languid tendency among the personnel. Once I had to wait for twenty minutes because the driver had not showed up. A bus ride in the city is eight cents. A transfer is three cents more. A halt at every stop is obligatory. Smoking is permitted inside a bus, causing additional discomfort to many. The bus that took me to Varadero had recently been imported from Czechoslovakia, and it was not bad at all, though a far from satisfactory job was being done of washing it and keeping it shiny and clean.

Another reason the bus engines keep breaking down is that the gasoline is of low octane content. The discharged fumes have given the air in downtown Havana a nauseating smell that never leaves. Gasoline used to be thirty cents a gallon. Castro doubled the price on the excuse that the people were using it for wasteful purposes. Cuba has no oil wells, but it has three refineries, two American and one British, which used to process crude oil from Texas. The reason Castro gave for nationalizing them in 1960 was that they had refused to process Soviet oil. Now crude oil from the Baku oilfields in the Soviet Union comes to Cuba from the Black Sea ports via the Dardanelles, and is processed at these refineries. When I was in Cuba, the Fidelistas were confident that very soon Venezuela would go Red and start sending its oil to Cuba. They were basing their hopes on the forthcoming elections in Venezuela, which they thought would never be held because of the Red terrorist activities. They were hoping that the Reds would soon be in the ascendency in Venezuela. But events proved the Fidelistas wrong, and Cuba has been unable to solve the problem of her serious oil shortage.

The taxi situation is worse that the bus problem. Not one new cab has been imported since the revolution, and of the old ones, more than half are out of commission. The rest just clatter along. The bumpers are missing, the seat covers are torn, dirty jute mattresses line the floor, the doors don't shut and sometimes a piece of rope is used to keep them in place. Things such as speedometers, clocks, and windshield wipers have long ago ceased to work, and cabs are allowed to have only one light on at night.

The cabs have not been nationalized, but their operation is subject to strict rules. A driver can operate only during the hours assigned to him, and can pick up passengers only in the area that is his. He is not free to buy as much gasoline as he needs. He gets only a fixed amount, and has to present to the authorities a mileage account to justify each gallon. Whenever there is a parade, he has to drive free for the government, and he is expected to contribute to fund-raising drives. In the name of volunteer contribution, much money is taken away from him. But if he is a good contributor, he can get priority in the allotment of gasoline and parts; and if he has pull, he can even get extra gas.

He finds no shortage of customers. At the big hotels, people have to wait in line for a cab. "But what good?" one cab driver said. "I have no petrol, or gas, as you Americans say." I have no idea why he mistook me for an American. Maybe he was thinking of the U.S. all the time.

The cab drivers I talked with did not know what they would do once their cabs gave up the ghost. "I have been keeping my baby running for two years," said one. "Two years ago it should have become matter for the junk. I hope the government gets some taxis, and I hope I get one."

One Western diplomat, preparing to leave Havana, said he could easily sell his old Plymouth to a cab driver for $10,000, but the rule was that he could sell it only to the government.

I must say that I found Cuban taxi drivers extremely honest. The fare is paid by the zone. A driver could have cheated me at any time by driving all over town before coming to the address I had given, but this never happened. Only once did a taxi driver try to charge me extra fare, but it was on a route with which I had become familiar, and I did not let him.

As everywhere, cab drivers in Havana are a source of gossip. They are also a source for supplying women. But you have to know them first, or at least you must be able to convince them that you are not an undercover agent for the government and are not out to trap them. The slightest suspicion, and you are frozen out. But once the confidence is established, the driver will go out of his way to tell you where women can be had, and to describe them to you, and to tell you how much they would cost by the hour or by the night.

He will also tell you, if you tip him, how to get the price reduced. "You like Argentino women? Big in front. Very big," one driver said to me. Another said that he could put me in touch with a young girl who, he assured me, would never say quit. "Never. Never," he repeated. I asked the man where I could meet her. He replied that she was a student at Havana University, and she would wait for me near the Admissions Building, and I would be able to recognize her by her blue dress. "But lot of money," he said. "Lot of fun, lot of money." I declined the offer. I was sure that Scripps-Howard would not have approved nor sanctioned the item in the expense account.

Cab drivers also supply whisky, cigarettes, and stockings. Dollars could be sold on the black market through them; they charged a 25 percent commission. Some undoubtedly have become informers for the government. I am sure that the driver who brought me from the airport to Havana was an informer. Before the revolution, the cab drivers were notorious for being Batista's agents. Because of their contacts with the people and the opportunity they have to mix with the citizens, the revolutionary government did not crack down on them. Instead, it offered to take them into its service. Some just switched sides, as they would if some other government came to power.

Private cars are hard to find because most persons who had cars fled the country and their cars were confiscated by the government, to be assigned to the various ministries. I was shown a shipment of about a hundred Czech Skoda cars that had recently arrived, but was told that they would be allotted to doctors, factory managers, and others with urgent needs. The common citizen, even if he has the money, can't buy a car.

The only good-looking cars in Havana belong to the diplomats. Whenever one is seen on the street, people turn around to stare at it as if it were something wonderful. The very top men such as Castro and Guevara have new American cars, imported from Brazil. Each man has a car for himself and several for his bodyguards. When I was in Havana, Castro was presented with a new Zil automobile by the Soviet ambassador, but the picture of the car that was published in the papers did not give a full view of it, and I heard people say that was because the car was too small compared to U.S. cars.

I found that railroads are having many difficulties. Passenger service is down to the minimum. One diplomat's wife told me that her maid wanted to go to Camagüey, and had asked permission to go to the station twelve hours in advance to be sure of getting a ticket. About 80 percent of the passenger cars have broken down. The dining cars are out, and lounge cars no longer run; I was told that some of the latter were turned into freight cars, whose number also is diminishing. No new railroad engines or boxcars have come into Cuba since the revolution. The Cuban gauge is wider than the Soviet gauge. Before the revolution all railroad equipment was imported from the U.S. The difference in gauge prevents the Soviet equipment from taking its place.

During all my meandering in Cuba, only once did I see a train— and I counted twenty-three cars in it. Six cars were open and being used to transport tanks. The railroad tracks are still there, but they are now overgrown with shrubs; rust is corroding the metal, and worms are eating the ties. Most surface transportation is now by bus or truck.

The trucks are all Russian, and there are thousands of them. They are used for both military and civilian purposes. It is not unusual to see a truck transporting volunteer workers to a farm, and also dragging a piece of artillery. Because of rough, constant usage and poor maintenance, these trucks are out of service much before their time.

Theft of parts from government trucks is very common. The drivers and workers pilfer them and sell the parts in the black market. The workers, although they are not supposed to, use these trucks for private purposes, such as for transporting furniture or carrying the family around. The head man always looks the other way, because he is equally implicated.

"Why don't you take better care of this truck?" I asked the driver.

"Why should I? I'm not a mechanic," he replied.

"But it's your truck now. It belongs to the people," I said.

"You mean, I use it. Yes. And I thank Fidel for it," he answered.

I have already taken some note of the government-owned Cuban Airline, with its monopoly on air travel. It flies to Prague and Moscow. Mexico City is the only place in the free world to which it travels. Most of its planes are Bristol Britannias. They too are aging rapidly. The Cubans were hoping to get some more Britannias or at least spare parts for the old. The government had bought two Soviet Ilyushin 18's, and was making a big show of them. These planes have a small range and so their serviceability is limited. The two recently bought were flown from Moscow to Conakry, Guinea, and from there to Bridgetown, Barbados, where they refuelled for the last leg to Havana. A Cuban crew was sent to Russia to learn how to fly these planes, but Russian mechanics came along, too. Plane travel within Cuba is still possible, but it's very difficult to get a reservation. I tried to fly to Camagüey, but was told that all tickets had been sold for two weeks.

Castro and the other top officials do a lot of flying, but they always travel in military planes. There was some talk of Khrushchev's presenting Castro with a plane for his personal use, but I don't know whether one was actually presented or whether the talk was just propaganda.

The Cuban "merchant marine" is under one operation—the Lineas Mambisas. It has only two freighters, the *Camagüey* and the *Bahia*

Santiago. I was told that they operated mostly between Canada and Cuba. I have already mentioned my vain efforts to get passage on them. The line has no passenger vessels. Nor had the government any money to buy ships. But the Cubans were hopeful that Spain would build a ship or two for them in return for sugar. I was told that negotiations to this end were already in progress. The Cubans were also trying to get the Russians to have one or two ships built for them in Finland, under a war-reparation agreement that the Russians have with that country. The idea was born when the Finns built two ships specially for the U.S.S.R.-Cuba run, but these two ships are Soviet-owned.

22. *The Prisons and the Prisoners*

THE young Cuban woman, working in an Eastern embassy in Havana, was strikingly pretty. I don't think she was more than twenty-five. She had large black eyes, a round face, and long, tapering fingers. I had a lunch date with the ambassador, and that was how I met her. The first thing I noticed about her was her lack of vivacity. I soon learned the reason. Several months ago the police had broken into her house at two in the morning, rummaged and looted it, and had taken her husband prisoner. She still did not know what had happened to him.

"Don't you know anything about him? Don't you have any clue?" I asked.

"No," she replied.

"Have you seen him even once?"

"No."

"Didn't they tell you where they were taking him?"

"No."

"Are you allowed to write to him?"

"What address should I write to?"

"Isn't there someone—some place to whom you can go?"

"Who?"

"How about Castro? You can write to him. Have you tried?"

"I have. No answer."

We had talked thus far when she became silent. "Please tell me more," I pleaded. She said no, because I could be a government spy. I assured her that I was not, and that I would soon be out of Cuba.

"You swear?" she asked.

"I do."

She told me then that before the revolution her husband had had a small hardware store. It had been left to him by his father, and he had been working in it since he was a child. "It was his life, the only thing he lived for . . . except me, of course," said the woman. When the revolution came, the store was nationalized. He was not given compensation, but he was made manager of it and a small salary was fixed for him. The salary was not much, but it was enough to get by on. For a year, the two lived on the salary. But then her husband was accused of having submitted an incorrect tally of goods. He was given no chance to refute the charges. No investigation was made, and he was planning to take the case to the people in the upper echelon in the Ministry of Industries when the police descended on him.

When the nighttime knock came at his door, he thought it was some neighbor calling. He went to the door, clad only in his under-clothing. He found himself staring at a dozen heavily armed policemen. In the dark, he could see their armored vehicle on the road. These men rudely brushed him aside and entered the house. He asked the officer in charge for identification, which, technically, he had the right to do. The answer he got was a blow on the head with a stick, which knocked him to the ground. "Traitor! Bandit!" shouted the officer. The man was lifted to his feet, and, at a nod from the officer, handcuffs were put on him. The policemen now began searching the house. The wife had emerged; she tried to help her husband, but they wouldn't let her. He was standing in a corner, and she joined him there. They were too frightened to argue.

The officer accused the husband of conspiring with the enemies of the revolution and of sabotaging the state by trading in the black market. He tried to explain, but his explanations were brushed aside. The men who were supposed to search his house were actually wrecking it. They were ripping the pillows and the upholstery, turning everything upside down, and pocketing the valuables. The husband tried to protest, and was beaten again. The wife, trying to protect him, was also roughly handled. When this "search" was over, the man was hustled away. He was not even given a chance to get dressed. His wife was left sobbing on the floor.

She ran to her brother-in-law's house, and when I met her she was still living with him. Her own house had been confiscated. She tried getting work with the government, but was told that the only job she could have was as a farm worker. By sheer luck, she was able to land the embassy job as secretary.

Such arbitrary arrests are common in Cuba. They were very frequent during the first two or three years of the revolution. When I was in the country their number had lessened, but they still constituted a menace.

"There are no more opponents to arrest," one Cuban said. "They are all in jail."

"Where is the big jail?" I asked.

"There are many of them. I don't know the biggest."

Others said that the biggest jail, the Cuban Devil's Island, was the Isla de Pinos (Isle of Pines), lying about fifty miles to the south of Cuba. This beauiful island was the setting for Robert Louis Stevenson's *Treasure Island*. I made several attempts to get to it. The Cuban Airline runs planes to Santa Fe, the main town on the island. When I tried to make a reservation I was told that all seats were booked for weeks to come, but I could not help feeling that I was being put off.

I was told that I could go down to Batabanó, a port in the south of Cuba, by bus, and take a ferry there to Nueva Gerona, the main port of the island. But I was warned that the ferries don't run regularly, and that I might have to wait several days in Batabanó for one. I was told that it was just possible that I would be refused passage, because the government keeps a careful watch on persons wanting to travel on the ferry.

INIT, the tourist office, told me that it was organizing a tour of the island, but I learned that while one would see a lot of the island's natural scenery, he would get no opportunity to meet the people or visit the prison. Even the INIT tours aren't regular; there is one only about every two months.

One diplomat estimated that there were 10,000 prisoners in the island prison. From him and other sources I was able to learn something about conditions there. All were sure that the conditions were subhuman. I was told of some unique forms of punishment (or torture) developed by the government.

In one, a prisoner is stripped naked and pushed into a deep pit from which it is impossible for him to climb out. The pit is open to the sky, and food is lowered in a basket. But in the pit he is also drenched regularly with water. There are no pipes in it for water to drain out. It remains in a pool on the floor until the sun evaporates it. The pit is not broad enough for the prisoner to lie full length. He can just roll himself into a ball on the floor when it is dry, and sleep as best as he can. The chances are that the moment he is asleep, water will be poured on him. If there is already water on the floor, the only way he can sleep is by leaning against the wall. He has to perform all his physical functions on the floor. He is not taken out for days or weeks from this solitary confinement. He is not given anything to read. The result most often is that in ten days he goes mad, begs for release, and is willing to do anything for it.

Nobody had any good words for the guards, who seem to have been chosen for their sadistic tendencies. They derive pleasure from beating the prisoners just for the sake of the beating. They normally use a small water hose or a water pipe for it, and hold competitions among themselves to see who can beat the longest and the hardest.

There are a number of women in the prison. They are subjected to sexual abuse, especially if they are young and good-looking. The guards often rape them. These women, some of good families, are locked up with Lesbians and professional prostitutes. The guards, I was told, also use the boys among the prisoners for homosexual acts.

There is no bar or check on what the guards can do. The theory is that the prisoners are the enemies of the revolution, and, as such, any misdeed committed upon them is justified. It does not matter that nothing has been proved against them, that their cases have not come up before any court of law for a proper and impartial hearing, and that they have not been legally sentenced. The food given the prisoners consists mostly of rotten beans that set them gagging. When a prisoner is ill, little or no medical care is available. He is not segregated from those who are well, and there are no sanitary arrangements to keep the cells clean.

I learned that planes are not allowed to fly over the prison on the Isle of Pines, and people approaching it are stopped a mile or more from the wall. The outer area is also mined to prevent escape. The guards have orders to shoot all the prisoners if there is an invasion of the island.

Conditions in other prisons aren't any better. The execution of the prisoners is arbitrary. The guards have the right to shoot any prisoner at their discretion, and are not accountable to a higher officer for a shooting. But they do have to submit a report, in which they are required to write down the cause of the shooting; if they just say that the prisoner was causing trouble and was unrepentant, that's considered sufficient reason for the shooting. Or a charge can be made that the prisoner was trying to escape. The guards are not required to submit proof.

In some cases, troublesome prisoners are produced before a court composed of prison officers, who can pass the death sentence at will. The sentence of death by shooting is carried out in the prison compound, and all prisoners are forced to watch. A condemned man is not given a last wish. He is not even given a cigarette to lighten his last hours. No priest is brought to him. The actual shooting is never done while he is standing still or tied to a pole. He is never blindfolded.

Sometimes the shooting takes on a macabre aspect. A gate is thrown open, or the lock and the bar removed from it, and the prisoner is told that he is free to walk out of it. If he hesitates, he is pushed toward it with rifle butts. He is thus forced to run, and is shot while he is running. He falls. Perhaps the bullet is not fatal, and he gets up and begins to run again. Again he is shot. The game goes on until the man is dead, shot in a dozen or more places.

All this is done while members of the firing squad are laughing and joking and taking bets among themselves on who will be able to put the bullet through the knee, the elbow, or the rectum. The dead man is dragged to a pit, unceremoniously dumped into it, and covered with mud. His name is erased from the register. The prison authorities are not obliged to inform the dead man's family. If some prisoner is set free, and someone in the family of the deceased knows him, he may get in touch with him and try to get some information. But what usually happens is that the man who is released is too frightened to talk. If asked about prison conditions, he asserts that they are good. He dare not tell the true story. But his haggard appearance and disease-ridden body are enough for the observer to draw the true conclusions.

In Havana itself, El Príncipe is the most famous prison. It lies on a hill not far from the university. It is housed in an old Spanish fortress, and the dungeons and the various rooms in it are used as cells. These cells are damp, and infested with rats, mosquitoes, and cockroaches. Prisoners wake up in the morning to find their bodies covered with blotches. I could not find a cab to take me to the prison. One morning, I walked up the narrow, winding road to the prison gate. I was not allowed to enter it. When I told the guards that I wanted to see the superintendent, I was told to go away.

When I was in Havana, the Cubans were also talking in low

whispers of a new place, Guanahacabibes. It is located in western Cuba, and is called "Rehabilitation Center for the Workers" by the government. In actual fact, it is a concentration camp for workers who are condemned for not having the proper attitudes toward the revolution, and for slowing down production.

Such a worker is charged with "crime against production," or he can even be accused of sabotage. A worker can be sent to Guanahacabibes for as long as ten years. Every morning the prisoners are divided into two groups. One group spends the day cutting trees; the other, breaking rocks. In the evening, both groups have to listen to political indoctrination. It was estimated that several thousand workers were confined to this camp.

One reliable estimate was that the total number of prisoners in Cuba was 75,000. This means that almost one percent of the country's population is in jail. It is a problem, guarding so many people, and, in many places, teen-agers have been recruited, equipped with light rifles, and assigned guard duty.

Who are these 75,000 persons who are in jail? Many are men who fought Castro when he was leading the rebellion against Batista. Others are men found engaged in sabotage, men who refused to be indoctrinated and who clung to their individualism, men who once used to spy on Castro, and those who were found too outspoken in such things as belief in God and Church attendance. Included are persons who once were on Castro's side, but who fell away because he went back on his promises, and because of the excesses committed by his government. Also in jail are members of the old Cuban Communist party, who thought they could use Castro and depose him after he had driven Batista out.

Factory managers unable to meet their quotas, student leaders found making the wrong speeches, professors caught teaching the wrong things, writers who dare to dissent, persons whose "criminal activities against the state" who are "unmasked" at reunion meetings, pickpockets, hoods, dope suppliers and dope addicts, persons guilty of petty larceny or homicide, the perverts, the professional pimps—all end up in these prisons.

There are no separate classes in the prisons for the various types of prisoners. Thus a political prisoner will find himself sharing a cell with a deranged sex criminal. There is no such thing in Cuba as a petty crime. The official attitude is that all criminals should be treated alike. The length of detention can vary, but it is never in days or weeks or months. It is always in years. No one is released on bail. Once a person is in jail and the gates close behind him, no appeal is possible, and no relatives can ever visit him or write to him.

23. The Lively Arts

A MOVIE I saw in Havana was called *Cuba Dances*. It was in Spanish, but I did not find the story difficult to follow, even though I could not understand the dialogue.

The movie had strong political overtones. It was about a young girl from a rich family who wanted to fraternize with proletariat boys and girls of her own age, but whose parents prevented her from doing so. Again and again she breaks out of her father's mansion, and joins the proletariat younger set at dance parties in public halls. But each time, the sour-looking, tuxedo-clad father, and the grim-faced mother clad in a gown imported from New York, come along and take her away. The mother is represented as an exceptionally mean woman, with more than her share of harshness. The story ends with the girl's finally having her own way and marrying her proletariat sweetheart. The parents give in, and agree to help their son-in-law along in life.

This movie and others like it, produced and directed by the Cuban Institute of Cinematographic Art and Industry, referred to as ICAIC, are the standard fare at Cuban movie houses. They have hardly any artistic value. The story is almost always the same: the struggle between the bourgeois and the proletariat elements in society; the eventual defeat of the former and the inevitable triumph of the latter. All films are in black and white. The acting is bad, the direction worse; the photography and the sound tracks leave much to be desired.

The ICAIC lacks both talent and money. Its movie-making budget for 1963 was about $1.5 million. The institute's director, Alfredo Guevara, a former classmate of Castro, has ambitious plans, which include the building of a film city outside Havana and the purchase of expensive movie-making equipment from abroad. But these plans are hamstrung by the shortage of money. The institute publishes a magazine, *Cine Cubano*, which is not badly edited. It is a review of forthcoming productions, and also carries articles on movies from behind the Iron Curtain.

In spite of the mediocre quality of Cuban movies, attendance at movie houses has increased considerably. Before the revolution, there were 520 movie houses in Cuba. Most of them are still in operation, although about 400 had been nationalized by 1963, and the rest were to be taken over soon. The government has built no new movie houses of its own, but it has acquired about sixty mobile projection units, and these visit the state farms once a fortnight. In the outlying areas, their coming is always an event. The women and children wait for hours for the unit to appear, and the operating staff always gets a rousing welcome. The government estimates that yearly attendance at movies is six or eight times the population of Cuba. I don't doubt the figures, because movies are one of the few remaining forms of popular entertainment left, and people take full advantage of it. Admission can be anything from one dollar in the cities to twenty cents in the outlying villages.

I was pleased to find that Hollywood movies are still extremely popular in revolutionary Cuba. There were more than a dozen distribution companies before the revolution. All were nationalized in 1960, and their stock of movies was confiscated. All movies which showed the United States at an advantage, such as those about American war heroes, were removed from circulation, but pictures such as *Lady Possessed*, with James Mason, were allowed circulation. Walt Disney cartoons were also retained. On Sunday mornings most movie houses in Havana have special shows of Disney cartoons, for children. Lines of ticket buyers are sometimes four blocks long.

Marilyn Monroe movies were the most popular, but the people did not know that she had died. When I told some Cubans about it, they expressed genuine surprise and regret. They wanted to know how she had died. I told them that she had committed suicide. This shocked one of my listeners, and he began mumbling something which I thought was a prayer. But his friend slapped him on the back and said: "Don't worry, Enrique. I would forgive her. She is so pretty that she will go to heaven."

"But I don't want her in heaven. I want her here," the man moaned.

The Cuban film diet also includes Swedish films directed by Ing-mar Bergman, unexpurgated French movies, and movies from Italy and Japan. I tried to get a ticket for *The Naked Island* (Japanese), but gave up after waiting in line for forty-five minutes. This import of films from non-Communist countries is not fully approved by Cuban leaders with a rigid, doctrinaire approach to Communism. But Alfredo Guevara is considered a liberal in this matter, and his attitude is that Marxism does not limit the search for artistic perfection, and as long as a film does not preach anti-Communism, and, even though it is from a non-Communist country, it's okay for a good Communist to see it.

But the biggest import of films is, of course, from behind the Iron Curtain. Soviet, Polish, and East German films, some of them with Spanish dialogue dubbed in, were being shown, not only for their propaganda value but also because they were easier to get. In addition, Czech and Russian production units were busy in Cuba making films in cooperation with ICAIC. I read in *Cine Cuba* that the famous Soviet director, Mikhail Kalatozov, was due in Cuba to make a film there.

Like everything else in Cuba, radio and television are state-owned. Cuba has powerful medium- and short-range transmitters that beam propaganda broadcasts to Central and South America, and also drum up a lot of propaganda for home consumption. This takes the usual form of long speeches by the revolutionary leaders and by so-called "politi-cal analysts." On occasion Castro is interviewed on TV by a group of newspapermen, but this kind of live "press conference" sometimes takes an unusual twist. Often, one person in the panel will ask Castro a long, carefully written question; Castro then takes two hours to answer it, and that ends the "conference."

Of course, no commercials are broadcast, but their place has been taken by excerpts from the writings of Marx, Lenin, Khrushchev, and Castro. Every ten minutes a program is interrupted, and a paragraph from these writings is read. The theme is always the same: exhortation to the people to work more, to be on guard against the enemies of the revolution, be prepared for a *yanqui* invasion. Often the announcer gives a long list of increases in production, or reads stories about how the factories are meeting and overfulfilling their quotas.

Or a story is read about some unknown farmer or worker who wins some sort of recognition for his adherence to work. Such a story often has this ending: "Comrade Enrique will fly next month on six weeks' vacation to the Soviet Union and Czechoslovakia, where he will be the guest of the workers in those two fraternal and socialist countries. We feel very envious of Comrade Enrique. We congratulate him on his success. He has set himself up as a shining example of a Cuban worker, an example which everyone should emulate." Again, when Comrade Enrique comes back from his tour, he is interviewed on TV and asked to render an account of what he saw and how well the revolutionary Cuba is looked upon by the Soviet Union.

Often live interviews with the common people are put on the air. These take the form of an announcer going to a pedestrian and asking him what he thinks of the revolution. The man always has good things to say. If he has any criticism, it is very mild. I could not resist the suspicion that all the pedestrians who are questioned are hand-picked and carefully schooled in what to say. Visits of a camera unit to state farms or to new factories are given much prominence. New housing and roads, schools and hospitals, are extensively publicized.

One propaganda medium is called "Radio Free Dixie." It is beamed to the Negro population of the Southern United States. It is in English, and is dedicated to the "gallant freedom fighters" opposing the Southern racists. The principal announcer is an American Negro extremist, Robert Williams, who is under indictment for kidnaping in North Carolina. He fled the country and sought refuge in Cuba. Williams goes to extreme lengths in criticizing the U.S. He says that the U.S. Federal government is just as racist as the government of Mississippi, and that the people of the U.S. are being fooled in the same patterns as the Germans were fooled by Hitler.

But not all programs have a propaganda value. Quite a few are purely for entertainment, and except for interruptions for the reading of the political excerpts, they don't seek to convert. When I was in Havana, there was a TV series based on the Robin Hood legend. It was for both children and adults. The musical programs on radio use many American records. One that was played frequently during my stay was "Unchained Melody." I heard no jazz or twist or bossa nova. That's because the policy of the government is to check American dance forms. But the young Cubans do not like that, and some I talked with thought there was nothing objectionable in the twist and bossa nova.

The networks are making their first faint attempts at inaugurating educational television and radio. This is in the form of lessons in physics and simple mathematics. Lessons in the Russian language are given for the adults. In addition, women are taught cooking, how to solve housekeeping problems, and how to do simple repair work around the house.

Carnivals remain an integral part of Cuban life. Once the big carnival of the year was Mardi Gras. It was celebrated in February over a period of six weeks, with a gaiety and abandon unknown in New Orleans or anywhere else. The institution is still there, but its old name is gone, and the pageantry is subdued. Also, it has been given a pronounced revolutionary tint. But it continues to evoke feelings of warmth and joy, and again and again I was told that I should come back to Havana for it. Now it is organized under government auspices. Mass displays of athletics and long lines of marching youths, carrying huge banners, flags, and portraits of the revolutionary leaders, are an important part of the parade. The streets are lined that day with thousands of people, all in a gay, holiday mood. They sit on the sidewalks for hours prior to the parade, and talk about it for days afterward.

Even in revolutionary Cuba, a carnival queen is chosen. Once she was chosen from the rich, socially prominent families. She was usually a social butterfly herself, used to the ways of the French Riviera. Now care is taken that the queen come from a working-class family, and that she personally qualify as an ideal woman of the new Cuba. The various youth organizations and unions select their own queens. These are presented before a jury, which makes the final selection. Good looks are important, but a candidate is also judged on her record as a militiawoman and party organizer. Married girls are qualified to compete. If a girl's husband is prominent in the revolutionary set-up, the chances are that he will pull strings for her.

Search for recognition is as natural with the Communist as it is with the non-Communist. Human nature never changes. Marxism modifies it, but the basic factors in it remain the same. The French Revolution in the eighteenth century sent the old dukes and counts and viscounts to the guillotine. But when Napoleon Bonaparte came to power, he created his own nobility from among the ranks of his trusted generals. The same has happened in Cuba, just as in other Communist countries. The Castro revolution shot or exiled the old bourgeoisie, but its place is now being rapidly filled by a new bourgeoisie—the factory managers, the technocrats, the party big-wigs. And these latter are as eager for social recognition for themselves and their wives and daughters as were their "thieving" predecessors of "accursed memory."

The annual selection of the national carnival queen is the closest thing to a beauty contest in Cuba. It takes place in the dining room of some big Havana hotel. Admission is free, but rowdy elements are barred. Seats are reserved for various groups—students, workers, writers. The girls who make the finals parade before a jury, under a spotlight, in one-piece bathing suits. Cheers and whistles ring through the hall. Each girl's name is announced over the microphone, and a statement about her background and political reliability is read. The girls parade a second time in evening dresses. Then the judges retire to another room, and after an hour's deliberation announce their decision. The queen's attendants are chosen in the same manner. The government newspapers take great pains in publicizing the proletariat origin of these girls. Long revolutionary statements of the usual pattern are attributed to them.

The pageantry sometimes lasts for four weeks. It includes dancing in the streets, folk shows, and other cultural events. Since the revolution, teams from other Communist countries have been participating in the events. The parade has the usual floats, but they don't represent the various business organizations or the clubs. They now represent the government departments and the unions, and extol the achievements under Castro.

There also are floats for pure entertainment. One open truck that drew much praise in 1963 represented a group of jet black Fiji Islanders with fuzzy hair. They wore hula skirts, had bones tied to their heads and carried primitive spears and shields with pictures of fierce-looking gods painted on them. On a separate float were a group of Fiji women standing around an artificial palm tree and waving and winking at the spectators, who winked and waved back.

The biggest event of the carnival is the announcement of Cuba's "Heroes of Socialist Labor." A new group is chosen each year from those who get the highest rating in their work, either at farms or in factories. Their reward is a six-week, all-expense-paid trip to the Soviet Union.

Parades on a smaller scale are staged in memory of some of the saints.

They, too, include floats depicting achievements since the revolution.

statues of children clustered about him. It seemed odd that the statue of a militant atheist should be carried with the statues of the saints— but then, this was Cuban Communism.

Like the movies and everything else, sports are under strict governmental control in Cuba. The first thing I noticed in Havana was the building of a number of large sports stadiums. They are in a huge area, called Sports City, not far from the Marianao beach. One characteristic of all dictatorships is the stress they lay on sports and stadiums; Castro's is no different. All sports are under the direction of the Cuban National Institute of Sports. Its director is José Llanusa, and one of its projects is the building of a factory to produce balls, bats, and gloves for baseball, which continues to be the favorite Cuban sport, quite as popular as in the United States. The government makes no effort to suppress it because of its American origin. In fact, the Institute does everything to encourage it. One reason could very well be that Castro himself used to be a pitcher during his college days; he continues to be a baseball fan, and attends almost all the games. At all stadiums there is a special box reserved for him, but quite often he joins the newsmen in the press box. He often gets up and takes a hand at pitching or batting. Newspapers and magazines regularly publish pictures of him playing baseball.

I was not in Cuba during the baseball season, but several times I saw teams of boys playing the game in sandlots. Teams exist in all schools, colleges, factories, and farms. Before the revolution, the main team was the Havana Sugar Kings, which held a franchise in the International League. There were also other leagues in which U.S. players used to participate.

Not long after it came to power, the new government abolished professional baseball. Today there are four main teams in the country— the Occidentals, the Orientals, the Sugar Makers, and the Industrials. They have thirty players each. The Industrials are the champions, but the Occidentals are hot on their heels for the pennant. The 120 players in the four teams are picked from the local leagues. They don't play baseball for a living, and are mostly farm or factory workers. They don't receive any additional pay for playing baseball, but they get leave of absence for the national series that lasts two months. During this period they continue to receive their regular pay, plus free food and lodging.

I did not see much evidence of other sports. Football, as it is known in America, is not played, but I was told that some colleges still have soccer teams. Golf is frowned upon; Castro considers it a rich man's sport. In all Havana, there is only one golf course left.

Shortage of sports equipment is a major problem. Some equipment is bought in Canada, but the dollar shortage is preventing additional buying. Homemade bats and balls are of inferior quality.

I was amazed at the popularity of chess in Cuba. In the evenings, people gather in parks and play chess. Recreation rooms in all college dormitories are provided with several chess sets. The newspapers publish regular chess columns. Cuba now is making its own chess sets. The squares are not black and white, but orange and white. (Orange now has become the unofficial color of Cuba.) The pieces are crude, but they meet the need. This pouplarity, no doubt, is due to the Russian influence. Ernesto Che Guevara is considered an able chess player, and takes a personal interest in making the game popular.

24. The Hard Life of the Diplomats

A FRIEND from a Western embassy drove me around the Miramar area in Havana, where most of the foreign embassies are located. We drove past the embassies of Mexico, Bolivia, Chile, and Brazil. I saw that a large number of tents had been set up in the compounds of the first three of these embassies, and people were living in them. Women chatted in groups in the sun, and children played hide-and-seek between the tents.

"These people look like refugees," I exclaimed. "Who are they?"

"They *are* refugees. Cuban refugees, who have sought asylum at the embassies," my friend replied.

Before the revolution, Cuba had diplomatic ties with all Latin American republics. When Castro came to power, a few of them refused to recognize his government, but there was no total diplomatic severance. It was only when Castro announced that he was a Communist that these relations were broken off one by one. Today, among Latin countries, only Mexico, Chile, Bolivia, and Brazil maintain embassies in Havana.

It was the policy of these embassies to grant asylum to fleeing Cubans. A Cuban could just walk into their compounds, let the authorities know that he was seeking refuge, and refuge would be given to him. To house these persons, tents were set up in the compounds.

Getting them out of Cuba always took time. Sometimes, more than six months were required. The embassies set in motion the procedure to confer their respective citizenship upon the refugees, and only when the paper work was completed and regular passports issued could the refugees safely leave the compound and board a plane to take them out of Cuba. Sometimes the host country even sent a special plane to pick up its new citizens.

There is no denying that the Cuban government did not like this arrangement. In this way, many of its noted enemies have been able to leave the country. But, apart from lodging stiff protests, there was nothing it could do. It could sever the diplomatic ties and ask the whole embassy staff to leave, but that still would not give it the right to send its militia into the embassy enclosures and arrest the refugees.

The four embassies have given refuge to hundreds of fleeing Cubans. But the embassy of Brazil stopped the practice early in 1963 when two of the persons to whom it had given refuge were killed in a fight over a woman. The other three embassies have not announced that they are stopping the practice, but they are not taking in any more refugees. The reason they give is that they must first get those already under their protection out of the country before they take in others.

Canada is the fifth and last country in the Western Hemisphere with an embassy in Havana. But it does not have a policy of giving refuge to Cubans. "If a Cuban comes to us for refuge, we won't admit him," a spokesman told me.

The staffs of these five embassies do not find a friendly atmosphere in Cuba. All the five countries are anti-Communist, and their embassy staffs are tolerated by the revolutionary government as a necessary evil. The Canadians are treated a bit differently, because Cuba is able to buy consumer items from Canada, but no warm feelings of friendship are shown to them.

The Fidelistas are proud of the fact that their government has been able to win the recognition of such important nations as Great Britain, France, Japan, and India. Relations with these countries are on the ambassadorial level.

"So what if the *yanquis* don't recognize us?" said one member of the Young Communists. "The rest of the world recognizes us. And the great and glorious socialist camp recognizes us. We have nothing to fear."

A person of importance in Cuba is Ambassador John Hugh Adam Watson of Great Britain. The Cuban government went out of its way to provide various kinds of facilities for him and his staff. It hoped that Ambassador Watson would recommend to his own government the resumption of at least some trade between Cuba and Great Britain. Every member of his staff was given super-VIP treatment. The envoy went about Cuba making innocent speeches about peace and good-will and the importance of international harmony. But he often took care to stress that Britain was on friendly terms with the United States.

That did not deter the Cubans from hoping that he would come out in favor of trade with them. "You are a trading nation," the Englishmen were told by fawning officials of the Cuban Ministry of Foreign Affairs. "Your life depends upon trade. Your greatness depends upon trade. You need sugar. Your people need sugar for their tea. We can give you plenty of sugar, if you give us machinery." And so the talk went.

When the embassy people hinted that they would like to see Cuba pay compensation for the three British oil refineries confiscated by the government, the Cubans never said no. In drawn-out diplomatic language, they replied that the matter was open to negotiation, which could be held at the appropriate time. I got the feeling that the Cubans were using the negotiation promise as a lever for trade resumption.

The Cubans held out the same carrot—trade—to the Japanese. Realizing the supreme importance of trade to Japan, the Cubans were promising their guests from across the Pacific that they had much to gain in selling machinery to Cuba. Next to the British, the Japanese were the most feted persons from the non-Communist world.

I saw groups of Japanese living grandly in all the main hotels of Havana. They were given whatever they asked for. If they ordered whisky, the hotels provided them with it, in spite of its acute scarcity in the country. When they traveled, they were given priority. I learned that a delegation of the Japanese Communist party was purposely given second-class treatment to avoid irritating the Japanese embassy and government.

The Cubans were also proud of recognition by India. Before the revolution, the Indian ambassador in the United States was also accredited to Cuba. But since the rise of Castro, the Indian ambassador in Mexico is accredited to Cuba, and the Indian consulate at 1003 Fifth Avenue, Havana, is run by a chargé d'affaires. It was doing valuable work in countering the Red Chinese propaganda against India in Cuba. Every day groups of Cuban students would call at the consulate to pick up literature stating the Indian case. But the Cuban government realized that it could not sell its sugar to India, because India produces its own sugar.

Another embassy of great importance in Havana was the Spanish embassy. The Cubans still look upon Spain as their "mother country." They cannot forget that Cuba was discovered by Christopher Columbus for Queen Isabella of Spain, and colonized by Spain. There exist today powerful sentimental and racial ties between the two countries. Culturally, Cuba remains Spanish. One estimate was that there were 50,000 Spaniards living in Cuba, and it is true that there is hardly a family in Spain that does not have relatives living in Cuba.

I found the Spaniards openly in favor of trade resumption with Cuba. An official of Iberia Airlines in Havana told me that but for American opposition, his company would be operating three or four flights a week to Havana, instead of one a week. The Cubans were aware of this feeling, and the government went out of its way to be polite and courteous to members of the Spanish embassy.

Hopes for trade and other political advantages were also behind Cuba's wooing of the diplomats from such countries as France and Sweden. Every action of French President Charles de Gaulle toward greater freedom for his armed forces from control by NATO was played up and applauded in Cuban papers. The Cubans were hoping that through such flattery they would be able to persuade France to sell much-needed industrial goods to them. Their wooing of Sweden was based on the fact that Sweden does not belong to NATO and follows a more or less neutral policy in the struggle between East and West. Among African countries having ties with Cuba were Egypt, Algeria, and Guinea. The Cubans wooed them all, because they realized that the more commercial and political ties they had with these nations, the weaker the effect of the American political and economic boycott.

"It takes nerve to stand up to America," one Cuban said. "All these nations that recognize us are proving that they have nerve."

When Castro emerged victorious in the struggle with Batista, the Soviet Union was one of the first countries to extend recognition to his government. Eastern European nations were quick to do the same, and Castro's recognition of them, and their recognition of Castro, were acts that were done almost simultaneously. Within the first few months of the take-over of Cuba by Castro, Hungary, Romania, Bulgaria, Albania, Yugoslavia, Poland, and East Germany had all opened missions in Havana. The Red nations of Asia were equally quick to follow the Soviet example. North Korea, Outer Mongolia, North Vietnam, sent missions rushing to Cuba.

There was a Nationalist Chinese embassy in Havana. It did not take Castro long to boot it out of the country. The moment this was done, the Red Chinese came in—dour, sardonic men, wearing heavy pants and high-collared coats. Methodically, they went about establishing an embassy and exploring the ways in which they could increase their influence with Castro. Nations that can be called Communist fellow travelers, such as Cambodia and Indonesia, also had no qualms in the matter. And while the Latin American embassies were being closed one by one, and it appeared to be just a matter of months before the U.S. embassy would close its doors, these new nations were acquiring buildings for their embassies in Havana with utmost rapidity.

The Red Chinese came bearing gifts in cash and long-term or deferred credit. In the early days of the Cuban revolution, these gifts were gratefully accepted. The rift between Red China and the Soviet Union was not very pronounced at that period, and the Cubans found it easy to get along with one without embarrassing the other. But as time passed, and the rift became serious, the Cubans found themselves in a fix. The tendency of Castro was to side with the Soviets, but unlike some countries of Eastern Europe that took an anti-Red Chinese posture, he tended to soft-pedal the rift. He was urged to adopt this position by his minister of industries, Ernesto Che Guevara, who, like Mao Tse-tung, believes in the forceful overthrow of governments.

At the time of the 1962 missile crisis, when Castro discovered that he was being used as a pawn by Soviet Premier Nikita Khrushchev in the latter's maneuvering to capture West Berlin, he found solace in the support given to him by the Red Chinese.

One Western diplomat interpreted this play of power politics to me in this manner:

"Have you read the story of Sinbad the Sailor and the old man who got upon his shoulder and would not come down? In early 1963, in the wake of the showdown over missiles, that was what Castro became to Khrushchev. He could not let go of him, because he found, much to his consternation, that if he did that, the Red Chinese would be only too willing to take him into their fold, and that would mean that the Red Chinese influence over Communist parties all over Latin America would increase. Castro did a superb job of playing the Russians against the Chinese. He knew that if the Russians left, the Chinese were too far away to take their place, but he also knew that the mere hint that he would go over to the Chinese would bring him additional Russian aid, and he got it in tons upon tons of goods and millions upon millions of rubles."

At the time I was in Cuba, it had become too difficult for the Cubans to deal with the two Communist giants without appearing to be partial toward either. Castro and the other revolutionary leaders took every opportunity to thank the Soviet Union for the aid they were getting, but they never joined in condemning the Red Chinese in any way whatever. This irked and irritated the Russians, but there was nothing they could do about it.

I also noticed that the irritation of the common people and some of the students toward the Soviet Union was based on the fact that the Russians had a "holier-than-thou" attitude, and were adopting a posture of superiority. But nobody ever complained to me that the Chinese also behaved in the same manner. Every dormitory of the "scholarship students" had a dozen or more students from Red China. These latter lived in the manner of the Cuban students. They wore the same kind of shabby clothes, ate the same food, did their stint of guard duty, and worked on the state farms on Sundays. This ability to mix with the people to the point of merging with them was creating a very good effect upon the Cubans.

And when these young Chinese opened their mouths to criticize the Russians, the Cuban students listened attentively and respectfully, without attempting to contradict. The reason was that the Cubans weren't really sure on whose side they should be in the Sino-Soviet conflict. It did my capitalist heart good to see this happen again and again during my visits to Havana University and the dormitories.

Havana newspapers published most of Khrushchev's speeches, but deleted the portions criticizing the Red Chinese. In editorial comment, the papers kept scrupulously neutral, and in no way whatever did they betray their feelings toward the schism.

I asked a young Cuban student: "What is your attitude toward the rift between the U.S.S.R. and China? What do you think of it?"

"Oh, don't worry about that," he replied, trying to appear casual. "It's only a family quarrel. There is nothing serious about it. It will be settled."

I learned that at diplomatic receptions the Soviet and Chinese diplomats do not speak with each other. On my third evening in Havana, I was at the Hotel Habana Libre where a reception by the North Vietnamese ambassador was being held. I tried to gate-crash, but was firmly stopped. The party was over at nine o'clock, and I watched all the guests coming out. The Soviet diplomatic contingent (it was easy to recognize them from their facial features) came out in a group. The Red Chinese were the last to emerge. Later I asked a

Western diplomat about the reception. He said that the Russians and Chinese don't even nod to each other at such parties, and take care to stay in separate corners of the reception hall.

"What do the Cuban leaders do on such occasions?" I asked.

"Well, some hang around the Russians, and some hang around the Chinese," he replied with a laugh. "If some big Cuban leader is attending, he takes care to shake hands and spend some time in idle chitchat with both."

I asked whether the two embassies put out literature denouncing each other. He answered: "Yes, they do. Even if Khrushchev's speeches pouring fire and brimstone on the Chinese are not published in Havana papers, Spanish translations are distributed by the Soviet embassy. In the same way, the speeches of Red Chinese bosses calling Khrushchev a rat cannot be read in Havana papers, but can be had in pamphlet form at the Red Chinese embassy."

He said that both embassies send free copies of such literature to all schools and colleges, and it can be bought for a few cents at all hotels and bus stations. I wondered about the attitude of the Cuban government toward the mailing of this literature. He replied that the mailing was a source of great embarrassment to the government, but there was nothing it could do to check it. "It could and did caution moderation, but this it does only indirectly, because if it takes an open stand against the mailing, it could be interpreted to mean that it is neutral in the struggle. It *is* neutral, but it takes care not to parade its neutrality."

But all diplomats I talked with stressed that they considered Havana a hardship post. This was because of the scarcities in the country, and the prevalence of a revolutionary atmosphere. All diplomatic personnel were given ration cards, but they didn't use them, because they preferred importing their own food. Every embassy brought in its own supply of everything it needed, from razor blades and shoelaces to salt and flour. One chargé d'affaires told me that when he traveled within the country he took his own food and a supply of boiled water. "You can't get food in the interior of the country, and I don't think that water outside Havana is adequately purified. Of course, there are thousands of persons who drink it, but they have become used to it," he said.

Another diplomat, a young man who had seen diplomatic life in Washington and London, complained that it was impossible to meet good-looking girls and strike up a friendship with them on the "cocktail circuit." He said: "First, there is no cocktail circuit worth the name in Havana. Every party is shabby. Second, those who come to the parties are always so darned serious and tense that you can't relax with them."

I remarked that at least his life in Cuba did away with all chances of his falling into the clutches of a female spy. "Oh, there are Cuban *señoritas* around, with whom you can flirt if you want to," he said, "but it does not take you long to figure out that they have been planted by the government, and the moment you realize that, you keep away from them."

Free-nation diplomats bring their wives and small children with them. They leave behind daughters old enough to go to a party. Communist diplomats bring their whole families. But the girls are taught to be very careful at diplomatic receptions. Sometimes they are so careful that they become bores.

The diplomats find it hard to analyze the political and economic situation in the country for the benefit of their own governments. That is because there are no reliable statistics available, about anything. They don't find it difficult to get in touch with the Ministry of Foreign Affairs and the other ministries. The normal channels of contact are still open, but there is no guarantee that the Cuban officials receiving a diplomatic note would really know how to handle it. "They don't have the experience," one diplomat said. "They don't know what to do with a note, how to take action on it, how to send a proper reply. The filing system in the Cuban ministries leaves much to be desired. It's downright inefficient. Sometimes we get a reply on the second day. Sometimes we have to wait for weeks."

Another diplomat said: "The Cubans want to buy machinery from us. Some time ago we received an official request for it. Attached to the letter was a list of the items they wanted. But some items they requested could be of no use to them, because before you can use them, you have to have the proper industrial base for it. I could not for the life of me see what the Cubans would have done with such things. They just did not know. When we pointed this out to them, they accused us of stalling. I talked with the appropriate official in the Ministry of Industries. He did not know his business. He kept repeating the official line."

The Cuban government says that it prefers to receive diplomatic notes in Spanish. Before the revolution, it used to receive notes in

English and French, as well as Spanish. Now, Russian has been added to the list of languages in which one can write to the government.

I felt sorry for the diplomats. Their governments should give them some bonus for serving in Havana. It's a tense, frustrating job—holding a diplomatic post in Cuba.

25. The People and the U.S.

AN old Hollywood movie I saw in Havana was *Julius Caesar*, featuring Marlon Brando as Mark Antony. The film was, of course, preceded by a newsreel. The first shots were of Fidel Castro making a speech. He was waxing hot on the good things done by the revolution. Then he switched to comparing Marxism's virtues with the evils of the free-enterprise system in the United States. As if to illustrate his point, shots from a grade-C Western were flashed, showing Indians being mowed down by white men.

"This is how the Americans conquered the West," said Castro. Then came shots of a dam in the U.S.S.R. and of Soviet workers entering a factory. "And this is how the people of the Soviet Union are winning their frontier lands today," he said. The hall was full, but the newsreel did not cause much stir. The audience was used to such comparisons.

In Cuba the government's anti-American campaign has never diminished in pitch. The screaming against the *"yanqui* monopolists" has never abated. Some choice names given to the Americans are: Wall Street warmongers, lackeys of capitalism, CIA bloodsuckers, stooges of oil barons, and bread-robbers. Billboard advertising has disappeared with the establishment of state monopoly over trade. But the place of giant posters advertising Coca-Cola, Krispy Corn Flakes, Ford cars, has been taken by giant posters showing Uncle Sam in various undignified postures.

The Cuban way of drawing Uncle Sam, I noted, was a bit different from ours. In the Cuban version, the face had been changed to that of President John F. Kennedy, complete with the large shock of hair. The bony hands looked like the talons of a bird of prey, and the famous Kennedy grin had been changed to a hideous grimace. The teeth still showed, but they reminded one of the teeth of a cannibal chief being bared at the sight of a cooked man. Also, the band in the top-hat had swastikas on it instead of stars.

It was amazing the way every human activity had been given an anti-American twist. On Havana's Plaza Civica was a huge drawing put out by INDER, the government's sports institute, meant to encourage athletics. The drawing showed a happy-looking Cuban javelin-thrower aiming a javelin at Uncle Sam. The latter was running away with the tails of his coat flapping in the air. One javelin had already gone through his top hat, and lifted it from his head. Between the drawings were the words: *"Derrotemos al Imperialismo"* (Get Rid of Imperialism), and a second reading *"Practica Deportes"* (Practice Sports). Such posters are all over the country; a fortune must have been spent on printing them. If rain spoils a poster, it is very soon replaced.

No government leader, no minor-league speaker ever gives a speech or makes a statement without including gibes at the United States. Radio programs are interrupted for the same reason. A play is on. All of a sudden it is stopped, and someone is heard denouncing the United States in choice expletives.

"How do you like these snipes in place of the commercials?" I asked a Cuban in my hotel lobby, who was listening to a program.

"Both are bad," he replied lazily.

My observation was that when an anti-American gibe is inserted in a program, the listeners sigh resignedly, look vacantly into space, and begin tapping their feet in impatience.

The government has changed the history books. Now the Cubans are taught that the United States did not play a decisive role in the winning of Cuban independence from the Spaniards. American intervention in the Cuban independence war is interpreted as a means of superseding the Spaniards. President Theodore Roosevelt and the exploits of his Rough Riders are downgraded in the new history books, and it is asserted that the battleship *Maine* was blown up in Havana harbor by the Americans themselves to find a pretext for intervention. The *Maine* Memorial facing Havana Bay is still there, but the American eagle has been removed from its top. Castro announced that a dove of peace would be put in its place, but so far that has not been done.

The attitude of the government is that everything American is bad; it views nationalism as synonymous with hatred of the U.S. With some ardent Fidelistas, the hatred is genuine. I questioned several of them on what they thought of the U.S. The impression I got was that the reasons for this hatred were mainly psychological. Before the revolution, Americans owned about 40 percent of the sugar mills of Cuba. They also owned much land and a large number of industries, banks, and utilities. This gave them physical control of about one quarter of the Cuban economy. In addition, the business and social relationships between the U.S. and the native Cuban businessmen were strong. The result was that a great sense of economic inferiority developed among the Cubans.

It was further complicated by the merchandising of Cuban sugar. Cuba was the largest producer of sugar in the world. It sold to the U.S. annually a fixed proportion of its crop at prices above the world-market price. The monetary advantage of this arrangement to Cuba was considerable. But sugar dominated the economy of the whole country, and such things as railroads, roads, and ports were built around that one industry. This situation gave the U.S. an immense indirect power over the affairs of the island.

Then there was the matter of the world-market price of sugar. It was determined not in accordance with production. The main buyers, besides the U.S., were other advanced capitalist countries. Their demand for sugar set the price. A lot of economic shenanigans went into the fixture of this price, and the victims were the Cubans. Their reliance upon the commodity was such that a variation of a few cents in the price meant the difference between hunger and plenty. The overall result was that while one part of the Cuban economy was directly at the mercy of the U.S., the rest of it seemed subject to the foibles of world capital, which itself was dominated in a large measure by the U.S.

The Fidelistas also made a strong point of the cultural domination of Cuba by the U.S. They claimed that before the revolution Cuba was the most Americanized country in Latin America, and that it slavishly followed the Americans in everything they did, ignoring its own cultural heritage and letting it rot, instead of trying to develop it. The Fidelistas, in a great burst of national pride, said that Cuban culture —its poetry, art, sculpture—was in no way inferior to that of any country in the world, and so it should not be allowed to get buried under American culture.

At one government office, I was given a copy of a speech by Nicolás

Guillen, president of the Writers and Artists Union. He explains the point of cultural domination:

> The bourgeoisie, in short, made Miami its tourist Mecca and New York its special obsession. English expressions and slang were substituted for Spanish words in current usage: "OK" for "*correcto*," "thank you" for "*gracias*," etc. Children were educated at Yankee schools, in the U.S. or Cuba, for there was hardly an important city on the island without an American school. Many officers of the national army were educated at West Point, and even our children's stories and games originated in texts in which the heroes were born in the U.S. and had a mentality based on brute force and racial superiority: Buffalo Bill, Nick Carter, Superman.

Another Fidelista increased the list by including in it fashions, hair styles, songs, pinball machines, and many other things.

But in making all these points, the Fidelistas conveniently ignored the positive aspects of the alleged domination. They refused to dwell on the fact that the financial and economic contacts with the U.S. had made Cuba a consumers' paradise compared to the primitiveness of other Latin American countries, and that the necessities and luxuries of life used to be present in Cuba in abundance. This contrasted sharply with revolutionary Cuba, in which the luxuries had disappeared and the necessities had become scarce.

The Fidelistas forgot that, before they took over, Havana was known as the Paris of Central America, and that the revolution had changed it into a dull, drab town of decaying buildings needing both plaster and paint. They ignored the fact that before Castro the per capita food intake in Cuba had the highest calorie count in Latin America, and that the revolution had cut the count by 30 percent.

Their one song was that America had cheated them into economic and political subjugation, and that they had smashed this subjugation. To them, "freedom" meant freedom from both American capital and a capitalist economy.

"If in 1959 America had given you economic aid, would you have accepted it?" I asked a member of the Young Communist organization.

"No," he replied with disgust.

"But Fidel Castro went to Washington to look for it."

"Fidel is no fool. He went to get the feelings of the American people toward our revolution. We have created a new society. We don't want to have anything to do with dying and decadent capitalism."

However, I was glad to notice that this blind hatred of the U.S. is not shared by the ordinary Cubans. I talked with cab drivers, shoeshine boys, waiters, elevator operators, mailmen, paper carriers. No one among them had a bad word for the U.S. In fact, they were genuinely sorry at the cleavage, and they looked upon the anti-Americanism being fed to them as some sort of nightmare that would soon be over.

One shoeshine man, a cripple about thirty years old, told me that before the revolution he used to earn twenty dollars a day from tourists, but now he was lucky if he made two dollars a day. He said that in those days he owned ten suits, but now most of them were worn out, and he did not have the money to buy a new one. One minor office head was very critical of the U.S. when he was in front of his colleagues. But when he and I were alone, he asked me whether I would do him a favor. He wanted me to look up his relatives in New York.

The main reason Castro's propaganda has been unable to instill mass hatred against the U.S. is that so many Cubans have visited this country, and lived and worked here. They know from personal experience that all the bad things the government says against America just aren't *correcto*. Many Cubans recalled to me the days when they could enter the U.S. freely, make money here, and send it home. A doctor's assistant told me that she had worked in New York for ten years. I asked her what she thought of America. She replied: "Oh, I am sure that Cuban relations with America will get better. They'd better. We need America. America needs us."

A man in my hotel lobby told me that in 1954 he drove a laundry wagon in Chicago. He wanted to know whether I had been to Chicago. I said I had. He began to reminisce about it, and told me that he had been paid a dollar an hour, and had been able to save money. With a touch of nostalgia, he asked whether the Buckingham fountain still played. I replied that as far as I knew it did. He said: "It will always be there. It will never stop playing." One Cuban told me that he had been a cab driver in Washington in the early 1950's and used to drive senators around. He had warm praise for Senator Tom Connolly of Texas, and when I told him that Connolly was dead, his sorrow was genuine.

I had a long chat with Dr. Josefina Yarini, head of the English department at Havana University. She is a graduate of Barnard College, New York, and a most pleasant woman. She asked me to make inquiries in Canada on the possibility of sending Cuban youths there for education under an exchange program. I did not detect in her a spot of hostility toward the West or the U.S.

One evening at the public library I caught an attendant behind the counter reading a bound volume of old copies of *Coronet* magazine. When he saw me, he quickly hid the volume, and kept it hidden all the time I was in the room.

I found that the desire to know more about America was widespread. People kept asking me all kinds of questions. At several such meetings, it became very difficult for me to hide my connections with the U.S.

"All I know of America is based on American papers I used to read in Canada," I would say.

"Ah-ha. You read American papers. *New York Times?* Do they still publish Blondie cartoons?"

I said that the *New York Times* runs no cartoons. But the Cubans thought that that was beside the point.

Many wanted to know more about President Kennedy and Mrs. Kennedy.

"Is Jacqueline really '*a bonito*'? You know, oomphie?" one Cuban asked.

"Very oomphie," I assured him.

"Has she five children?" he asked, raising five fingers to his face.

"No. Two."

That caused a moan of disappointment. Large families are still considered desirable.

One woman wanted to know the color of Mrs. Kennedy's hair and her style of wearing it. She was delighted when I drew a picture of the pillbox hat made famous by the former First Lady.

In Canada I had been told that I would have no language problem in Cuba because, I was assured, half of the population speaks English. This was largely true, but I noticed that many persons who could speak English were wary of admitting it. It is more fashionable to pretend ignorance of the language of the hated Yankees. I would ask a person whether he knew English. He would say that he knew very little of it or none at all, but then we would converse freely in the language for thirty minutes.

One proof that the ordinary Cuban has no real hatred for America was that dozens of them asked me to help them to get to this country. Planes that fly into Havana from Madrid and Mexico City are always three fourths empty. Planes that fly out of Havana are packed to capacity.

I visited the American embassy building, a beautiful structure in glass and concrete, overlooking Havana Bay. It has seven stories, was patterned after the United Nations building in New York, and cost $1.2 million to build. American diplomatic relations with Cuba were severed on January 4, 1961, and the building was put under the charge of the Swiss embassy. Early in 1963 Castro announced the building's confiscation. That was against all diplomatic practices, because international law states that even if diplomatic ties are cut, the embassy building remains inviolable.

The Swiss chargé d'affaires, Charles Masset, told the Cubans that he would not surrender the building, and that if the Cubans wanted it they would have to use force. Just before I was in Havana, one Swiss officer, during the absence of Masset, began flying the Swiss flag over the building. When Masset returned, he had the flag hauled down to avoid unnecessary provocation. Now a few Swiss officers and thirty-seven Cuban employees manage the building. It opens for just a few hours on working days. All but ten rooms are kept locked. The American emblem can still be seen carved on the outside wall, and many times I saw wandering Cubans halt, gaze at it for a few minutes and go away. To a large number of them, I am sure, the emblem remains a symbol of hope.

At the time of the revolution about 50,000 Americans were living in Cuba. Within a year of Castro's ascendancy, all but a few had left. When I was on the island, there was living in Havana, as far as I knew, just one American, J. Niven Alleyn, whom I have referred to earlier. He is eighty-nine years old, and he has lived in Havana since 1898. He is known to be trenchant in his criticism of Castro, but the government does not bother him because of his age.

W

26. Future Prospects

HEN all is said and done, I don't think I would like to live in revolutionary Cuba. I know that if I were a Cuban I should be proud of the fact that the island has acquired an importance in world politics far in excess of its size and population. Since the revolution it has hardly been out of the headlines the world over. But I don't care for that sort of notoriety.

I would not be happy with a situation in which the per capita production has gone down 20 percent and the per capita intake of food has dropped by several hundred calories.

I would not like to see my leaders making grandiose promises and fulfilling only a small percentage of them. I would believe them at first, but very soon I would see through their guile, and do something about it.

I would not like to wait for hours in a line to get a moldy tube of toothpaste. I would not like to have to use the backs of propaganda pamphlets for note paper. If I were a laborer, I would like to retain my right to strike, and the right to change jobs, and the right to hassle with my employer over my wages. I would want to feel free to go to a church, read the Bible, talk with my God. I would want my children to cultivate such character traits as decency, honesty, a true sense of proportion, fear of God, and respect for their parents and elders.

I would not like to read only what the authorities want me to read, or to watch only the regime-sponsored TV programs, or listen only to government-approved broadcasts. I would want to know what's happening in the rest of the world, what the leaders in other countries are saying, and what new horizons of the mind have been traversed by thinkers in other countries. I would want all this information exactly as it is, and not in an edited or adulterated form, for I believe in what the poet says:

Let there be many windows to your soul,
That all the glory of the universe
May beautify it.

And faced with the world's variety and richness, I would want to do my own thinking, instead of having someone else do it for me. I would like to make up my own mind about things, instead of others doing it for me. I would like to listen to what others who disagree with me have to say. I know that I am not so brilliant that I can never be wrong. For all I know, the person who is disagreeing with me might be right. I would like to live in a society in which I am free to make my own friends, and to talk with them without the fear of being overheard and reported. I would like to visit them unhindered, and I would like them to visit me without being shadowed. I would like to form a social club of my own, if I wanted to; and I would want the right to join other social clubs.

I also would like to see other parties in existence besides the Communist party, and I would want the right to belong to a non-Communist party without the fear of being thrown into jail or losing my job. I would want the right to vote. I would want the laws of my land drawn up by a properly elected assembly, and I would want the president of my country also to be properly elected, instead of ushering himself into office through the support of the military and tricky maneuverings within the party.

I would want the rest of Latin America to quit treating me as a pariah. I am related racially and culturally to the peoples of the Latin American republics, and I would never forget that my welfare is linked to their welfare, that they are my people, and that I cannot harm them without harming myself.

I would like the friendship of all the world, instead of just the dubious friendship of the Communist nations. I would hate the way my country has been taken over by the Russians. I would strive for freedom from them. I would follow international conduct of good behavior which forbids fostering revolutions in other countries. I would hate to see Cuba treated as a pawn in international politics by the men in the Kremlin. I would rebel at my island's political isolation from the mainstream of world events.

But if these things are denied me, what good is it if my island makes the headlines every day? There are a few things that are very clear to me: Castro set out to bring economic progress to the country, but under his regime the country is worse off economically than at any period in its history. Castro set out to end exploitation of the many by a few. He has driven out the exploiters, but in their place he has created a new set of exploiters whose methods are far more vicious. He set out to rid the country of what he called domination by the United States. But he has substituted domination by the Soviet Union to an unparalleled degree. Never was "Yankee exploitation" of Cuba as great.

I did not like the Castro regime. I did not like the things I saw. I was not impressed by them. I thought they were abhorrent, disgusting. I said to myself, if this is Communism (and Cuba was the first Communist country I had visited in my life) then I can do without it.

And yet I could not avoid the impression that the Castro regime was very firmly entrenched. It was strong militarily, it had Russian arms and Russian troops to back it up, and the flow of Russian goods showed no sign of decreasing. Food was scarce, the diet was abominable, but nobody was starving. The calorie count was low compared to five years ago, but I recalled that in most Asian and African countries the calorie count of the diet of the people is even lower. The Cubans dressed shabbily, but I have seen Asians and Africans even shabbier.

What I saw in Cuba can be described as a supreme example of Machiavellianism. The method is to promise the people a hundred things, get them only twenty, and then blame your failure on Yankee imperialism. If the people begin to get restless, get them five more things, and at the same time make ten newer promises. Keep the people guessing, expecting, but just see to it that the breaking point is not reached. Also, don't forget a frequent show of military might. Suppress your opponents ruthlessly, flatter the people when need be; sometimes even discreetly acknowledge your own mistakes and solemnly promise to do better next time. Do all these things, and you will come out fine.

The impression I got was that it would not be easy to overthrow Castro. I think it will be difficult—very difficult—to get rid of him. But my visit also convinced me that it would be a folly to reconcile ourselves to this presence of a Red regime ninety miles from our shores. It would be wrong of us to quit doing anything about it. That would be victory by default for the Fidelistas. There is no denying that Castro is a menace to the freedom of the rest of the Western Hemisphere, and that his regime represents a dangerous breach by Communism in Latin America. If we aren't careful this breach can be widened. If we quit harassing Castro, this is exactly what we would be doing. We would be contributing toward the widening of the breach. A fact of life is that Castro is here. He is like a cancer. Through taking no medication, we can let the cancer spread; or, through medical care, we can confine its growth and hope that eventually it will be eradicated.

There are two methods of getting rid of Castro: internal insurrection or invasion. In a previous chapter I discussed the difficulties that lie in the path of an insurrection. This leaves us with invasion as the best method. But the invasion must not be of the harum-scarum type, as it was in 1961. It must be very well organized to succeed. In tactics and logistics, it would require as much care (though not on the same scale) as the Allied invasion of Europe during World War II. Also, the invaders must have a plan as to what they would do if they succeeded, because if they don't have such a plan, the anarchy in Cuba would be tremendous, and it would provide the soundest possible reason for the triumph of a counter-counterrevolution.

The chances of such an invasion appear vague. I don't say that there are no chances at all. There *are*, although no conjecture is possible as to its scale. The thought of an invasion is what is keeping the Castroites very jittery. Their big fear is that the invaders would be able to secure American air cover and even some American troops, which would directly involve the United States in the venture. The administration in Washington has repeatedly asserted that it would take no part in an invasion, but the Castroites don't believe that. However, if we examine the matter coolly, we realize that the possibility of U.S. involvement doesn't exist for several reasons. First, there still are Soviet troops in Cuba, and if American troops are involved in an invasion, they would also be fighting the Russians, and this could lead to a situation that would result in world war. Second, it would set in motion all over the world a wave of anti-Americanism that would lead to our isolation. Third, it is doubtful whether our military allies would go along with us. That matter would undoubtedly come up for vigorous debate at the United Nations, and our NATO allies would be in a dilemma. If they support us, that would be in opposition to world opinion. If they don't, that would mean a weakening of NATO ties. The whole pattern of international relations would be affected, and there is no predicting the course the events would take.

In considering the overall situation, it must not be thought that Castro's regime has no weak points. The truth is that it has several, and some are serious and costly to his existence. He knows that the threat of a new invasion is not past. He realizes that for an invasion to succeed it has to be on a very big scale. But he cannot afford to let down his guard. He is forced to keep on spending a large part of the nation's revenue on defense, because a weakening of the island's defense posture would invite invasion and foster insurrection. There are few governments in the world that depend more than Cuba on the army for staying in power. But Castro cannot go on spending such a large portion of the revenue on arms year after year. Sooner or later, a point will be reached when the burden will become unbearable, unless, of course, he is able to increase the revenues. The chances for such an increase are not bright, at least not in the near future.

This also raises the question of manpower committed to defense. Castro needs men on the farms. But he is forced to keep them armed and on the alert against an invasion. For years now, they have had no duty except to drill interminably and go on practice maneuvers. One Western diplomat said: "Look at these men in the guard and combat militia and the army. They aren't doing a thing. They are needed for planting the fields and harvesting the crops. It is really a terrible drain on the work force having them in uniform." Of course, at cane-cutting time, a large number of soldiers are assigned to the cane fields, but national economic interest demands that they stay there permanently. Thus, Castro cannot really afford to engage in any real harassment of the United States, because that would mean an additional shortage of farm labor, and a new drain on the already depleted financial resources of the island.

A second and more important chink in Castro's armor is the uncertainty of his relations with the Soviet Union. When he first came to power, and even until 1961, Soviet relations with Red China weren't as bad as they are now. They grow progressively worse, and Castro has come to realize that this conflict is forcing the Soviets to adopt a conciliatory attitude toward the West, and to refrain from endorsing his jingoism. In other words, with the Chinese peril just across the border from Siberia, the Russians cannot afford to keep up their former antagonism toward the West over the Cuban problem. In 1961, at the time of the Bay of Pigs invasion, Khrushchev openly threatened to rain his missiles over New York on behalf of Cuba. It is not at all in the cards now that he would repeat the threat today. The Chinese peril is also compelling the Russians to cut down their military aid to Castro for fear of further annoying the United States, and Castro knows that without this military aid he would have a difficult time maintaining his power. Arms aid has to be continuous, because arms become obsolete and must be replaced.

Castro is also aware of the fact that the rest of Latin America, although still economically backward, is not stationary, and that the urge and the movement is present in each country to get ahead. The pace of development in these countries is slow, but the situation is not getting worse, and the overall picture is that at least *some* advance is being made. Revolutionary Cuba could have set herself up as an example of the success of Marxism if it had been able to give actuality to the promises it had held out. But these promises have remained unfulfilled, and Cuba has lost the allure it had hoped to gain as a model for advancement on Communist lines.

The result has been that the rest of Latin America continues to regard revolutionary Cuba as an outcast, and refuses to have anything to do with it. Things Cuba could have gotten cheap from Venezuela, Brazil, and Argentina, she is now forced to import from the far-off Soviet Union. The moral support Cuba had hoped for from Mexico and Brazil has failed to materialize at the councils of the Organization of American States and at the United Nations.

Castro's efforts to foster Red revolutions in other Latin American republics have so far failed miserably. Cuba is still training revolutionaries, and some have been sent out to create trouble, but the trouble has been easily checked. One cannot say that there won't be any more trouble in the future, but Castro is being forced to draw back somewhat because of his economic troubles. He has by no means given up the idea of fostering armed insurrections elsewhere, but the pell-mell urgency has gone out of the project. He has come to realize that unless he succeeds in making Cuba a showcase of Communism, his pronouncements on the worth of Communism will have no meaning. Talk can be good up to a point, but action, too, is required, and solid results are imperative if talk is to be believed for long.

Then again, it must not be forgotten that the Soviet Union has lost to a considerable extent its earlier crusading zeal to spread Communism. When it was first established, it lacked material wealth, and it is always easy to talk of revolution and war when you have no wealth to lose. Now the Soviet Union is better off than it was in those days, and although it is currently faced with economic difficulties, it realizes that they cannot be surmounted nor its wealth increased or preserved if it continues propagating world Communist revolution.

Red China, on the other hand, is a new entrant into the world of Communism. So is Cuba. These two still retain the old Marxist zeal for revolution at any price. But without Soviet material wealth and armed might behind what they preach, their talk appears hollow.

Today the position of the U.S.S.R. is that it will welcome a Red revolution in a country if one occurs. It will even render some help toward causing it. But it will *not* risk its own prosperity, or neck, in making it an actuality anywhere on earth. Latin America is one of the spheres in which the U.S.S.R. has lost interest as far as a Red revolution goes. She appears unwilling, at least for the time being, to go along with Castro in fostering upheavals. And Castro on his own, although he can cause immense trouble, cannot do anything decisive.

Let us look at the Cuban attitude toward the Sino-Soviet conflict from the Soviet angle. I have mentioned in an earlier chapter that it is easy for Castro to force the Soviet Union into giving him more aid by threatening to go over to Red China's side. In the past the threat did not matter much, because the Sino-Soviet conflict was not very acrimonious. But when I was in Cuba, the conflict was reaching the point of no return, and the Cuban neutrality was not to the U.S.S.R.'s liking. If I were a Russian, I would not like it either. I would say to myself, Cuba exists because of the aid my country gives it, and so it is Cuba's moral duty to support me openly. The Russians are no fools. They realize that if they pulled out of Cuba, Castro would be left stranded, and that it would be futile for him to depend upon Red China, because Red China does not have enough resources to take over the Soviet role in Cuba. The Russian displeasure is quite understandable. It's odd—when the United States gives aid to its allies, all of them receive it on condition that there will be no political strings attached to it. The U.S. always goes along with this request. "No strings," it says in effect. "You can have all you want, and we will not try to guide you in your political decisions, and no matter how much you get from us, you will be free to follow your own course."

But Russians are different. They don't have such scruples.

These uncertainties are compounded by rivalries within the Cuban hierarchy. At present Castro seems to be the top dog; it appears that his position is unassailable. It seems that there is no one inside the revolutionary leadership strong enough to oust him. But it is one of the vagaries of Communism that often the leader who seems to be the strongest turns out to be the weakest. There is always a strong undercurrent of hostility against him. Problems of personality and differences over methods can and do lead to serious upsets in a Communist society. This is because each leader's power rests on force, and hardly ever on love and respect. The moment a rival spots a weak point, he hits at the leader of the day, and topples him from his pedestal without much ado. One can never tell what will happen next in a Communist society, and Cuba is no exception.

Frequent trials in Cuba highlight every day the uncertainty that Castro feels. Today he has devoted colleagues in the persons of President Osvaldo Dorticos, Minister of Industries Ernesto Che Guevara, and his own brother, Minister of Defense Raul Castro. But it must be remembered that even Khrushchev was once on friendly terms with Stalin; and Beria and Malenkov and Bulganin were all buddies, drinking toasts to each other, wishing each other prosperity and health, until the chance came for each to stab the other in the back.

There is no guarantee that such a thing cannot and will not happen in Cuba. There have been too many defections within the ranks of Castro's followers. He is at odds with the orthodox Communists. Any one of them, on finding the opportunity, would not lose time in striking at the "ultimate leader."

This brings us to the question of what effect the U.S. blockade is having upon the economy of Cuba. My observation was that the effect has been considerable. Before the revolution Cuba depended upon the U.S. for 90 percent or more of its supplies. The U.S. was its natural market. These supplies all of a sudden ceased coming. In addition, the U.S. embarked upon a policy of prohibiting foreign ships carrying cargo to Cuba from using American ports and refuelling facilities. The U.S. also forbade its own ship users from chartering a vessel engaged in trade with Cuba.

The embargo and the blockade have not been 100 percent successful. Ships of the free world continued going to Cuba, but at a very reduced rate. A Western diplomat told me that between January and August, 1963, not more than two hundred free-world ships anchored in Cuba. The goods they brought were hardly enough to fill the vacuum created by the cut-off of U.S. goods. The result was that very soon everything required to keep a modern economy functioning disappeared, and the economy of the island was reduced to a primitive state. This was only partially offset by the Soviet aid.

Things would have been better for Cuba if the geographical distance between it and the Red bloc were less and the Red bloc had a larger maritime fleet. But a whole ocean and several seas lie between Cuba and East Europe, and two oceans lie between Cuba and Red China. The oceangoing tanker fleet of the world numbered 3146, only 58 of which belonged to the U.S.S.R. The Reds were then left with no choice but to charter free-world vessels, even at increased cost. It was pointed out to me that these terms were so good that a growing number of free-world shipowners were falling for them in spite of U.S. restrictions. These Soviet bloc supplies averted total collapse. They could not prevent hardships, but they at least kept the country going.

Today in Cuba, Castro's race is with time. He needs time to consolidate himself, time to correct the mistakes of the past; time to make further breaches in the economic and diplomatic wall thrown around the island by the United States; time for the Cubans of the younger generation to train themselves adequately and fill the places left vacant by the exiles. Cuba has been making efforts to lessen her dependence on Soviet goods, and to enter into trade pacts with free-world nations. The success of her efforts in this direction depend on her foreign-exchange resources, and these depend on how much sugar she is able to put into the world market.

Castro's problems are to make the workers put in a greater effort, to improve the administration, and still to maintain a "revolutionary spirit" within the country and among the people.

The U.S. blockade and the hardening of U.S. attitude toward trade with Cuba by U.S. allies are hindering and hampering Castro's consolidation, and are keeping the country off balance and its rulers nervous and uneasy. That there should be no change in this policy is necessary for the containment of the Communism that has been planted in Cuba. If the United States comes to terms with it, gives it respectability by recognizing it, ends its efforts to hamstring it, it would get a chance to spread outside the borders of Cuba and enter into the other Latin American republics.

Let there be no mistake about it; no matter how much Castro might wish for a normalization of relations with us, he is our enemy and an enemy of the economic and political system that is ours. His wish and effort is to destroy this system. He cannot do so by directly attacking us. He knows he would be wiped out if he did that. But he can still weaken us, deprive us of our friends, isolate us, by weaning away other Latin American nations from the free-enterprise system, and making them assume a militant posture toward us.

In my opinion the current U.S. policy toward Cuba is the best policy under the circumstances as discussed in this chapter. If the castigation of Cuba continues, and the Red rulers of the island do not get a chance to perpetuate their power, there is still hope that the chances of an insurrection or invasion will gain momentum, and the Cuban people will regain the freedom they lost in substituting Castro for Batista.

27. Good-bye to Cuba

THE time for me to leave Cuba was now at hand. I wanted very much to prolong my stay, but I was advised not to do so. I had a plane reservation from Havana to Madrid for September 14. The airline (Iberia) said that if I wanted I could have my reservation moved to some other date, but they made it clear that it could not be before the first week of October, because an International Conference of Architects was due to begin in Havana in late September and the orders of the Cuban government were that Iberia give priority to the conference delegates.

"You have a reservation," one diplomat friend said to me. "For heaven's sake, make use of it and get out of here. Don't tempt your luck, or we will have you on our hands and will have to strain ourselves to get you out."

I also checked on my wallet, and found that I was very short on money. I had been spending fifteen to twenty dollars a day, and there was no way for me to get money from my newspaper. Of course, I could have asked a certain free-world diplomat for more money, and he would have given it to me, but because of the plane reservation problem I decided not to prolong my stay.

On Iberia's advice I had secured my exit permit from the Cuban Immigration Department on my third day in Havana, and on September 12 I went to the Iberia ticket office in Vedado to get my boarding pass. The office had not opened, and I sat down on a bench in the gallery. There were other persons, too, waiting for the office to open. One middle-aged Cuban kept staring at me in a peculiar manner. I was about to ask him what he wanted, when he came over to me and asked whether I was going to Madrid. I said yes. He asked whether I had a reservation. I said yes. He then offered to buy my reservation for 200 pesos. I said I was not willing to sell. He raised the price to 250 pesos, then to 300 pesos. I was just getting interested in him when a militiaman showed up and the man slunk away. Later on I recounted this incident to an Iberia official. He said that such offers were very common, and that I should forget it. He said further that Iberia ran only one flight a week out of Havana, but he had a waiting list of 5000. These people had pesos and were willing to pay handsomely for a reservation.

After rechecking on my ticket, I went to the bank to get a certificate that as a tourist I had been spending ten dollars a day. At the bank, I had a touching experience.

I was accosted by a very pretty receptionist. I thumbed through my phrase book and came up with a sentence I had been using often in my meetings with the Cuban girls. It was, *"Usted es muy hermosa,"* meaning, "I think you are beautiful." I wrote it on a piece of paper and gave it to her. Immediately she brightened. Resting on her desk was a toy giraffe made of colored wires. She gave it to me. Through an interpreter she explained that she had made it herself by twisting and joining discarded wire, and that she wanted me to have it as a memento of my visit. I was affected by this spontaneous gesture of friendship. I still have the giraffe, and shall never part with it.

On September 14 I got up early and did my packing. My biggest problem was where to hide my notes. I had avoided taking notes in a book. Instead, I had been jotting down my impressions on small pieces of paper. I remembered that a British correspondent several years ago had gotten his notes out of Cuba by hiding them in his shoes, but I thought that method too clumsy. Discovery would have meant a long interrogation and a delay in my departure. I hit upon another method. The various government offices had given me a lot of propaganda pamphlets. I distributed my pieces of note paper between the pages of these pamphlets, and tied the whole bundle with a string. This bundle I decided to carry in my hand. I put my trip diary in my suitcase. It had no suspicion-arousing entry, and I was, in fact, eager for the Cuban authorities to read it, because it contained such phrases as "Had a very nice time at . . ." and "The Immigration people were very nice to me."

I wanted to buy presents for my friends in Washington and Cleveland, but lacked money. I left twelve dollars as a tip for my room waiters and elevator boys. I gave the money to the hotel manager, and he divided it equally among them. All were very happy to receive these few dollars. It was obvious that they had not been tipped for a long time. At nine o'clock in the morning I took a cab to the airport. The plane was not going to leave until seven that evening, but Iberia had told me to be at the airport eight hours ahead. It took me two hours to get there, because halfway to the airport the cab had a flat tire. The airport was jammed with people, relatives of the Cubans who were to fly out with me. Traveling bags had been put in a long line before the customs office. I put my own bag in the line, and prepared for a long wait.

The plane had not yet arrived. It was somewhere between Santa Maria and Barbados. It was the same one on which I had come. It was due at one o'clock, and was to fly back after a stop of six hours. The airline was keeping a careful check of the course it was following, and every hour or so its location was announced over a microphone. We heard the announcement that it had landed in Barbados, and everyone cheered. Then we heard that its departure from Barbados had been delayed by an hour. A big groan of disappointment. Things were so uncertain that it would not have surprised anyone to be told that the plane had been ordered back to Madrid, or that it would come to Havana but would not be allowed to board passengers, and would be returned to Madrid empty. All of us had tickets and reservations, but that didn't mean a thing. The feeling was that only when we had actually flown out of Cuba could we really say we were leaving the country.

Cheering rent the air again when it was announced that the plane had left Barbados and its next stop would be Havana. I looked around and saw an old woman on her knees, praying for its safe arrival. It was a moving spectacle. Those who were leaving were both happy and sad; happy because they were getting out of Cuba, sad because they knew they would probably never see their relatives again. And the relatives must have been wishing that they, too, were leaving.

Among the passengers were many babies and children. The latter played in the waiting room. I even saw one climb into the lap of a militiawoman. But how unaware the children were of the great drama going on around them! The babies slept, or their chattering mothers took them to the washroom to change their diapers.

Most of the passengers were young men, either single or with their wives. They had a grim expression upon their faces. The older passengers seemed to be in a daze. It is not pleasant to be plucked out of one's home in one's old age and begin a new life somewhere else.

The Cuban government technically places no restrictions on the migration of its people to other countries. One joke going around Havana was that if a bridge were built between the Cuban capital and Miami, 90 percent of Cuba's population would migrate. Another joke was that Cuba is the biggest country in the world; its capital is in Moscow and its population is in Miami.

But the hitch lies in the actual getting out. During the first few years of the revolution, world air and shipping lines maintained service to Cuba, and the earlier exiles were able to leave the country in this manner. But now there are only a few plane flights a week out of the country, and no passenger ships are going to Cuba at all. Some hardy souls run the danger of providing themselves somehow with a small boat and sailing it ninety miles across the water to Florida. They have to risk attack from Castro's gunboats. Some make it to Florida, some don't.

Those who are lucky enough to get a plane reservation are not allowed to take many possessions. A migrant's house and all his belongings are taken away. Each man can carry with him only one suit in addition to the one he is wearing. Each woman is allowed one extra dress. Valuables such as watches, fountain pens, silver tie clasps or cuff links, women's jewelry—even a wedding ring, if it's an expensive one—art objects of ivory and wood, all are confiscated. Children are allowed to take only a single toy. No person can carry out more than five dollars. The airline rarely accepts payment for a ticket in pesos. Most of the Cubans who flew with me were provided with tickets by relatives and friends in Madrid or elsewhere, who had paid in dollars or Spanish currency. Before a Cuban can leave for Spain, he has to be sure that there is some friend or organization in Spain willing to take care of him. Unless he has such a sponsor, he won't get a Spanish visa.

The Customs people got busy with the luggage at about eleven o'clock. Each suitcase, each box, was thoroughly searched. The owner was asked to lay out everything on a table. Then the Customs men felt the sides of the suitcase to ensure that no gold or silver had been hidden there. Each shirt, each jacket, was unfolded to make sure that nothing was concealed in it.

Of course, the pockets of the clothes each person was wearing were searched too. One man wanted to take a statue of Christ. It was shaken again and again by several officers for fear that jewelry might be hidden inside it. There was a golden orb in the statue's hand. It was scraped with a knife to make sure that it was not real gold. Even babies' rattles were examined to find out whether they were hiding anything. The searching of each suitcase took twenty minutes. There were only three Customs officers, and they didn't seem to be in any hurry to get the work finished. It was stifling in the airport. The air-conditioning had broken down, and the ceiling fans weren't working, though the Customs officers had a table fan to keep them cool. Finally, someone thought of bringing ice water, and it was distributed free.

The plane was sighted at two o'clock. Everyone rushed to the windows and glass doors to watch it land. Its coming was indeed a pleasant spectacle; one of Cuba's few remaining links with the free world. Many people rushed to the roof for a better view. When it actually landed, a tumultuous shout of welcome went up. I had heard the same shout when I first arrived.

Now there was a speed-up of the search process. My suitcase was thoroughly searched, though I was not asked to lay out everything on a table. An officer leafed through my trip diary, read a few entries, nodded in approval, and put it back. He asked me about the tied bundle of pamphlets. I told him what they were, and offered to untie the string. He said I didn't have to.

I was then subjected to a few routine questions. The first was: "Did you like our country?"

"I liked it very much. I wish I could come back. Maybe I will," I replied.

"What did you like most?"

"The zeal of the people to make the revolution succeed."

I was, by now, well able to take care of such questions. I had lost my awe of them and they didn't frighten me. I told the officer exactly what he wanted to hear. Each answer appeared to please him immensely. He came out from behind his desk, shook hands with me warmly, embraced me, and wished me good luck.

I was then told to proceed to another window to have my money checked. I showed the man behind the counter the bank statement I had secured, and it satisfied him. I had about twenty pesos, and they were exchanged for American dollars. The dollar bills I got were so old and wrinkled that I wondered where they had been all the while. I wanted to take some pesos and Cuban silver out of the country, but was told it was against regulations. One man endorsed my exit permit, and a second man put the departure stamp on my passport. I was then told to join a group of passengers who had gone through all the formalities and been cleared.

Joining these people was heartrending. Their relatives were on the other side of the glass wall, waving, or just looking. There was sadness in every face, and many of the men and women were weeping. There was one young girl who was leaving Havana with her husband. Her mother and father were staying behind. Both women were crying their hearts out, and the men were having a hard time consoling them. The two couples were aware that they would probably never see each other again. Their fevered outpourings cast a gloom over the entire scene.

We still had to wait several hours. We weren't allowed to step outside, and an old woman fainted because of the heat. Some of us wanted to go out and buy food, but we weren't allowed to do so. There was nothing to read. No one seemed to be in any mood for talking. The relatives began to leave one by one, but some lingered. They couldn't talk with the passengers, because of the glass wall. They just stood and watched, grief etched on their faces. The sun went down, and in the distance we could see our plane being refuelled. A few members of the crew joined us, but they did not know how much longer the Cuban authorities would take to issue the flight permit.

"Can the flight be canceled?" I asked a crew member.

"Yes."

"For what reason?"

"Many reasons."

"Has there been any indication of cancellation?"

"I don't know."

Our waiting continued. I tried to doze off in a corner, but could not. In my mind I tried to compose a lead for the first of my stories. I could not think of any. I tried looking out of the windows. There was nothing to look at. I gave my seat to a woman. There was a big table in the center, but those who were standing could not sit on it, because some of the babies had fallen asleep and their mothers had laid them on the table. I can honestly say that that wait was the most excruciating of any in my life. I have never gone through anything like it. The Cubans who were leaving the country were now worse than outcasts, pariahs, and lepers to the authorities, and as such deserved no consideration or kindness. We could step out of the room only to board the plane.

"The airport authorities could at least send a hand truck with food," I complained to a Spanish crew member.

"What for? These people don't have any money," he replied.

Finally, at 9:30 P.M. we heard the announcement that we could board the plane, and a door was opened to the Tarmac. With armed militiamen standing guard, we began to file out of the room in twos and threes. A small girl was asleep on the center table. With her mother's permission, I lifted her in my arms. She awakened briefly, and fell quickly asleep again as I carried her.

Inside the plane it was a problem for the stewardesses to get everyone seated. Many of the passengers had never flown. They had to be escorted right up to their seats and shown how to fasten the safety belts. When all passengers and everything was in, I found that the plane was packed to capacity. Excess luggage was piled on the rack over the seats and on the floor between the seats. We were undoubtedly overloaded. Some of the relatives were now out on the Tarmac, and the passengers crowded around the windows for a last look, a last wave.

At last the door was closed, and I heard the steps being wheeled away. Then we heard the captain's voice bidding us welcome. The runway lights were lit, and the plane began to move. I looked out of the window, and saw the relatives walking slowly away. The plane began to gain speed. Soon it was too dark to see anything. Only when we were cruising between the clouds with the tossing, inky sea under us did I breathe a sigh of relief.

Index